The Tory Winning Machine

Why the Conservative Party
keeps winning elections
and what we can do to stop them

Adam Herriott

© Copyright Adam Herriott 2023
All rights reserved.

The content contained within this book may not be reproduced, duplicated or transmitted without direct written permission from the author or the publisher.
Under no circumstances will any blame or legal responsibility be held against the publisher, or author, for any damages, reparation, or monetary loss due to the information contained within this book. Either directly or indirectly.

Legal Notice:
This book is copyright protected. This book is only for personal use. You cannot amend, distribute, sell, use, quote or paraphrase any part, or the content within this book, without the consent of the author or publisher.

Disclaimer Notice:
Please note the information contained within this document is for educational and entertainment purposes only. All effort has been executed to present accurate, up to date, and reliable, complete information. No warranties of any kind are declared or implied. Readers acknowledge that the author is not engaging in the rendering of legal, financial, medical or professional advice. The content within this book has been derived from various sources.
By reading this document, the reader agrees that under no circumstances is the author responsible for any losses, direct or indirect, which are incurred as a result of the use of the information contained within this document, including, but not limited to, — errors, omissions, or inaccuracies.

To the memory of my mother,
Catharine Herriott (1947-2021)

CONTENTS

Introduction 1

PART 1: BRITISH POLITICAL OVERVIEW 7
1. The British Political Playing Field 9
2. Overview Of Tory Success Since 1900 23

PART 2: THE TORY PARTY'S MAIN OBJECTIVE IS WINNING ELECTIONS AND POWER 39
3. Select Leaders Most Likely To Win General Elections 41
4. Staying United In Public Above All Else 45
5. Adaptability And Pragmatic 51
6. Quickly Regain Power Following A Defeat 57
7. Effective Party Organisation 61
8. The Party Of The Rich 67

PART 3: HOW THE TORIES GOVERN TO ENSURE THEY WIN THE NEXT ELECTION 77
9. The Tory Party Presents Itself As the Natural Party Of Government 79
10. Tory Statecraft 89
11. Project Governing And Economic Competence 99
12. Manufacture Tory Voters 105
13. Distract, Invent Enemies, Dirty Tricks, Crush Opponents 117

PART 4: HOW THE TORIES WIN MORE GENERAL ELECTIONS — 131
14. Appealing Electoral Programmes And Manifestos — 133
15. Effective Electioneering Techniques — 139
16. How the Right-wing Media Helps The Tories Win Elections — 155
17. Factors Influencing Voting Behaviour — 181
18. The Tories Are Better At Building Voter Coalitions — 191
19. Why Do People Vote Tory? — 199

PART 5: WEAK AND DIVIDED OPPOSITION — 219
20. The British Labour Party — 221

PART 6: STOPPING THE TORIES — 245
21. How To Stop the Tories At The Next General Election — 247
22. How To Stop The Tories In The Long Term — 255

Conclusion — 281

Acknowledgements — 285
Notes — 287

INTRODUCTION

The Tory Party is a disgrace. Tory governments operate to defend the interests of the wealthy and British capitalism at the expense of ordinary people. This results in various issues that adversely impact the country and its people.

The Tories weaken trade unions, workers' only serious protections from predatory employers. The Tories fail to run the economy in the interests of ordinary people and instead base policy on the interests of the wealthy and large corporations. They want to reduce the state's size and taxes, reducing public spending. This undermines the public services we all rely on. In reality, 13 years of this Tory government's low economic growth have meant the Tories have recently put taxes up to the highest levels since the Second World War. It is clear to most that the Tory Brexit is a disastrous act of economic self-harm. The Tories' economic mismanagement has resulted in a cost of living crisis, with millions in poverty and going hungry. Millions of workers are forced to work meaningless, low-paid jobs with short-term contracts.

Tory housing policy ensures their voters benefit from a nationwide housing shortage (especially new builds in wealthy areas) to push up house prices and protect landlords so tenants suffer from substandard and insecure housing. The Tories operate a racist, authoritarian, populist immigrant policy that scapegoats entire communities to distract from Tory misrule and shore up their voting coalition. The Tories say the right things on important issues such as equality for women, trans acceptance, racism and climate change but fail to do anything practical to solve these pressing problems and make life better for ordinary people in Britain. I would argue the Tories are actively operating against solving these issues as resolving them goes against the interests of many of their supporters, namely Tory voters and Tory funders.[1] The Tories are attacking our democracy by taking away the right to protest and practising voter suppression by making it more difficult for people to vote by requiring ID cards.

If all this is true, how is it that the Tories are the most successful and dominant political party in Britain? There is a lack of accessible books analysing why the Tories keep winning. This information is scattered across old books, online articles and youtube. To collectively beat the Tories and limit the damage they can do in the future, we need to understand our enemy.[2]

A weak opposition in parliament handicaps those that oppose Tory misrule, the right-wing media and a voting system that is tilted in the Tories' favour. The Labour Party is generally less focused and committed to winning elections than the Tories. Labour has many factions and traditions that its leadership struggles to keep united. The First Past the Post electoral system puts those parties on the left and centre-left at a disadvantage, forcing them to fight over the same voters, leading to 'splitting the vote'. The Tories generally do not have to compete with other parties on the right, which gives Tory MPs and candidates an easier path to victory.

In this book, I have brought together all the knowledge and analysis of why the Tory Party has kept winning general elections over the last 123 years when they govern against the interests of most people. I will explain why the Labour Party is so weak and how pro-democracy and anti-Tory individuals and groups outside the political parties can take action to stop the Tories. The Tories are currently far behind the Labour Party in opinion polls, and a Labour government after the next election looks likely. But we can't take this for granted, as the polls will narrow between now and the next general election, likely 2024. So we must do everything possible to remove them from power. In this book, I will also describe the details of an achievable strategy to stop the dominance of the Tories in the future once they have been removed from power.

My name is Adam Herriott, and I've been campaigning for social change for over twenty years. I'm part of the team that launched the https://stopthetories.vote/ tactical voting website for the 2023 local elections. For a long time, I focused on raising awareness about climate change. I worked in Westminster in the late 2000s for an environmental NGO and saw the underbelly of our political system. In 2016, I realised that those of us who want a better world would only make progress if we changed our politics. We need multiple electoral and constitutional changes, and the significant roadblock to change is the Tory Party, so I've been thinking, researching, discussing and campaigning against the Tories since then. It is clear that simply electing a Labour government is not enough; we will need to apply pressure on the Labour Party to push them towards the world we want.

I want to share what I've learned so you better understand what we're up against and how to make change happen. We can improve the dire state of British society with the correct knowledge, analysis, strategy and action. Many developed Western countries have a much more functional state that better protects the less fortunate in society. Sure, all countries have problems, but Britain has extreme levels of inequality and a broken political system. However, it does not have to be this way.

The pro-democracy and anti-Tory movement is gaining momentum in Britain across dozens of organisations, groups and campaigns. Thousands of people across our country have had enough of Tory misrule. They are ready for our political system to be transformationally changed. This book is a contribution to this vital movement. I want to encourage you to take heart that you are not alone and that there are people who feel the same up and down the country. There are campaigns and roles for everyone if you are ready to take action. My aim with this book is so you are fully equipped with the knowledge of what we are up against and what we can do about it.

Those of us who want a better society have a unique opportunity to take steps to lay the groundwork over the next year while the Tories are still in office, to prepare for the next Labour government because that is when the hard work begins. Sadly, a Labour government will not do what is necessary without us demanding it. I understand that with the Tories far behind Labour in the polls, it is tempting not to take action, but this is a mistake. If we want progressive change for our country, we must take proactive action now, or we'll miss our chance.

I have read and listened to everything I can find on why and how the Tories keep winning and what we can do about it. Every chapter of the book will provide you with that information in a concise, accessible way. If you read this book, you will gain an in-depth understanding of what we are up against and what you can do to help get our country on a better path.

Structure Of The Book

I will use 'Tory Party' and 'Conservative Party' interchangeably in this book. There are 6 parts to the book and 23 chapters and a conclusion. Part 1 gives an overview of the British political context. Chapter 1 describes 2 key political concepts, the 'left-right political spectrum' and the 'centre-ground of British politics'. This chapter also unpacks the British electoral system of First Past the Post. Chapter 2 provides a history of the Tory Party's success since 1900. This chapter includes a history and analysis of why the Tories dominated during certain periods or won specific general elections.

Part 2 describes the features of the Tory Party as an organisation that helps it keep winning. Chapter 3 looks at how the party selects leaders that win elections. Chapter 4 focuses on how the Tories stay united in public to keep winning. The adaptable and pragmatic nature of the Tory Party is discussed in Chapter 5. Chapter 6 describes the Tories' ability to regain power quickly following a defeat. Finally, chapters 7 and 8 illustrate the effectiveness of the party's organisation and fundraising from the rich.

Part 3 focuses on how the Tories use the advantage of being in power most of the time to improve their chances of winning future elections. Chapter 9 describes how the Tory Party presents itself as the natural party of government. Chapter 10 explores Tory statecraft, which is the ability of the party to win elections from opposition and stay in power. A component of Tory Statecraft is the Tories' ability to project governing and economic competence, described in Chapter 11. In addition, the party has proved highly effective at manufacturing Tory voters throughout its history, as examined in Chapter 12. Finally, Chapter 13 discusses how the Tories hid their governing failures by distracting voters, inventing enemies, and dirty tricks and crushing their opponents.

Part 4 explores how the Tories run effective, strategic, dirty and disciplined election campaigns. Chapter 14 examines how the Tories produce more appealing general election programmes and manifestos than their opponents. The Tories' effective electioneering techniques are described in Chapter 15. Chapter 16 outlines how the right-wing media help the Tories win elections. Chapter 17 unpacks the factors that influence voting behaviour, which helps explain how the Tories are better at building voter coalitions, covered in Chapter 18. Finally, Chapter 19 describes why people vote for the Tories.

Part 5 digs into why we have a weak and divided opposition to the Tories. The main focus here is the British Labour Party, covered in Chapter 20. Part 6 outlines what we can do to ensure the Tories are removed from power and what we need to do to stop them from dominating in the future. Finally, the conclusion summarises the 17 factors that help the Tories win more elections and how we can stop them.

THE TORY WINNING MACHINE

PART 1:

BRITISH POLITICAL OVERVIEW

1

THE BRITISH POLITICAL PLAYING FIELD

Before we dive into all the history and politics, it is important to give an overview of the political playfield field in Britain that political parties are operating within. I will reference the right and left throughout the book, so the first section of this chapter will briefly explain the left-right political spectrum. The 'centre ground' of British politics is another important concept, where parties position themselves to appeal to ordinary voters. The final section of this chapter describes Britain's voting system, First Past the Post (FPTP). I will also explain the problems with FPTP and how it benefits the Tories.

Left-Right Political Spectrum

The left-right linear political spectrum is a simplistic way to identify political positions, ideologies and political parties. The terms 'left' and 'right' date back to the French Revolution and the seating arrangements adopted by the political groups at the first meeting of the Estates-General in 1789; those that sat on the left supported equality and common ownership, and supporters of meritocracy and private ownership were on the right. The labels stuck.

Ideology is defined as a set of ideas that are the foundation for political activity. This activity could be to maintain, change or overthrow the existing power structure. Ideologies have three features. First, they provide an understanding of the current context through a 'world view'. Second, they promote a vision of a desired future that is seen as a 'good society'. Third, ideologies explain how political change can be achieved and how to get from the present to the desired endpoint.[1]

Those on the left are associated with equality, rights, progress and social change, progressive reform, and internationalism. Political ideologies of the left include socialism, communism, anarchism, left-libertarians, feminism, environmentalism, anti-racism and trade unionism. Those on the right are associated with tradition, duty, authority, hierarchy, nationalism, capitalism and private property. Political ideologies of the right include conservatives, fascists, reactionaries, right-libertarians, neoconservatives, nationalists, imperialists, monarchists and traditionalists. There are also several political movements and groups that do not fit the left-right spectrum. In between the left and right are centrists or moderates; the ideology of liberalism is located here.

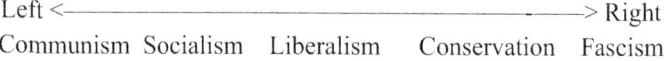

Left <———————————————————————-———> Right
 Communism Socialism   Liberalism   Conservation   Fascism

The Tories are on the centre-right, although recent Tory governments have moved further to the right than the party's position in the twentieth century. The Labour Party is on the centre-left, but since the New Labour government of the late 1990s and 2010 has shifted to the right of the Labour Party in the twentieth century. The Liberal Party and Liberal Democrats are in the centre. The Scottish National Party, Green Party and Plaid Cymru are on the centre-left. The UK Independence Party and Reform UK (previously the Brexit Party) are on the right.

The left-right political spectrum also applies internally to political parties. Each political party is a coalition of individuals and groups with different priorities and ideologies. As a result, different wings of political parties dominate at various points, which impacts their appeal to voters and success in elections.

The Centre Ground Of British Politics

The centre ground of British politics is not a fixed point but where parties position themselves to make an appealing and broad electoral offer to build a voter coalition. As well as locating the centre ground and claiming it, Prime Ministers can create and modify the centre ground. Elections are not an intellectual debate about what is best for the country. To win, parties must align with most voters on the centre ground.

Following the Second World War, the centre ground moved to the left to form the post-war consensus with the welfare state and full employment. The economic problems of the 1970s shifted the centre ground rightwards around trade union reform and opening up the UK economy. In the 1990s, the Labour Party (New Labour) accepted and worked within the Thatcherite arrangements. In the 2010s, under leader David Cameron, the Tories continued New Labour's social liberalism, combined with austerity and shrinking the state. The 2016 Brexit referendum shifted the centre ground rightwards politically again, and Tory leader Johnson needed to promise to tackle regional inequalities by 'levelling up' to win the 2019 general election.[2]

The Electoral System - First Past The Post

First-past-the-post (FPTP) is the electoral system that elects Members of Parliament (MPs) to the House of Commons in Westminster. It is formally known as 'single-member plurality voting' (SMP), but no one calls it that. The country is divided into 650 'constituencies' with roughly the same number of voters in each. Constituencies are also called seats. It works by voters casting their one vote for a candidate of their choice at a polling station or by a postal ballot. Only one MP will represent each constituency, so only one candidate from each party is on the ballot.

Ideally, voters choose a candidate they prefer, but if they think their preferred choice has a low chance of winning, they can select a candidate with a better chance of stopping a candidate they dislike from winning. This is known as tactical voting. For example, if someone supports the Liberal Democrats, is against the Tories but lives in a constituency with a Tory MP, with Labour in second place and the Liberal Democrats are a distant third. The voter might then vote for the Labour candidate to remove the Tory MP. I strongly advocate tactical voting to remove Tory MPs. More on this later.[3]

The candidate that receives the most votes wins the election even if the top candidate does not get 50 % of the vote. All other votes are disregarded. Tory MPs are regularly elected on less than 50% of the vote when Labour, Liberal Democrat and Green Party candidates collectively get more than 50% of the vote and 'split the vote'.[4]

Voters vote to elect a local MP, and the party with the highest number of MPs nationally generally forms the government, with the party's leader becoming Prime Minister. However, if the election is close, the party with the most MPs may not have a majority of MPs, resulting in a hung parliament. In this situation, the largest party has three options. One, it can form a coalition government with a smaller party, such as the 2010-15 Coalition Government between the Tories and Liberal Democrats. Two, it can form a 'minority government' with a 'confidence and supply agreement' with a smaller party, which will support the government to get necessary votes through parliament, such as the budget. The most recent confidence and supply agreement was between the Tories and the Northern Irish Democratic Unionist Party following the 2017 general election. The third option is that the largest party gives way and lets the next largest party form a minority government. The last example is in 1923, when the Tories got the most seats but let Labour and the Liberals form a government.

What is a working majority in the House of Commons?
650 MPs in the House of Commons represent each part of the UK. There is a Speaker of the House of Commons and 3 deputies. They manage parliamentary business and do not vote. By convention, 2 are drawn from the governing party and two from the main opposition. Additionally, Sinn Féin in Northern Ireland won 7 seats in the 2019

general election. They reject the British state, so they do not take their seats. So we can subtract 11 from 650, leaving 639, which means a government needs at least 320 MPs to have a working majority of 1. In the 2019 election, the Tories won 365 seats, and since then, this has been reduced to 354 MPs due to losing several by-elections.[5]

Features of FPTP

A party may get millions of votes, but if they are thinly spread out nationwide, they may only get a few or no MPs. In recent elections, this happened to the Green Party, the UK Independence Party and the Brexit Party. At the same time, the Tories and Labour get twenty or thirty thousand votes in multiple seats and hundreds of MPs. This results in the number of voters that parties get not matching up with the number of MPs they get. This results in two large parties that can form governments, the Tories or Labour, as smaller parties without strong support bases in multiple seats struggle to gain many MPs. Nationalist parties with a strong geographical base in a small part of the UK benefit from FPTP, the Scottish National Party is a good example. They got half the votes in Scotland in 2015 and 95% of the seats. Generally, FPTP means that parties can form governments on their own but sometimes on a tiny share of the vote. In 2005, Labour got a large majority of seats on 35% of the vote, with a low voter turnout of 61%. In 2015, the Tories got a small majority of 37% of the over, with a turnout of 66 %.[6]

FPTP in Britain results in two types of seats. There are 'safe seats' that rarely or never change parties, and this covers most seats (roughly 500). There are also 'swing seats' or marginal seats, where the current MP won the seat at the last election by a few hundred to a few thousand votes. These marginal seats are vulnerable to opposition parties and decide elections, including about 100-150 seats. Therefore, Political parties focus all their campaigning in these marginal seats, attempting to win over a few thousand 'swing voters' in each. Policies in party manifestos are designed to appeal to these swing voters meaning that millions of voters in safe seats are mostly ignored.[7] General elections are normally decided by 100,000 to

300,000 voters in these marginal seats, about 1% of the UK population.

Types of voters
There are four types of voters from the perspective of political parties. First are those that don't or rarely vote. They are disillusioned with politics and don't see the point. Young people are a good example. Politicians ignore them. Second are those that vote for parties that have no chance of winning. They are more engaged in politics but ignore the reality of our voting system. Politicians also ignore them because they do not use their votes to influence the outcome of elections. Third are those who vote for a party or candidate with a realistic chance of winning. Either the voter is fortunate that their preferred candidate has a good chance of winning in that seat, or they make a pragmatic choice and vote tactically to stop another candidate they dislike from winning. Their vote is consistent from election to election, so they don't influence elections either. Fourth is the swing voter, who will vote for one party in one election and a completely different one in another. They will review which candidate or party is best for the near future, unconcerned about their record in government. These voters might look well-tuned into politics but know little about politics, so they believe different parties can be the best choice in different elections. The last group of voters decides the balance of power in parliament.[8]

These swing voters in marginal seats are the Tories and Labour's 'target voters'. These target voters have a superficial understanding of politics. They don't pay that much attention to current affairs and will vote but not think deeply about it. They are target voters because they are open to changing who they vote for based on the government's performance, how viable the opposition is, election campaigns and media influence. Therefore parties need to focus their campaigns on a few clear messages to cut through and appeal to these voters.[9]

Arguments for FPTP

The arguments for FPTP are that it is simple to understand and that ballot papers are easy to count so that the results of elections can be quickly declared. Another perceived benefit of FPTP is that it generally produced clear overall winners from the two main parties in the UK, the Conservatives and Labour. The thinking goes that these strong single-party governments can enact policies from their manifesto without compromising with smaller parties in a coalition. The claim is that this results in more stable governments than other voting systems. Another claim is that FPTP prevents extremist parties like the BNP from getting representation. Supporters of FPTP like that it results in one MP per constituency, so there is a strong link between MPs who know the local area and those they represent who live in a constituency (constituents). It is argued that constituents would be unclear who to contact for support if we have multiple parliamentary representatives.[10]

Problems with FPTP

There are several different problems with FPTP listed below. The biggest problem is that about 32 million people vote in general elections, but the result is decided by 100,000 to 500,000 voters in 100 to 150 marginal seats out of 650. Your vote is wasted if you do not live in one of these seats. This is a weak and undemocratic way of deciding who runs the country.

This results in the Tories and Labour focusing their policies and campaigning in these marginal seats and at those swing voters in those seats. Brexit is a good example, it is now apparent what an economic disaster it is, but the Tories and Labour can only change their position once these swing voters come out against Brexit. Labour leader Starmer campaigned vigorously for remaining in the EU, so he is likely sticking to 'making Brexit work' because opinion polling tells the Labour Party that their target voters in marginals still want Brexit to work.

FPTP is unrepresentative in several ways.
1. FPTP fails to reflect the national popular vote in the number of MPs that parties get. Therefore, it is irrelevant to the final result the total number of votes each party receives; all that matters is which party managed to win the most votes in small arbitrary geographical areas.
2. FPTP creates 'false majorities' and 'minority rule' by over-representing larger parties and those with strong regional support so that parties can get a majority in parliament on a minority of the vote (under 50% of votes).
3. FPTP leads to two parties dominating, failing to represent British politics' multi-party nature in the twenty-first century. Political diversity is suppressed; the winner-take-all nature of FPTP means that smaller parties struggle to win seats. Smaller parties receive millions of votes but get few or no MPs.
4. Millions of voters are misrepresented because their representative in parliament is an MP they did not vote for and disagree with. One perceived benefit of FPTP is the constituency link, but is this valid if you have drastically different views of your MP? In 2019, 14.5 million people, 45% of voters, voted for candidates that did not win and are therefore represented by MPs that do not share their political views.
5. FPTP results in millions of wasted votes, either cast for the losing candidates or excess votes for winning candidates, known as 'vote mountains'. In the 2019 election, 71% of votes were wasted in both ways.
6. FPTP means that not all votes are equal. For example, at the 2019 election, it took 26,000 votes to elect an SNP MP, 38,000 to elect a Tory MP, 50,000 to elect a Labour MP and over 800,000 for the Green Party. On the other hand, the Brexit Party got over 600,000 votes and had no MP to show for it.

There are some geographical problems with FPTP. It benefits parties that can concentrate their voters in a small geographical area. The SNP in Scotland is an excellent example of this. However, FPTP in the UK has resulted in uneven representation across the country. FPTP in the UK results in hundreds of safe seats, either Tory or Labour, that always stay the same, resulting in the MPs feeling immune from electoral pressures and not behaving in the national interest. FPTP fails to consistently link total voters to seats. Parties can gain votes nationally but lose seats or lose votes and gain seats. It is only important what happens in marginal seats; changes in the number of voters in safe seats are irrelevant. Since 1952, 213 seats have been held by the same political party.

FPTP can result in wrong-winner elections, also known as 'majority reversal', where the party that gets the most voters nationally loses the election and another party receives more MPs and forms the government. This happened in 1951, with the Tories forming a government, and in February 1974, with Labour forming a government.

The high number of wasted votes with FPTP results in tactical voting. Voters' approach to voting changes from "Who do I want to represent me?" to "Who's best to vote for to keep out the candidate I dislike?" This form of negative voting distorts elections. Voters are confused about who is best to vote for to keep out candidates. It gives a lot of power to the media when working out which candidates to vote for. In the 2017 and 2019 elections, there was an increase in tactical voting, with 20% planning to vote tactically. This was an increase from 9% in the 2015 election.

FPTP has negative impacts on political parties and society:
1. FPTP only sometimes leads to good and fair government, working in the national interest. It can cause parties in government to ignore areas where they don't have MPs and only govern in the interest of their supporters. This has led to divisions and tensions between the regions and nations in the UK.

2. FPTP leads to short-sighted, confrontational politics. Politicians exaggerate their differences and constantly discredit political opponents instead of working together in the national interest to solve the country's problems.
3. It can lead to extreme politics. The failure to give extreme parties and their voters representation in parliament can lead to voters joining mainstream political parties and resulting in a radical faction gaining control, which we have seen in the UK with the Tory Party since 2019.
4. Most voters are entirely against the governments we get because most politically engaged people do not get a voice in elections. This can lead to disengagement from politics and low voter turnout.
5. FPTP is also vulnerable to 'gerrymandering', where the party in government changes the boundary lines of seats to give them an advantage at the next election. FPTP is based on hundreds of small geographical areas (seats) that can be modified, and the national popular vote is irrelevant.
6. Research shows that FPTP has a bias favouring right-wing governments, so they are in power 63-75% of the time. At the same time, countries with fairer proportional systems have progressive governments three-quarters of the time.
7. FPTP forces Labour to the right on issues such as immigration and climate change action. Most people support these issues, but these voters are piled up in vote mountains in primarily urban areas with only a third of seats. So Labour has to appeal to voters in the other two-thirds of seats with more right-wing views.[11]

How the Tories Benefit from FPTP

In the 2019 election, 16.2 million people voted for progressive political parties (Labour, Liberal Democrat, Green, SNP, Plaid Cymru), and only 13.9 million voted for parties on the right (Tories, Brexit Party, UKIP). But the Tories won an 80-seat majority because our undemocratic voting system helps them. Boris Johnson in 2019 only got 270,000 more votes than Theresa May in 2017, a 1.2% increase. But gained 47 seats and claimed this a landslide. Since 1945, 19 of the 20 elections have had the progressive vote outnumber the right-wing vote, but the Tories have won 12 elections and the progressives 8. The Tories know that most voters are to their left, so they must keep FPTP in place. Below are five ways the Tories benefit from FPTP.

1. Only one party on the right; the left vote is split between multiple parties
Through the last 123 years, the Tories have had little competition on the right of the political spectrum. The Tories have been able to assume they will get the right-wing vote so they can focus on the centre ground. This is not the case for Labour, and it has to fight for the left and centre-ground votes against other centre-left parties.

The left's vote is constantly split. In the first half of the 20th century, the Liberal Party and Labour Party competed for votes and went into government together. From 1945 to the 1970s, the Liberal Party got 1-5 million votes and 6-13 seats. Then, in 1981, four Labour MPs split from the party and formed the Social Democrat Party (SDP), and formed an alliance with the Liberal Party and won 23 seats in the 1983 election, 22 in the 1987 election on 7-8 million votes. Splitting the progressive vote helped Thatcher win three general elections on a share of the vote that would have lost general elections for most other postwar elections.

At the 1997 election, Labour and the Liberal Democrats worked together to beat the Tories with tactical voting. However, tactical voting declined for the 2010 and 2015 elections, splitting the left vote. The Scottish National Party had a very successful election in 2015, winning 56 in Scotland and taking seats from Labour and the Liberal Democrats. In recent elections, UKIP and the Brexit Party have been a potential threat to the Tories, but this has not materialised, and the Brexit Party stood down hundreds of candidates in the 2019 election in safe Tory seats.

Some Liberal voters are strongly anti-socialist, so they will vote

Tory to stop a Labour candidate and government. This was certainly the case during Corbyn's leadership of the Labour Party. Sadly, these voters fail to see that they generally have more in common with Labour policies than the Tories.[12]

2. The Tories' vote is distributed more efficiently
The Tories understand how to take advantage of FPTP by efficiently distributing votes across many seats, winning these seats by a few thousand votes. In 2019 Johnson only gained 270,000 more votes than May in 2017 but gained a large majority, whereas she had lost her majority. Of the 66 most marginal seats the Tories won in 2019, they each had a majority of 5,000 votes or less.

The Tories have a strong, loyal, stable base of voters between 20-30% of voters, which is spread efficiently across hundreds of seats. This allows the Tories to benefit disproportionately when they are popular and hang onto second place when they are unpopular without a serious threat from smaller parties. Historically, if they don't win an election, they are guaranteed second place, with roughly 200 seats, so they are in a good position to win next time.[13]

Research in countries that use FPTP shows that a feature of FPTP is to punish political parties with geographically concentrated support. This affects centre-left parties like Labour, which piles up voters in urban areas.

3. FPTP leads to voter disillusionment and low turnout, which benefits the Tories
The problems with FPTP include that it is unrepresentative, with millions of wasted votes and its generally negative impacts on society and politics, which result in disillusionment and disengagement with voting; and low turnout. Throughout the 20th century, turnout was always above 70%. But since 2001, voter turnout has dropped to 60-70%. This drop in turnout is among the young, ethnic minorities and people experiencing poverty, who are more likely to vote for Labour or other progressive parties. Older voters have always been more likely to vote and to vote Tory, and that trend has strengthened

in the 21st century. So the Tories target their policies to older voters. Labour and the other parties have to chase swing voters in marginals, which causes many young people, ethnic minorities, and people experiencing poverty not to bother voting because politics doesn't help them and 'nothing changes'. This helps the Tories keep winning.[14]

4. Seats are vulnerable to Gerrymandering through boundary changes
Boundary changes to parliamentary constituencies over the last 123 years have generally benefited the Tories. This is because the Tories are in power more so get to influence boundary changes to their advantage. Boundary changes in 1918 expanded the seats in the Tory voting Home Counties and disadvantaged the Liberal Party. With the formation of the Free Irish State in 1921, 80 Irish MPs were removed from the House of Commons. These MPs had opposed the Tories, so removing them increased the Tories' balance of power in parliament. Boundary changes just before the 1950 election are believed to have benefited the Tories by 25 seats, helping reduce Labour's majority from 146 in 1945 to 6 in 1950. Boundary changes in 1974 cost Labour 30 seats and in 1983, another 30 seats. Seats decreased in the north and increased in southern counties and suburban areas.[15]

5. Bias in the electoral system
Since the Second World War, the bias in the electoral system has fluctuated between the Tories and Labour. In the 1950s, the bias was against Labour, so the Tories benefited. There was little bias in the 1964 election, but in the 1966 and 1979 elections, the bias was against the Tories. The 1980s saw a bias against Labour, and the 1992 election had a bias against the Tories. The 1997 election saw bias against Labour. By 2010, the Tories had a slight advantage from the electoral system. The Tories increasingly benefited from the electoral system through the 2010s. In 2017, on average, a Tory MP was elected with 43,000 votes and Labour 49,000. This became extreme for the 2019 election, with a significant bias for the Tories. If the Tories and Labour had an equal share of the vote nationally at the

next election, the Tories would have had 23 more seats, which means that a Tory MP was elected with 38,000 votes and Labour 50,000.[16]

2

OVERVIEW OF TORY SUCCESS SINCE 1900

This chapter gives a historical overview of the Tories' success since 1900. If you don't want a history lesson, skip to the next chapter. Between 1900 and 2023, there have been 31 general elections, and the Tories have won 17 of them. The Liberals won 4 elections in the early twentieth century, and Labour won 10. This has meant that during those 123 years, the Tories have been in government 81 years, the Liberals governing on their own for just 6 years, and the Labour Party has been in government for a total of 38 years. The Tories have held power alone, sometimes in coalition with the Liberals and National Labour. They generally dominated the coalitions they were part of and habitually undermined or absorbed their coalition partners.[1]

During this period, the Tories had only had three intervals when they were out of office for more than six years: 1905-15, 1945-51, and 1997-2010. Mostly, when the Tories lose power, they are back in office at the next election, or they regain seats at the next election to set them up to retake power at the election after that. In each period of Tory opposition, the party changed its political programme to broaden the party's appeal. Many of these times in opposition have seen the party innovate how the party organisation operates.[2] For the rest of the chapter, I have summarised the Tory Party's success during the last 123 years, broken into eight periods.

Transition 1900-23

The 20th century is called the 'conservative century', but it didn't start well for the Tories. They were in government from 1900 to 1906 but failed to implement popular policy over pensions and trade union legislation. This resulted in them losing the 1906 election and failing to win a general election on their own until 1922, and they did not form a confident government until 1924. The liberals held office from 1906-14. They introduced much-needed reforms such as pensions, free school meals, medical inspections for children, health insurance for workers, support to help the unemployed find work, and a minimum wage. During this time, the Tories worked to block these reforms, modernised the Tory Party's organisation and experimented with policy.

The Tories returned to government in 1915 as junior partners under Liberal leader Asquith. The Liberals split in late 1916, with Lloyd George taking over as Prime Minister and the Tories becoming dominant partners in this coalition government. The Tories and Liberals stood on a joint ticket for the 1918 election and formed another coalition government. The Tories won 382 parliamentary seats so that they could have formed a government independently. However, they played it safe as they were concerned about threats from changes to the voting system (universal suffrage), trade union unrest, the Communist revolution in Russia, and the Labour Party, which had won fourteen by-elections between 1918–22.

Pressure within the Tory Party to end the coalition with the liberals increased in 1921, and in late 1922 Tory MPs voted to end the alliance. Liberal Prime Minister Lloyd George resigned, and a general election was called, in which the Tories got an 88-seat majority. Tory Prime Minister Bonar Law failed to lead effectively and had health problems, so he stepped down in 1923 to be replaced by Baldwin. Baldwin advocated protectionism (restricting imports from other countries), a change in Tory government policy, so the Tories called a general election in 1923. The Tories got the most seats but not enough to form a majority government. Baldwin rejected forming an anti-

Labour government, and Labour formed a minority government under Ramsay MacDonald.

This period saw the Tories focus on resisting Liberal reforms and then working to weaken the Labour Party. However, the Tories benefitted from superior organisation, wealthy backers, an appeal to women, the perception of a national party and credibility to govern.

The Dominance Of Baldwinian Consensus 1924–40

The Tories won significantly in 1924 due to an appealing policy platform and the Labour Party and Liberals lacking credibility. The Tories had tried reactionary and protectionist policies at the start of the century, which had not proved popular. So Baldwin adapted and introduced pragmatic and selective state interventions in the economy and social policy. Four significant achievements were: a pension for widows and injured workers; housing and slum clearance; moderate handling of trade unions to reduce militancy and avoid a severe social conflict; and further electoral reform, bringing women's voting age to 21, the same as men. Other policies included reorganising the coal and cotton industries to make them more efficient, setting up the Central Electricity Board and national grid, establishing the BBC as a public corporation, and reorganising local government rates to help agriculture and industry so they could take on more workers. This all resulted in a decrease in unemployment. However, a significant economic mistake was made in returning Britain to the Gold Standard in 1925, resulting in exports becoming overpriced and increased interest rates.

At the 1929 general election, the Labour Party won the most seats without a majority, forming a minority government under Prime Minister MacDonald. This was terrible timing for Labour, with the Great Depression hitting the same year. The Labour cabinet was divided on how to deal with the economic crisis. To resolve the issue, MPs from different parties formed a new Labour National government in 1931 to work together to tackle the economic crisis caused by the Great Depression. Most Labour MPs refused to serve in this government, so the cabinet comprised mostly Tory MPs and a few Labour and Liberal MPs.

At the 1931 general election, the Labour Party suffered heavy losses, only winning 52 seats, while the Tories won 470. The Labour national government continued from 1931-35, with MacDonald as Prime Minister, but the Tories held most key cabinet positions. Moderate economic interventions and social reforms continued under the Labour National government. The 1935 general election resulted in a Tory National government forming with Baldwin as Prime Minister. It contained Liberal and Labour MPs in the cabinet. In 1937, Neville Chamberlain replaced Baldwin as Prime Minister.

Seven reasons the Tories were so successful from 1924-40:

1. The leadership by Baldwin, who voters saw as decent, trustworthy and popular. The Liberal and Labour opposition leaders were not particularly popular;
2. The Tories offered mild reforms, stability, patriotism, and order in an unstable world. However, the opposition could not compete, Labour's programme was seen as too radical by many, and the Liberals saw their policies stolen by the Labour Party;
3. The Tory Party's organisation and finances were better than the opposition. The Tories formalised the Shadow Cabinet reformed local constituencies; improved communication within the party, education work and propaganda; and strengthened fundraising from members and supporters;
4. Party membership increased, which included many women who volunteered for the party;
5. The Tories benefited from divisions between the Liberals and Labour during this period. The Liberals split in 1916 and Labour in 1931;
6. The electoral circumstances helped the Tories. Boundary changes in 1918 benefited the Tories, to the Liberals' disadvantage. Following the formation of the Republic of Ireland in 1920, eighty anti-Tory Irish Nationalist MPs left the House of Commons. The Northern Ireland MPs that

remained mainly supported the Tories;
7. On social class, the Tories had the backing of the wealthy and influential, bringing money and expertise to the Tory cause. Also, during this period, the Tories attracted more working-class votes than Labour. This is attributed to many of the working-class desiring stability and status and their support for patriotism and national unity.

Transition In War And Reconstruction 1940–51

The Tory National government ended in 1940 and was replaced by a cross-party coalition government (with Tory, Labour and independent MPs) for the war years. Much to the surprise of the Tories, they were heavily defeated at the 1945 general election, with a Labour majority government elected under Prime Minister Attlee. The electorate thought the Labour reconstruction programme and welfare reform programme looked more appealing and credible. The Tories were also blamed for not doing more over interwar unemployment and Chamberlin's lack of action to tackle Hitler before the Second World War started.

The Attlee government had five main planks: the mixed economy (some nationalisation), full employment, harmony with the trade unions, a commitment to equality, and the welfare state. These went on to form the basis of the post-war consensus that the Tories adopted.

The Tory Party's organisation had been neglected during the war, and by 1948 was made fit for purpose again. By 1951, Tory Party membership reached 2.8 million, an invaluable resource at election time. Candidate selection was reformed, and political education was prioritised. The policy was updated to respond to the electorate's shift to the left. There was a focus on convincing voters that the Tories' progressive policy on social reforms, a mixed economy and full employment were credible.

The 1950 general election saw the Labour majority reduced to 6. Attlee called another election in 1951 to increase his number of MPs, but Labour lost. This put the Tories back in government, with Churchill as Prime Minister again. The Tories' ability to adapt in opposition proved highly effective.

Postwar Conservative Domination 1951–64

This 13-year period of Tory dominance saw a weak challenge from the opposition, with general elections in 1955 and 1959 seeing the Tories increase their majority each time.

Churchill led a moderate government backed by a united party. Spending on health, education and housing increased. By 1954, the Tories were building 300,000 houses a year. However, Churchill's health deteriorated, and he retired in 1955 to be replaced by Anthony Eden, who won the general election that year.

The Eden government struggled with economic problems. Eden's ill health and temperament meant he was not up to the job, plus he presided over the disaster of the Suez crisis. Eden resigned in 1957 and was replaced by Harold MacMillan. The Suez crisis had deeply divided the Tory Party. MacMillan's charm and reassurance and the party's desire to put the Suez crisis behind them brought the Tory Party together. In 1958, the cabinet strongly desired to make government spending cuts. These were resisted by MacMillan, who was concerned about increases in unemployment that might follow and therefore damage future election success. He was accused of risking inflation by not cutting spending. By 1959, the economy was improving, so the Tories called a general election and won a surprisingly large majority.

The Tories had an excellent first year but went downhill after that. MacMillan looked tired and outdated compared to other world leaders like US President Kennedy. Other countries, such as France and Germany, were understood to be doing better than Britain. New entertainment and media made the establishment look laughable. The economy started to struggle, strikes increased, and the Tories lost a critical by-election. Macmillan replaced 5 senior cabinet members, but this looked desperate. MacMillan introduced three new policies:

increased self-government in the British colonies, further planning and government involvement in the economy to regenerate industry, and he applied for Britain to join the European Economic Community (EEC).

By 1963, the Tories were mired in the Profumo scandal; a Tory cabinet minister was having an affair with a woman who was also sleeping with a Soviet spy. MacMillan resigned due to ill health. A former House of Lords member, Sir Alec Douglas-Home, took over. He struggled under a disunited party and made little impact on the policy front.

Eight factors can be identified for the success of the Tories from 1951-64.

1. Leadership, all three leaders were popular at each general election. And the Labour Party's leaders, Attlee and Gaitskell, did not have the same widespread appeal;
2. Highly effective party organisation continued from the pre-war period of success;
3. The Tories had greater financial resources, so they outspent Labour nationally and locally;
4. The Tories offered an appealing government programme, having moved towards Labour on the economy and social policy. The Tories could also celebrate their successful record in government;
5. Changes to the electoral arrangement, including boundary changes and the introduction of postal voting, helped the Tories;
6. The Tory Party unity was solid for the three 1950s elections, with the Labour Party struggling to stay united;
7. Changing voting preferences based on social class helped the Tories. Many middle-class voters switched to Labour in 1945 and back to the Tories in the 1950s. However, the Tories continued to be supported by the wealthy and influential. In addition, the working-class vote was still more significant than the middle class, and new policies attracted working-class voters to the Tories, such as home ownership

and new towns;
8. This period saw a healthy economy, and the Tories took the credit. There is MacMillan's famous line "Never had it so good" from 1957. This resulted in general rising prosperity and an increase in consumer items, giving the perception of government competence. This also combined with economic growth, allowing government spending to increase without significant tax increases.

A Change Of Direction 1964–79

Labour won the 1964 general election with a small majority, and Harold Wilson became Prime Minister. Wilson was a more popular leader than former Tory Prime Minister Douglas-Home. The Tory Party organisation was struggling by 1964. Labour offered a more appealing government programme based on confident economic and industrial policies. The Labour Party was also united for the 1964 election, with Douglas-Home struggling with disunity, with only nine months between taking over as Prime Minister and the general election. Another significant factor was the general sense that the British economy was less competitive than Germany and Japan.

The new Tory Party leader was Edward Heath, taking over in 1965. The Party undertook a huge policy review but still wasn't ready for the 1966 general election when Labour increased its majority.

Heath generally favoured continuing the post-war economic policies of full employment and welfare reforms. The Tories under Health won the 1970 general election and introduced laws to restrict the unions instead of working in partnership with them. The Tory Manifesto proposed less government intervention in the economy and lowered taxes and public spending in the first year. By 1972 unemployment was rising nearly to 1 million, combined with extreme union militancy. Health buckled and introduced interventionist policies to bail out failing large businesses. He negotiated with the unions and introduced statutory income policies to keep control of inflation, breaking election manifesto promises. Government spending dramatically increased, and unemployment decreased. Health took Britain into the EEC in 1973. A global financial and oil crisis hit in 1973, resulting in high inflation in Britain.

The Tories lost the two general elections in 1974, with Labour elected and Harold Wilson returning as Prime Minister. However, labour formed a minority government at the first election, so Wilson called a second election to get a majority, which he achieved but only a majority of 3. The Tory Party elected Margret Thatcher as their leader in 1975, and she carefully noted Heath's difficulties and public opinion when developing policy.

Thatcherism's Conservative Dominance 1979–97

The Tories were elected in 1979, and Thatcher became Prime Minister. What came to be known as Thatcherism reduced the role of the state and government in the economy and prioritised the freedom of the individual. Thatcher deregulated the financial industry and implemented 'monetarism', an economic policy to control the money supply to reduce inflation. Thatcher achieved this by selective tax cuts and rises, increasing interest rates, privatising national industries and public services, cutting public spending and reducing the size of the welfare state. These ideas came from outside the Conservative Party, from Chicago-based economists and what later became known as neoliberals.

Thatcher's policies resulted in significant unemployment (3 million), high inflation and a deep decline in manufacturing output. Even so, Thatcher led the Tories to winning the 1983 and 1987 general elections with large majorities. The Falklands War in 1982 is seen as ensuring Thatcher won the 1983 election, as she struggled in the opinion polls before this. The labour movement militancy that caused problems for the previous Labour government was crushed during the 1984-5 miners' strike and through anti-union legislation. By the late 1980s, Thatcher claimed she had reversed Britain's economic decline to produce an 'economic miracle' in her words. Productivity and economic growth had increased in the south but unevenly across the country and sectors, so the north suffered.

Thatcher was removed from office by her MPs in 1990. A confidence vote in her leadership was held, which she failed to win convincingly, so she resigned. Criticism of her leadership had increased in the late 1980s, with economic problems, by-election losses, her anti-EU position and the disastrous introduction of the community charge (poll tax), which resulted in several cabinet ministers resigning. As a result, many in the party believed she would not win the next general election.

Four factors can be identified for the Tories' dominance from 1979-90.

1. A key factor was the lack of credibility of the Labour Party to hold office. The leftwing leader Michael Foot led the Labour Party to loss in 1983. He was replaced by Neil Kinnock, who lost the 1987 and then 1992 general elections. The 'union excess' of the 'winter of discontent' in 1978-9 and the miners' strike from 1984-5 were linked to the Labour Party in the electorate's mind;
2. A divided opposition, the Social Democratic Party and Liberals split the anti-Tory vote in 1983 and 1987, giving Thatcher an easier ride and resulting in Tory majorities of over 100 seats in those general elections;
3. On social class, an increase in home and company shares ownership solidified Tory support, with 43% of skilled workers voting Tory in 1987;
4. Thatcher did not win elections because she converted a majority of voters to her politics or because she was popular. Instead, her government delivered enough tangible benefits to voters in the correct places. Opinion polls showed that Thatcherism never inspired the majority of the electorate.[3]

Major replaced Thatcher in 1990. He removed the poll tax and replaced it with Council Tax. Major introduced the Citizen's Charter to make public services more accountable and user-focused. Also, in 1991 he sent the armed forces into the first Iraq war. The Tories fought the 1992 election during a recession but maintained the perception of economic competence by claiming they were the party of low taxes. Labour, by comparison, was seen as socialist, incompetent and would increase taxation and spending. The Tories got their highest number of votes ever, 14 million, and lost 40 seats but kept a small majority.

Major presided over an economic crisis in September 1992, known as 'Black Wednesday', when the Tories withdrew the pound from the European Exchange Rate Mechanism (ERM). The Tories had been slightly ahead in the opinion polls before this. However, following the ERM disaster, the Tories were at least ten points behind Labour until they lost the 1997 general election.

Major continued many of Thatcher's policies and came to be seen as incompetent and harsh. The railways and coal pits were privatised. Major's seven years saw significant disunity in the party over Europe. Major launched the 'Back to Basics' campaign to promote family values and social conservatism. It was followed by a series of Tory MP sex and financial scandals, so the campaign became a joke. Donations to the Tory Party dried up, and the party went into debt. Membership numbers declined, with those who remained being older. The Tories became very focused on Britain's relationship with the EU, but the public was more concerned about domestic issues. Most of the right-wing newspapers turned on Major by 1997.

New Labour 1997-2010

The 1997 general election saw the Labour Party win a large majority and end 18 years of Tory rule, with Tony Blair succeeding Major as Prime Minister. Five factors resulted in the Labour Party's victory.

1. The Labour Party under Blair was a strong opposition, with a charismatic leader, a strong policy offer, a united party, and an effective party operation that was well funded and focused on the centre ground, making it popular with voters;
2. The Tories were seen as incompetent at governing and managing the economy;

3. The Tories were disunited during the 1990s over Europe, which fed into them being seen as unfit to govern;
4. The right-wing media turned on them throughout the 1990s and switched support to the Labour Party;
5. This all fed into a general feeling in Britain that it was 'time for change'.

Hague was elected leader of the Tories in 1997. He was unpopular with voters and lacked authority. The Tories failed to assess why they lost the 1997 election effectively, so they continued with Thatcherite policies such as tax cuts, a smaller state and anti-EU policies. But the public wanted modest tax increases to increase spending on public services. The Tory 2001 election campaign lacked discipline and was disunited. It failed to appeal to the centre ground, leaving it open to Labour.

Following the 2001 election defeat, Hague resigned, and Duncan Smith was elected leader, which was a disaster as he was not up to the job. The Tories replaced him with Michael Howard in 2003 to recover some sense of competence. Howard was keen to move to the centre ground and modernise the party but came with right-wing baggage from his years in the Thatcher and Major governments. The Tories also lost the 2005 election. They ran a disciplined campaign that focused on cutting waste, tax cuts, spending increases, immigration limits, improving poorly managed hospitals, and reducing high crime rates. However, the public was unconvinced, and although Blair was no longer popular, Labour won this election with a reduced majority.

Cameron was elected leader of the Tory Party in 2005 and set about modernising the party and moving back to the centre ground on issues such as environment, civil liberties, education, and localism. His liberal Toryism was designed to appeal to women, many of whom had deserted the party for New Labour. Labour leader Blair stood down in 2007 to allow Gordon Brown to replace him. At the 2010 election, Cameron and the Tories gained seats but not a majority. They negotiated with the Liberal Democrats for the Coalition Government.

THE TORY WINNING MACHINE

Five factors led to the Tories winning the most parliamentary seats and forming the Coalition Government in 2010.
1. Cameron was a reasonably charismatic leader with a united, modernised Tory party;
2. The Tories ran one of the best-prepared, well-funded, most technically advanced campaigns ever launched by a British political party;
3. Brown and Labour ran a poor campaign;
4. Brown's mistakes over calling a general election in 2008 and perceived economic and governing incompetence didn't compare well with Cameron and the Tories;
5. Cameron had the support of the right-wing media.

Three factors influenced why the Tories didn't win a majority in 2010.
1. Leadership, although many voters were fed up with Brown and were open to voting for Cameron, they had doubts about the Tory Party and if it could be trusted in a recession to improve the economy, protect public services and the needs of ordinary people over the wealthy;
2. The Tories only had about 200 seats going into the election and would need to gain about 120 extra seats to form a majority government. The Tories have never won this many seats in an election before. Cameron gained 96 seats, which was a historical achievement;
3. Third, post-election polling showed that Tories under Cameron failed to modernise and move to the centre ground enough for many voters.[4]

The Ruinous Tories Are Back 2010-2023

Labour's bailout of the banks in response to the 2008 financial crisis created a large government economic deficit. The Tories cunningly blamed the crisis on Labour, claiming it could not manage the economy competently. Cameron and the Coalition government introduced austerity through public sector cuts, which they claimed would reduce the deficit. They failed to do this and instead rolled back the welfare state through 'welfare reform' with more NHS privatisation; school privatisation by introducing academy schools; privatised Royal Mail; made claiming benefits more difficult. At the 2015 election, the Tories achieved an unexpected victory, gaining a majority of 12, and could govern without being in coalition with the Liberal Democrats.

Nine factors led to the Tories winning a majority government in 2015

1. Leadership, many swing voters preferred David Cameron to the prospect of Labour's Ed Miliband as Prime Minister in terms of strength, competence and being good in a crisis;
2. The Labour offer to voters wasn't inclusive and appealing enough regarding economic growth, a more balanced economy and presenting an aspirational and hopeful vision for the country;
3. The Labour Party had not overcome the public's perception that their economic incompetence had caused the 2008 financial crisis. The Tories had a very effective negative narrative that Labour's economic incompetence and high spending had caused the crisis;
4. The Liberal Democrats' reputation was heavily damaged for being part of the Coalition government, so they went from 57 to 8 MPs. The Tories benefited heavily from this Liberal Democrat collapse in support, with Liberal Democrat voters not voting or switching to other parties;
5. The UK Independence Party (UKIP) got 3.8 million votes, and although they took many votes from the Tories, they

hurt Labour more. Due to the geographical spread of UKIP votes, they prevented Labour from taking or holding onto key marginal seats;
6. Voters were concerned about another hung parliament and preferred the prospect of a Tory-Liberal Democrat coalition to a Labour-Scottish National Party (SNP) coalition government;
7. The opinion polls before the election showed another hung parliament, resulting in a significant focus on a potential Labour-SNP coalition government. If the polls had been more accurate, there would have been more focus on the impact of Tory cuts on welfare and public services. This likely took the result from being a hung parliament to a Tory majority;
8. The Tories' ground game resulted in a more efficient distribution of votes than in previous elections. They lost votes in safe seats and gained them in marginal seats, resulting in the Tories taking twice as many seats from the Liberal Democrats as Labour and eight from Labour;
9. The Tories did well amongst certain demographic groups – the middle class and over-55s that voted in high numbers.[5]

A key Tory manifesto commitment was to hold a referendum on the UK membership of the EU. The referendum took place in 2016, and Cameron supported the UK staying in the EU. Following the slim win for the leave campaign, Cameron resigned as Prime Minister and was replaced by Theresa May. May was Prime Minister for 3 years, and this time was dominated by difficult negotiations with the EU for a Brexit withdrawal agreement. Her government combined a one-nation public face with authoritarianism and a more interventionist approach to economics.[6] May called a snap general election for June 2017 to increase the number of Tory MPs and strengthen her position to get a Brexit agreement. The Tories' election campaign was a disaster. May lost her majority in parliament and only continued as Prime Minister leading a minority government with the support of

Northern Ireland's Democratic Unionist Party (DUP). May failed to get a Brexit agreement through parliament and resigned following terrible results in the May 2019 local elections. Boris Johnson replaced her in July 2019.[7]

Johnson's premiership was dominated by Brexit, the Covid-19 pandemic, the Russian invasion of Ukraine in 2022, rising inflation and a cost of living crisis. He also presided over several scandals, and the most well known was Partygate, where he received a police fine for attending parties in Downing Street when the country was in lockdown to stop the spread of the Covid virus. Johnson called a snap general election for December 2019 and won a large majority, promising to 'Get Brexit Done' and 'Levelling-up' to tackle regional inequality. The Tories also made modest spending commitments regarding the NHS, extra police officers and nurses. The Tories had a charismatic leader and ran an effective and disciplined campaign against Labour leader Jeremy Corbyn, who was unpopular with swing voters.

Truss replaced Johnson in September 2022. Truss's chancellor quickly made an economic announcement, the famous 'mini-budget' of unfunded tax cuts that spooked the markets and caused an economic crisis. Truss sacked her chancellor and resigned soon after to become the shortest-serving UK Prime Minister. Truss was replaced by Sunak, who has brought some stability to UK politics but leads a disunited Tory Party. His chancellor announced an austerity budget in late 2022 to reassure the markets and recover some of the reputation lost over economic competence for the Tories that was lost during the Truss period. The 2023 local elections were a disaster for the Tories, losing over 1,000 Councillors.

PART 2:

THE TORY PARTY'S MAIN OBJECTIVE IS WINNING GENERAL ELECTIONS AND POWER

Due to the Tory Party's long history and success, it is seen as the most successful political party in the world. The party's main objective is winning general elections and holding onto power. The Tory Party is organised and operates in several ways to help achieve this. First, it selects leaders that are most likely to win general elections. Second, Tory party MPs and members know that the party has to stay united to keep winning. Third, the Tories are adaptable and pragmatic. Fourth, the Tories are quick to regain power following a defeat. Fifth, the Tories consistently have an effective party organisation nationally, regionally and locally. Finally, the Tories are Britain's best-resourced and funded political party.

Why do the Tories want to win elections and form the government? They are motivated to be in power to maintain the social order and to stop Labour from forming governments that threaten this goal. Specifically, the Tories want to maintain the power and legitimacy of the elite and the wealthy and prevent the redistribution of wealth. They do this by using their time in government to force their values and interests on society and blocking their opponents, Labour, from promoting their values in government.[1]

3

SELECT LEADERS MOST LIKELY TO WIN GENERAL ELECTIONS

Between 1900 and 2023, the Tory party had 20 leaders, and 17 became Prime Minister. The three that didn't make it were during the New Labour years. That is quite an achievement. Tory MPs and the Conservative Party's membership's main criteria for selecting their leader is based on which candidate has the strongest chance of winning the next general election. There are, of course, exceptions, but the Tories are much more consistent at this than the Labour Party.

The Tory Party is a top-down hierarchical organisation. The leader and his inner circle have full control of strategy and policy. When a leader is replaced, the new leader removes the previous personnel and replaces them with their people. The Cabinet or Shadow Cabinet have limited input. They will meet to agree on the leader's plans and provide input, but the leader has the final say on everything.[1]

What Makes A Successful Tory Leader And Prime Minister?

What do we mean by successful? For the Tory Party, a successful leader wins general elections and keeps winning them. In addition, whether a Tory leader works in the country's interests, is popular and leaves a legacy, these things are desirable but of secondary importance.

Tory Party leaders need to be ambitious, make sacrifices in their personal life, work hard, and be thick-skinned to the criticism of rivals. The desire for power is a hugely powerful force that is required to make it to the top. Once they reach the top successful Tory leaders need to stay in touch with colleagues and the broader party to maintain their position.[2]

Tory Party leaders that have lasted have put the health and unity of the party before the government and country. They have left a legacy such as Bonar Law, Macmillan and Thatcher. Those that wanted to use the Tory Party to become Prime Minister for its own sake and weren't concerned with the party had problems. These include Neville Chamberlain, Churchill, Health, Cameron, Johnson and Truss.[3]

Anthony Seldon identifies ten rules that Prime Ministers must follow if they are to be successful. One, is their support staff, who must be loyal, competent and stable to manage government policy and presentation. Two, they need an effective relationship with their chancellor to manage the economy well. Three, they must be someone that the country can relate to. Four, they must have one policy or issue they make their own, which will be their legacy. Five, successful Prime Ministers must manage their time effectively. Six, they must manage their ministerial team well. Seven, they must not be 'media-driven' and stick to their strategy. Eight, they must respond appropriately to big events. Nine, must run effective government operations, avoiding regular reshuffles and relaunches. Ten, they must act with decorum and behave like they are representing the nation.[4]

Tory Party Leaders Generally Have Broad Appeal

Tory Party leaders are generally more popular and have wider appeal than Labour leaders. This allows the Tories to widen their appeal and build strong and durable voter coalitions. Another key aspect is that many Tory leaders have relatable personalities, which means they can connect with voters in a way that causes voters to forget that the Tories represent the interests of the wealthy. Most Tory Party leaders are able to extend beyond their core vote, attracting a large number of working-class voters.[5] MacMillan and Thatcher appealed to aspirational working-class voters. Tory leaders must also not alienate traditional conservatives that see the Tory Party as there to look after their interests.

When the party has been struggling, the leaders have set it in a new direction by reading the changing context. Thatcher repaired the party after Heath's difficult years. Cameron rebranded the party to appeal to middle-class and pro-Europe voters, and Johnson with get Brexit done, moving on from austerity to levelling up.[6] New Tory Prime Ministers have shown an ability to reform the party while in government, going on to win the next general election. This took place in the 1950s and 2010s. The Tory Party have been very effective at changing leaders, taking advantage of a new face to present the administration as a fresh start and putting a problematic former leader behind them in voters' minds. New Tory leaders with a new strategy are Bonar Law, Thatcher, Duncan Smith, Johnson, and Sunak. Those with different outlooks and backgrounds are Bonar Law, Heath, Thatcher, and Major. And from the next generation were Heath, Hague and Cameron.[7]

The 1963 Tory leadership election was the last where the party leadership and MPs selected the leader behind closed doors. The aristocrat Bonar Law was selected and lost the 1964 general election. Leadership elections were introduced at this point to broaden the appeal of future leaders. The following three leaders, Heath, Thatcher and Major, came from middle-class backgrounds, educated in state schools. Cameron has taken credit for diversifying the Tory Party from 2005, resulting in the 2022 Tory leadership candidates being diverse.

Remove Failing Leaders Quickly

The Tory Party leader is almost a dictator when they are ahead in opinion polls and winning elections. But they depend on the support of Tory MPs and the electorate. When this belief in the leader goes, their power and authority go with it. Examples are Churchill being voted out in the 1945 general election or Thatcher being removed by Tory MPs in 1990. Because the Tory Party's main objective is winning elections, if it looks likely that the party will lose the next election, then the leader is vulnerable. Baldwin was under huge pressure to step down in 1911; Chamberlain was forced out in 1940; Churchill went against his will in 1955; Eden and Macmillan were struggling and had health problems which disguised their departures in 1957 and 1963, respectively; Health was ejected in 1975, Thatcher in 1990 and Johnson and Truss in 2022.[8]

The Tory Party's ruthlessness in removing leaders they think unlikely to win the next general election has increased in the last forty years. Thatcher was the first Tory leader that was also Prime Minister to be challenged and removed from office.[9] Since then, most Tory Prime Ministers have been challenged by their party, Major in 1995, May in 2018, and Johnson and Truss in 2022. Major limped on to lose the 1997 general election; May stepped down in 2019, and Truss stepped down in 2022. Cameron managed to avoid this by resigning after the Brexit vote in 2016.

One of the advantages of being a hierarchical organisation is that they can pick and remove leaders quicker than the Labour Party. The party picks leaders, and if they aren't up to the job, they remove them quickly. Whereas the Labour Party has a pattern of electing leaders unlikely to win general elections and finds it hard to remove them. The weakness of the Tories' membership over party matters makes it easier for the parliamentary party to remove unsuitable leaders, as seen in 2022.[10]

4

STAYING UNITED IN PUBLIC ABOVE ALL ELSE

Tories know they must project a sense of cohesion, unity and purpose to voters to keep winning general elections. A disunited political party is well understood as a way to lose elections. Disunity is a constant problem for the Labour Party. It's not that the Tory Party is more united than Labour; it's just that Tory MPs are much better at hiding internal conflict and maintaining party and message discipline. They know the party must look buoyant and confident to voters.

Any disunity in the Tory Party from rivalries and factions is generally visible to the party leadership and parliamentary party, and it is kept hidden so as not to damage the party's reputation nationally. As a result, the Tory Party successfully holds the different traditions and fractions together regionally and nationally. Membership numbers have dropped significantly since the 1950s, but the party has remained stable and cohesive.[1]

In the 20th century, there were only two periods when there were open splits in the Tory Party. The first was from 1906-11 over protectionism and tariff reform (import controls). The second was in the 1990s over Europe. The 2016 Brexit referendum could have easily split the Tory Party, but May and Johnson managed to navigate this to keep the party together. It looks unlikely that Sunak can hold the divided Tory Party together and win the next election.

Leaders Prioritise Party Unity

The Tory Party's biggest split was in 1846 over the repeal of the Corn Laws. The Corn Laws were introduced in 1815 to restrict the trade of imported foods such as wheat, oats and barley, known as corn. This was to maintain high corn prices to benefit domestic producers, especially landowners. This resulted in rising food prices and living costs for ordinary people, combined with the slow growth of the British economy, especially in the manufacturing sector. Following two years of the Great Famine in Ireland (1845-52) and increasing opposition in urban areas, the Tory Prime Minister Peel moved to repeal the laws. However, the Tory Party split on these issues, and Peel needed the opposition Whigs' support to continue. This split resulted in the Tory Party being unable to win a parliamentary majority for nearly 30 years. The Tories learnt an important lesson: Tory leaders must maintain party unity. This is a key factor in understanding the party's behaviour, explains the party's many U-Turns, and drives how the party operates – pragmatism over any ideological consistency.[2] Tories leaders effectively manage the factions inside the party to present the party as electable to voters.

When Thatcher was elected in 1975, she had not established her authority over the party. She had to go to great lengths to accommodate her critics in the Shadow Cabinet. To manage the moderates, known as the 'wets', she kept secret her radical plans for the economy and trade union reform to maintain the public appearance of party unity to ensure success at the next general election.[3]

In 2005, David Cameron was elected leader of the Tory Party after 7 years in opposition. Europe had been causing Tory Party disunity since the 1990s. To resolve this, Cameron made a small concession to the Eurosceptics by withdrawing the Tory Party from the European People's Party, a grouping of centre-right parties in the EU parliament. He then played for time and told the party to 'stop banging on about Europe'. By the mid-2010s, the Tories had lost millions of votes to UKIP, so Cameron made a major concession for the 2015 general election. He committed to a referendum on Europe to hold the party together. He did not expect the Tories to win a majority and, therefore, to have to go through with the referendum. He campaigned to remain in the EU and did not expect to lose that either. But all this worked to keep the Tory Party together, and they came out of the Brexit referendum in a stronger position than any other party.[4]

Cameron resigned, and Theresa May was elected Tory Party leader and Prime Minister. Throughout 2017 she managed to unite Tory MPs behind her position on leaving the EU. Tory MPs that wanted to remain in the EU had no choice but to follow the new Brexit consensus.[5] The Brexiteers in the Tory Party threatened to split the party if the UK did not leave the EU. May had a choice, see the country destroyed or the Tory Party destroyed. She chose to save her party (and her job as Prime Minister, although this didn't work out). Boris Johnson then had to take the UK out of the EU, Customs Union and Single Market to maintain the support of the Tory Brexiteers to keep the party together and to stay on as Prime Minister.[6]

Loyalty To The Leader

The Tory parliamentary party is generally loyal and respects the authority of its leaders. This has been crucial when quick policy direction changes are needed to maintain public support to win future elections. As a result, it is rare for Tory MPs to leave the party and join other parties. This is more common for Labour and the liberals.

The Tory Party membership and local constituencies are also consistently loyal and deferential to the leadership. This is prioritised over ideology, principle and procedure, especially compared to the Labour Party.[7] The weakness of the Tory Party's membership helps with party unity. It generally avoids the public factional infighting that weakens the Labour Party and reduces Tory members proposing unrealistic policies in public.[8]

During the post-war period of Tory dominance, Churchill and MacMillan moved the party to the left on economic policy to adapt to the Keynesian interventionist consensus. There was resistance from those in the party that wanted to increase public spending cuts, but this was managed internally. During the 1980s, moderate Tory MPs did not agree with Thatcher's economic policy direction, but this did not become an issue because they agreed with the government's general strategic direction. Thatcher also had significant authority due to her success at winning general elections. In 2005, Cameron was given a lot of latitude to modernise the Tory Party to regain power, even though many in the party didn't personally support Cameron or his policies. In 2019, Johnson was elected leader, even though most Tory MPs weren't confident in his competence to govern or suitability as Prime Minister because they recognised he was the best person to win the next general election.[9]

Party Unity And Leadership Elections

The main concern of the Tory Party during leadership elections is to avoid splitting the party. Tories ideally want a new leader most likely to unite the party and win the next general election. This was helped up to 1963 by the informal way the party selected its next leader. A formal leadership election was introduced in 1965, and then the rules were adjusted in 1975 and 1991 to meet these aims.

Between 1900 and 2023, there have been 20 leadership changes. For 7 of these, the replacement leader was a clear choice and mostly accepted by the party, even if not generally desired. In 13 of the changes, there was some form of leadership contest. Leaders that were picked to unite the party were Bonar Law in 1911, Baldwin in 1923, Macmillan in 1957, and Home in 1963. Since the introduction of the leadership election, most have had the support of the parliamentary party and membership. The winning candidates' rivals withdrew before the final ballot for the 1965, 1990, 2017, and 2022 leadership elections. In 1975, 1990, and 2003 the process was used to remove Tory leaders who no longer had MPs' support. Backbench Tory MPs have had the most influence on selecting leaders than the party leadership inner circle and, therefore, more influence over the party's direction.[10]

The Tory Party generally runs leadership elections with little fuss and damage to the party so they can move on quickly once there is a winner. Through the last 123 years, unsuccessful leadership candidates were prepared to accept posts in the Shadow Cabinet so the party could focus on winning the next election. Interestingly, the summer 2022 leadership election is an exception to this, with several highly damaging TV debates with candidates attacking each other and the Tory Party's record in government. This is combined with Truss's rival Sunak refusing to serve in Truss's cabinet and Truss removing all his supporters from the government.

The Tory Party are effective at moving on from leadership elections and uniting behind the new leader. Again many in the party may not be happy with the new leader but either accept them because they are seen as an election winner or because the party understands the importance of projecting unity to voters. Labour is very poor at this and can remain divided for years after selecting a new leader, such as with Corbyn. Following the summer 2022 leadership election, Michael Gove, a bitter rival of Truss, publicly supported her leadership.

5

ADAPTABLE AND PRAGMATIC

It is universally acknowledged that the Tories are a highly adaptable and pragmatic party with a flexible ideology. They also have an impressive ability to reinvent themselves in government and opposition to remain in office and win the next general election.

The Conservative Party does not have a written constitution, which helps it remain flexible. This allows it to be responsive to the changing political context. They are significantly more decisive than other parties. The dominance of the leader over the party makes quick policy changes easy. There isn't any internal democratic decision-making by the membership over policy. Leaders are generally selected quickly. The membership has only been able to vote to select the leader since 2001 and has no say in removing the leader.[1] The fact that most Tory leaders do not step down at a time of their choosing means it is a precarious position. This motivates leaders to remain flexible and adapt party policy as events and public opinions change.[2]

The Tories are more willing to take risks than their opponents. Regarding leaders, the Tories had the first bachelor and women Prime Ministers. On policy, Thatcher and Johnson implemented high-risk strategies to gain or keep power. Labour prioritises winning power less than the Tories, having ideological disputes in public. The Tories are not naturally innovative, with some in the party supporting social reform, but it's not a priority. It normally reacts to changes made by other parties. The Tories only make significant changes during national emergencies or to win or maintain power.[3]

The Tories learnt from the 1846 Corn Law split that no principle, individual or manifesto commitment is worth looking disunited in public and losing power. They do not value consistency. They practise what has been called 'lethal pragmatism'. This allows them to recover quickly from devastating election defeats to return to power at the next election and, on a few occasions, the election after that.[4] The Tories are quick at changing policies or leaders not serving the core aim of gaining or maintaining power. The removal of senior ministers or advisors is a common feature of Tory leaders.[5]

What are some of the issues the Tories have adapted around? A big one is the welfare state and public spending. Following losing to Labour in 1945, the Tories modernised and embraced Keynesianism, including full employment and the welfare state and returned to office in 1951. When the post-war economic boom ended, leading to stagflation and trade union militancy, Thatcher replaced Keynesianism with 'monetarism' to reduce inflation and maintain economic stability even if this resulted in high unemployment. When Major took over in 1990, he made commitments regarding public services to win electoral support for the 1992 general election, a departure from Thatcherism. In 2017, May changed direction from the previous seven years of austerity, increasing spending on public services. Then in 2019, Johnson made large public spending commitments focused on regional 'levelling up' to win the 2019 general election.[6]

On the Empire and Europe. Through the 19th and early 20th centuries, the Tories were the party of the Empire. From the 1950s, Macmillan adapted and managed the dismantling of the Empire. Macmillan was the first Prime Minister to apply for the UK to join the EEC, with Heath taking the country in during the 1970s. The Tory Party was 'the party of Europe' until the 1980s. It finally became an anti-Europe or Brexit Party in 2016 under May, Johnson and Truss. May and Truss voted to Remain in the referendum and went on to lead Brexit governments, with Johnson only leading the Brexit campaign to help him get to Downing Street.[7]

The Tories have had a flexible relationship with the trade unions over the last 123 years. At the start of the 20th century, the Tories went along with the Liberal reforms to not lose working-class voters. Following the General Strike in 1926, the Tories imposed trade union restrictions. Union strength grew from the 1930s, and by the post-war period, the unions were involved in government decision-making with Tory administrations. Union militancy and economic problems from the 1960s meant another change of position to reduce the power of unions again. Legislation to limit union powers was introduced in the 1970s and 1980s, significantly weakening trade union power.[8]

What Are The Tories Adapting Towards?

Mostly the Tories are very effective at adapting to the constantly changing 'centre ground' of British politics, either in government or in opposition. The Tories are adept at moving onto terrain seen as an area of strength for the Labour Party, such as public services, especially the NHS. When Labour created the NHS in the late 1940s, the Tories were completely against it and voted against it multiple times in parliament.[9] Once the Tories realised the popularity of the NHS with voters, they adapted and started to compete with Labour over being safe stewards of public healthcare.[10]

Over the last 123 years, the Tories have excelled at knowing when voters have moved, so the party needs to adapt to be on the centre ground to appeal to the largest number of voters. An example of this is social values. Britain and the Tories have traditionally been socially conservative on family values, with homosexuality being illegal until 1967. During the 1980s, the Thatcher government introduced Section 28, which banned schools from 'promoting homosexuality'. New Labour repealed Section 28 and introduced civil partnerships for gay couples. Many Tories opposed this, but the party identified that the public had shifted, and the centre ground of voters accepted homosexuality. As part of Cameron's modernisation of the Tory Party, his government brought in same-sex marriage.

Ideology Vs Pragmatism

The Tories have an ideology but are flexible enough to allow the party to adapt around it to keep winning. Tory ideology includes defending private property, and personal liberty from the state, maintaining the Tory Party in power, reducing state intervention, minimising or reversing the redistribution of wealth, and protecting the legitimacy of the British elite. Some of these have been sidelined throughout history to ensure domestic and national security in times of crisis and emergency. They believe the state should not get too large or spend too much, and Tory governments best ensure this over the Liberals or Labour. Over the long term, all other policies and issues are flexible. Tories believe it is more beneficial to compromise to stay in power or win a general election, even if this means stealing policies from opponents. Then once in power, they can bring in a weak version of the stolen policy that's just good enough to win target voters over. The Tory Party is most successful when it has leaders that can manage the tension between Tory ideology and what is politically necessary and pragmatic.[11] The Tories have dumped elements that were seen as key parts of their ideology in the past because they no longer appeal to voters such as laissez-faire economics, the House of Lords, Irish unionism, the Empire, industry and manufacturing, and agricultural interests.[12]

The Tory perspective is influenced by the period and context, which helps it adapt to the changing voter preferences. Tory members and voters do not generally have an idealised vision of the future. The conservative utopia is based on the past, which is mythical and aspires to a 'golden age' of social stability, which has been lost. This is more straightforward to find a consensus around and puts fewer restrictions and expectations on Tory governments. Conservatism is presented as 'common sense' with Baldwin's plain truths and Thatcher's 'household economics'. Tories focus on realism, which limits expectations, is anti-intellectual and suspicious of grand plans. The Tories promote getting on with ordinary life and dealing with issues as they come along.[13]

It is fair to ask how a so adaptable and flexible party remained coherent enough to be identifiable and distinctive to win elections. The Tory Party has advocated policies that, in the long view, look contradictory, such as free trade vs imperial protection, laissez-faire vs state planning, individualism vs collectivism, and liberty vs authority. It could be argued that its regularity and effectiveness at changing to maintain power is an ideology in itself.[14]

The Tory Party has another advantage in that its ideology has a broad reach across British voters, from one-nation centrists to anti-immigrant populists to open racists. Many party supporters have extreme reactionary views around race, sexuality, and immigration, but generally, they understand to keep quiet, support the leader and ensure the party keeps winning.[15]

One of the key parts of Tory Party ideology is the defence of property rights, and they have been very flexible in maintaining this through social and political reform and, at times, have used force. Challenges have come from radical democrats, Chartists, Socialists, the labour movement, and unrest by the unemployed. The party has also successfully adapted from being the party of aristocrats and land-owning property to gain support from industry, business and workers.[16] In the 20th century, the Tory Party adapted again from representing the interests of the owners of industry and manufacturing to those of finance in the 1980s under Thatcher.[17]

Drivers Of Tory Party Change

Changes to policy and leadership take place when in office due to the Tories being in office two-thirds of the time. Organisational changes to the party generally take place when it is in opposition. The two key factors that drive change in the Tory Party are defeat and leaders. See the following section on how the Tory Party regains power quickly after a defeat. Other factors include the dominant faction in the party; fear of losing the next election; not repeating the mistakes of previous Tory governments; resolving unfinished business from the last time in office; and stealing appealing Labour Party policies. Leaders greatly impact how the party projects itself and its policies. Macmillan, Health, Thatcher, Cameron, and Johnson have all driven change in the party. The party's membership has a limited impact on driving party change around organisation and policy.[18]

Several factors explain why badly defeated parties do not make rational and appealing offers to voters at the next election. Many of these apply to the Tories from 1997-2005. These include: underestimating new, smaller parties; the influence of party members and campaign donors, who do not see the party's policies as unappealing as average voters; more extreme policy platforms are distinctive so clearer to present to swing voters; lack of understanding by politicians that the policies are unpopular; a belief by politicians that they can convince enough voters to support less moderate policies; a belief that the party can include a few extreme policies if it seen as more credible than its opponent; inertia may be better than the challenging, time-consuming and risking business of change.[19]

6

QUICKLY REGAIN POWER FOLLOWING A DEFEAT

The long history of success for the Tory Party is due to its ability to overcome setbacks, adapt to changes in the economic, political and social environment and present itself as the only credible alternative to the Liberal or Labour government.[1] Following the defeat, the Tories quickly devised a strategy to regain power, such as for 1924, 1951, 1970 and 1979.

Several important factors must be considered for a political party to return to power from opposition. They can be divided into external and internal to the party in opposition. The external factors are more important, but the internal ones need to be in place to ensure the party in opposition is positioned to regain power. There are seven external factors:

1. government performance;
2. condition of the economy;
3. 'state of the nation', which relates to social stability and crime levels;
4. international crises and national security;
5. media support for the government;
6. the role of a third party in the balance of power;
7. any changes to the electoral system.

The first five factors relate to the overall effectiveness of the government in public opinion. It is highly damaging for the government to be seen as not in control of events, without the leadership and ideas to manage problems. This is more of a problem than being unpopular, which can be changed with a new leader or policies or an unexpected event. Another problem for governments is if they have been in office for a long period. A public feeling of a 'time for a change' can develop, especially if the government is considered ineffective and complacent.

An opposition that does not have government experience is not a problem if the public has lost faith in the government. The opposition must be credible, perceived as 'electable' and appealing to voters. An opposition will gain unity, popularity and confidence when a government struggles and fails to meet expectations. The government's actions and agenda drive the opposition's strategy. The most important thing for the opposition to do is not to make any missteps to damage its electoral chances. It must position itself to take advantage of the government's difficulties with policies that are popular with voters. The opposition has to regain the voter support it has lost in previous elections and gain support from new voter groups.

Five key internal factors apply to an opposition, so it is best placed to regain power:

1. a new leader or leadership team, ideally a change of generations;
2. party unity and discipline, which projects a clear sense of direction and effectiveness;
3. party's image that is based on a fresh program and policies that are different to the government's;
4. effective party organisation that is responsive to events and challenges;
5. adaptability includes a pragmatic desire to take office and the capability of taking advantage of opportunities as they appear.

The credibility of the opposition for voters is based on combining these factors and can be aided by local or by-election victories, wins in parliament and positive media coverage. The opposition must position itself between its long-standing supporters and swing voters. It must identify important areas to voters, critique government performance, and offer appealing alternative policies. This must be combined with presenting slogans and challenges that connect with voters.[2]

A new opposition leader must also decide to follow an 'active' approach, with a new program or policies or a 'reactive' position of waiting for the government to have problems and take advantage. For the 'active' strategy, the opposition has to be careful not to pick policies that alienate some target voters and attract others. The leadership must also decide if they focus on Tory policies of cutting taxes and public spending that its core voters will support or aiming for the centre ground and appeal to swing voters. The Tory Party's adaptability and desire to regain power led to the policy reviews in 1924, 1945-51 and 1975-79.

Another issue with an 'active' strategy is that if the opposition puts forward policies in enough detail to be seen as credible, the government will likely steal them. The opposition then loses the advantages of being in opposition: flexibility, a focus on general ideas and the big picture. But they do not gain the benefits of governing: credibility, patronage, and access to supporting institutions such as the civil service. Generally, Tory oppositions go for the reactive strategy of chipping away at Labour governments and waiting until they fail.[3]

Examples Of The Tories' Quick Recovery Of Power From Opposition

Labour formed a minority government in 1923 with the Tories returning to power in 1924. Baldwin presented a popular manifesto based on some state intervention in the economy and progressive social policy. The Tories also benefited from better party organisation, wealthy backers, and strong support among women, combined with a perception of being the national party with credibility to govern.

Following the defeat in 1945, the Tories improved their organisational effectiveness, which had suffered during the war. They also adopted Labour's economic policy of full employment. Following the narrow defeat in 1950, the Tories focused on reassuring Liberal and Labour voters that they could trust the Tories to manage public services. This was combined with new policies to challenge Labour on new terrain around reducing state restrictions and increasing living standards.[4]

Following the Tory defeat in 1964, the unpopular leader was replaced. There were some organisation changes, a change to electing party leaders, the party adapted to issue-focused and evidence-based policy development, greater focus by Shadow Cabinet members on their portfolios, improved financial controls and transparency, significant focus on key target seats, increased effectiveness around polling, advertising and broadcasting. Significant policy changes concerned controlling trade unions, major tax policy changes, a shift to targeted welfare benefits, and limiting immigrants.[5]

The Tories lost two elections in 1974, and Thatcher replaced Heath. She was ideologically driven and could be pragmatic when needed. A dynamic advertising agency helped with publicity.

Thatcher developed a radical economic policy to deal with the economic problems and developed appealing tax policies. Following the 1970s trade union militancy, the unions were seen as a problem that must be dealt with.

7

EFFECTIVE PARTY ORGANISATION

Through the last 123 years, the Tories have consistently shown superior party organisation abilities nationally, regionally and locally; compared to its opponents. It is generally better resourced and embraces new electoral techniques and technology to win votes. The three big defeats in 1906, 1945 and 1997 were not the result of a failing party organisation, but it was a significant factor. The party's effective organisation is believed to give it an edge in close elections in 1935, 1950, 1951, 1964, 1970, 1992, and 2010.[1]

The main aim of the Tory Party is to defeat its opponents and maintain power. To meet this aim, it must recruit volunteers and fundraise to campaign in elections effectively. The Tory Party prioritises unity and loyalty to avoid divisive incidents. Another key role of the party is to inform the leadership of the membership's views. The leadership must then keep track of the perspective of their supporters, accommodate them and ensure that any conflict is managed with the minimum public disruption. Other functions of the party organisation include creating and distributing party propaganda and presenting a positive image of the party in public.[2]

Voters' perception of the Tory Party is affected by its morale, unity and organisational effectiveness. A political party that lacks an effective national and regional structure will lose the support of the public. The appealing face of the Tory Party is constructed using several components: patriotism, national unity, the importance of self-reliance, moderation, and the importance of continuity between the past and present. However, national and local organisation efficiency is sometimes missed as a key factor for the Tories' success. This factor has resulted in the Tories being seen as the national party of government since the First World War.

In the months leading up to the general elections, the Tories spend large amounts of funds to carry out detailed analysis and planning of their campaigns. There is a clear division of labour. Tory Party leadership and national campaign function is to appeal to voters. The local party structures are to identify potential voters and get out the vote on election day. Tory candidates need the party endorsement, as many Tory voters support the party out of loyalty over the specific candidate. The local association pays for the candidates' campaign expenses and ensures the area of the parliamentary constituency is covered with canvasses and transport. Through much of the 20th century, the Tory Party's large membership made this easily achievable. However, since the 1990s, the party membership numbers have dropped significantly, with the average age increasing, posing problems for the party's organisational effectiveness.

Due to the UK's electoral system, First Past the Post, general elections are won or lost in a few marginal constituencies. Of the 650 seats today, elections are decided in 100-150. Since the 1920s, the Tories have been very good at focusing money and election agents on target constituencies. The 2010, 2015 and 2019 elections saw an efficient spread of Tory voters, so they won dozens of parliament seats by a few thousand votes. The key role of the Tory Centre Office is to direct the national propaganda campaign and ensure there are national arrangements to resource this. The national Tory Party is excellent at taking advantage of new developments in the voting system, such as increasing their vote from postal voting and expatriate voters, which increased the number of Tory seats in 1959 and 1992, respectively.

The Tories have also linked strong and weak neighbouring constituencies, sending volunteers to canvass between and during elections. In addition, local conservative associations provide transport to elderly voters to get them to the polling station. Tory candidate expenses over the years show that the Tories spend near or up to the maximum compared to their opponents in both safe and marginal constituencies. This high level of spending relates to greater amounts of propaganda and activities by Tory campaigns.

The superior Tory Party organisation for winning elections gives Tory campaigners a confidence boost, and their reputation has the opposite negative impact on opponents' morale. Following election defeats, the party's consistent organisational strength has ensured the party can regroup to give the party a fighting chance at the next election.[3]

Tory Party's National And Local Organisational Structure

There are four key features of the national and local Tory Party organisation. First, the party does not have a hierarchical structure; it is more complicated than this. The authority of the leadership is dependent upon the support of the membership, which must be convinced to follow instead of being forced. The party's principle of local autonomy minimises the power of the leadership. Second, as discussed earlier, the Tory Party is highly adaptive and flexible. Third, the party has had a consistently broad outlook through the last 123 years across its voter base, members, aims of the party, the functions of the different parts of the party and how the other parts of the organisation are managed and power distributed. The final feature is the effective coordination of the professional and voluntary parts of the party. This is not based on a written rule book but is influenced by middle-class behaviour and private-school culture. Debate about political theory is avoided; instead, there is a focus on common aims and practical activity, with unity and loyalty projected publicly at all times.[4]

The Tory Party comprises three parts: the parliamentary party of MPs; the professional party, those that work for the party; and the voluntary party, the membership. The Parliamentary Conservative

Party is managed by the Whip's Office. This enforces discipline, manages Tory MPs welfare issues and reports to the party leader. The parliamentary party also decides on policy through internal negotiations. The 1922 Committee is made up of all backbench Tory MPs. The committee has 20 executive members, selected by consensus from backbench MPs. It meets weekly when parliament is sitting. It is the party body that manages the selection of new Tory leaders.

The professional party is managed by the Conservative Campaign Headquarters (CCHQ) and leads on campaigning; communications, such as public relations, the media and propaganda; and research. It includes full-time staffers around the country. The CCHQ was originally called the Conservative Central Office (CCO) and was renamed in 2014.

Members join the party as part of a local Conservative Association based on parliamentary constituencies. The associations have some autonomy to decide the affiliation fee and are responsible for recruitment and discipline. Candidates are chosen based on party rules, and then the candidate applies to CCHQ to be included in an approved list of candidates. They will be informed which seats they can apply to stand in. A Tory MP can be deselected at a special general meeting following a petition signed by more than 50 members. All Tory councillors must be members of the Conservative Councillors' Association (CCA).

The National Conservative Convention decides the direction of the voluntary part of the party. It comprises the 800 highest-ranking officers, including association chairs, officers from areas and regional and representatives from the Conservative Women's Organisation. The Convention meets at least twice a year, during the Spring Forum and at Party Conference. In addition, it coordinates campaigning with other parts of the party.

The Conservative Party Board is the party's ultimate decision-making body. It is responsible for all operational matters, including the approval of the party's accounts, management of the national membership, including membership discipline and lists of approved candidates, organisation of party conferences, legal compliance governing political parties, managing the NCC and dispute resolution. The board meets about once a month and works closely with other parts of the party through several management sub-committees.[5]

The Conservative Party conference is a two-way forum between the leadership and membership. It gives the leadership an important opportunity to listen to its supporters to improve the party's chances of winning the next general election. It is not a policy-forming structure and mostly provides a social event for members and a public event to show party unity.[6]

Following the Tory defeat of 1945, the party focused on building a mass membership. The Tory Party membership peaked in the mid-1950s at 2.8 million. From the 1960s, Tory Party membership decreased due to the decline of class and community institutions, increased competition with new leisure activities and generational changes. By 2005, 198,844 votes were cast in the leadership election, which dropped to 134,000 by 2013, and 124,000 in 2018. In 2019 there were 139,000 members and at least 141,000 members for the summer 2022 leadership election.[7]

Fundraising

The Tory Party consistently raises more money than its opponents and can therefore outspend the Labour Party in between and during general elections. There are four areas to consider regarding Conservative Party fundraising:
1. the money that local associations raise;
2. the amounts that local associations pass on to central party funds;
3. donations by companies;
4. donations by individuals.[8]

The last two points, donations by companies and individuals, will be described in detail in the following chapter.

Before 1945, most local associations relied on the Tory MP or candidate to raise money to run their campaign for general elections. Following the defeat in 1945, changes were made, so local associations had to raise all the funds for general election campaigns in constituencies. It involved broadening local association members across society to recruit a mass membership of subscribers. In 1948, targets were introduced for each local association to contribute to central funds. This was very successful through the 1950s. By the 1960s, the number of associations failing to send over some or all of their quota increased due to inflation and a decreasing and ageing membership. This resulted in the party getting into financial difficulties in the 1980s. In 1990-1, £15 million was raised by local associations, and £1.5 million went to the Central Office from the quota system. This was 52% of assigned quotes and dropped to 45 % the following year. This provided about 10% of the party's central budget. During the 1980s, the average association target was £31,500. Most associations would raise £18,000-25,000, with safe seats raising £75,000-100,000 and safe opposition seats raising £2,000-5000. Money is raised from social events and membership fees, which increased to £10 in the 1980s. This was a large increase which offset the decreasing membership numbers.[2]

8

THE PARTY OF THE RICH

Stanley Baldwin, one of the Tories' successful Prime Ministers in the 1930s, is quoted as saying in 1927, "Our one great advantage: wealth. Let us use it. Its expenditure should be regarded as an insurance premium."

The Conservative Party is the main party of capitalism and the rich in Britain. The Tory Party is a voluntary organisation that works very hard to reproduce itself, win elections, out-manoeuvre its opponents, defend government power and authority, and maintain a forum for establishment individuals to network. This ensures that a new group of stable political elites replaces one set of stable political elites. The Tory Party is not against reform but sees it as the least bad option to ensure the current power and privilege arrangements continue. The party is a defensive organisation for corporations, businesses, and the financial and property sectors. It operates as a vehicle to unite the different groups that make up the upper classes so they can collectively maintain power through a public face that is appealing to the electorate so it can compete in a parliamentary democracy. The Tory Party is the political wing of these interests. The rich control the Tory Party, not Prime Ministers or MPs. The wealthy do this by donating or withholding funds to the party.

The Tories have supported social conservatism because these are the views of the rich through the 20th century. In addition, businesses that do not directly benefit from Tory policies support the party. An example is how the owners of industrial machine manufacturer JCB support the Tories' maintenance of elite power, even though the Tories have brought in policies over the last 40 years that have resulted in the decline of manufacturing and industry in Britain.

In the 1990s, major financial and commercial interests switched support from the Tories to New Labour after Blair committed to maintaining Thatcherite economic and political arrangements. These interests then changed back to the Tories once the 2008 financial crisis destroyed Brown's reputation for economic competence. Brexit complicated things for British capitalists, with many supporting Remain in the referendum. Capitalists with short-term interests and right-wing small-state views backed the Johnson government. These go against the interests of British capitalists in general.[1]

Tory Party MPs and members are generally better off financially than the average person and have a background of greater social privilege. Since Cameron, this has started to change, but Tory MPs from more humble backgrounds are generally ambitious and aspire to be better off. In addition, many Tory MPs have lucrative second jobs. All of this does make those in the party biassed towards supporting capitalism, corporations and businesses. And then, in turn, it is the billionaire and millionaires, corporations and companies that donate huge sums to the party.

The support of the rich is worth more than that of the poor. As well as money, wealthy and influential people can provide less tangible benefits, such as convincing many others that listen to them to vote Tory. Well-resourced Tory supporters can also provide professional skills and expertise in legal, finance, marketing, and publicity. Wealthy people own parts of the media and press that support the Tories.[2]

What do the wealthy get from donating to the Tory Party? The main one is stopping the election of the Labour government, which might introduce reforms that would threaten the interests of the rich. During the 1990s, the Tobacco Manufacturers' Association donated to the Tories to stop a Labour government that planned to ban tobacco advertising. A second reason is that the rich know that the Tories will notice their views more, especially if they donate to the party or threaten to stop donating. This is known as 'access' to the Prime Minister and ministers. A third reason is the history of Tory Party donors getting government contracts and money. Between 1978 to 1992, five construction companies got 42.5% of £1.37 billion of government spending on aid projects linked to trade deals. More recently, there was the Covid pandemic scandal of Tory donors getting access to government PPE equipment contracts through the 'VIP lane' and making huge profits.[3] A fourth reason to donate to the party is to get tax breaks such as the £100 billion in tax breaks given to the super-rich and big corporations in 2020, many of whom had donated millions to the party.[4] All of this is not lost on the general public. Recent opinion polls show that 50-60% of people think the Tories are close to the rich.[5]

Tory MPs Are Wealthier Than Opposition MPs

Through most of the 20th century, Tory MPs have come from families with social privilege, educated at private schools. Their occupations cover four main areas: landed aristocracy, the military, business (industrial, commercial, financial) and the professions (lawyers etc.).

Following the defeat of 1945, changes were made in the Tory Party so parliamentary candidates did not need to fund their election campaigns. However, the informal selection process continued until the 1980s resulting in selections continuing to be based on social position. A survey in 1974 of the Conservative Party found a lack of working-class people, with most MPs and local association members coming from the upper-middle-class.

The party elected three leaders and Prime Ministers from middle-class backgrounds and was state-educated: Heath, Thatcher and Major. In the last 13 years, Cameron and Johnson were privately educated at Eton, then Oxford University and came from money and are distant relatives of the Queen.[6]

There is also the issue of MPs' outside earnings. All MPs engage in this, but Tories make the most of it. For a long time, second jobs did not have to be declared. However, following several second job scandals, a register of members' financial interests was not created until 1974. In 1994 there was a 'cash for questions' scandal; Major set up the House of Commons Committee on Standards in response.

In 2021, it was found that of 360 Tory MPs, 90 had second jobs, collectively taking home an extra £4 million. This compares to only three Labour MPs having second jobs. The big Tory earners include Owen Patterson, £100,000 per year; Andrew Mitchell, £182,600 for 34.5 days' work; Geoffrey Cox, £1 million a year; Chris Grayling, £100,000 per year; John Redwood, £230,000 per year; Julian Smith £144,000 per year; Sajid Javid £300,000 per year.[7]

The Johnson government in 2022 had multiple super-rich ministers. Here are the top 10 and their net worth:

1. Rishi Sunak, Chancellor of the Exchequer: £200 million;
2. Jacob Rees-Mogg, Brexit Opportunities Secretary: Between £55 million and £150 million;
3. Nadhim Zahawi, Education Secretary: Up to £100 million;
4. Alister Jack, Scotland Secretary: £20 million;
5. Sir Geoffrey Cox, former Attorney General: £6 million;
6. Michael Gove, Levelling Up Secretary: Up to £3 million;
7. Priti Patel, Home Secretary: Up to £2.2 million;
8. Sajid Javid, Health Secretary: £276,000;
9. Boris Johnson, Prime Minister: £157,372;
10. Nadine Dorries, Culture Secretary: £157,000.[8]

Resourced By The Rich

The Tory Party is very secretive about internal processes, especially how the party is funded. The party is an unincorporated association, meaning that it has no legal status and has no requirement to publish audited accounts, so none are submitted. Since the 1980s, the Tories have brought in legislation so that trade union donations to the Labour Party have to be declared publicly. Political Parties in the UK have to declare donations of over £7,500 to the central party or £1,500 to local associations, which is easily avoided. Businesses can give donations to the Conservative Party without the knowledge of their shareholders. The money can be redirected through third parties such as overseas businesses, and the Tory Party has bank accounts in the off-shore tax haven such as Jersey.[9]

Now let's look at the history of how the Tories are funded by the wealthy. During the early 20th century, there were rampant 'cash for honours' arrangements, with the rich paying political parties, mostly the Tories, for peerages and knighthoods. There were also strong links between brewers/pubs and the Tory Party. Tories used pubs as meeting rooms and paid for drinks. In return, the brewers donated to the party to protect their interests from the Liberals, who wanted to bring in new licensing laws. In the 1910 general election, the Tories also received support from car companies through loaned vehicles to transport voters to the polling booth.

In the 1920s, there was a shift in the Tory party to more legitimate sources of funding, as the 'cash for honours' scandals were getting too much public attention. As a result, there was a focus on getting money from the finance sector in the City of London and businesses. However, it's likely that 'cash for honours' continued quietly. Maundy Gregory was the main Tory fixer connecting rich people who wanted a peerage with political parties. He was caught in the act in the 1930s but did not share in court any details of how he had helped the Tories. He got a 2-month prison sentence and then retired in France with a generous pension from the Conservative Party. The 1929 general election campaign cost the Tories £300,000. Over half came from donations, with £141,000 from a secret account raised from private individuals and undisclosed sources.

In 1948 as part of the party's reorganisation, it set up a network of eight 'river companies' that allowed anonymous individuals and businesses to make secret donations that did not show the final destination of the money in the companies' accounts. This also was a workaround to the problematic legal provision that money from trusts could not be left to political parties. One-third of the party's total income between 1954 to 1964 came via these river companies. This illegal practice was only made public by a leak in 1988. The 1940s also saw the creation of 'Aims of Industry,' a Tory front group which publicly promoted 'free enterprise' and was hostile to Labour's nationalisation proposals. It was well funded and staffed, spending £250,000 during the 1983 election.

In the 1950s and 1960s, the Tory Party established several 'cut out' organisations to launder secret donations. The British United Industrialists (BUI) was the most significant, set up in 1960. There was also the Conservative Industrial Fund. This hid the money donated from corporations from their shareholders and boards. It was a limited company until 1968. Following the Companies Act 1967, BUI became an unincorporated association, so it didn't have to produce annual accounts. By 1992, BUI received too much attention, so it was wound down. It is believed to have channelled £10 million to the party during its existence.

From 1979 to 1990, the Tory Party treasurer was Lord McAlpine. He raised over £100 million during that time, hugely helping the party's dominance during the 1980s. £23 million was raised for the 1987 general election. Between 1979 and 1993, the party received £1 million from United Biscuits and £800,000 each from Hanson, Taylor Woodrow, British and Commonwealth, and George Weston Holdings. The brewing industry donated an estimated £250,000 to the party before the 1987 general election. During this period, the Tories were believed to have received large donations from the Harrods owner Mohamed Al-Fayed. Tiny Rowland, the CEO of Lonrho, claimed that it was suggested that a donation of £150,000 to the party would ensure its smooth purchase of House of Fraser. This money also came from overseas via the 'Conservatives Abroad' grouping. The Telegraph newspaper reported in the 1980s that lunch with Thatcher cost around £50,000 for industry and business leaders, which was effectively 'cash for access'.

There were strong links between the party and parts of British industry, such as road builders, banks, insurance companies, brewing industries, tobacco industries, and arms manufacturers. Arms deals in the 1980s between the Thatcher government and Saudi Arabia were worth about £100 billion, and £30 million is believed to have been given to Conservative Party Central Office. In addition, cash for honours was taking place during the 1980s. Between 1979 and 1995, the Tories issued eighteen life peerages and eight-two knighthoods in relation to seventy-six companies that had donated a total of £17 million to the party.

In 1991, it was reported that Major spent 2 days in Hong Kong fundraising. He is believed to have received over £1 million for his trouble. In 1993, foreign businessman Asil Nadir claimed he gave £1.5 million to the Tory Party for a knighthood he never received. Following the collapse of the company Polly Peck in 1990, it was discovered that Nadir gave £440,000 to the party. Separately, it was found that following the takeover of Sovereign Leasing in Manchester, they gave £100,000 to the party in 1990.

In 1992, the party's Central Office cost £500,000 a week to run, and the 1992 general election cost £20 million. In the run-up to the 1992 general election, there was a lot of press interest in who was donating to the Tory Party. It received £19 million in gifts: £4 million from companies and businesses. The top ten donations were from: United Biscuits of £130,000; Taylor Woodrow £124,500; Hanson £115,000; Glaxo £102,000; P&O £100,000; Rothmans £100,000. In addition, £15 million was donated from 'undisclosed and anonymous individuals'. It was reported that £7 million of this was from foreign sources. This related to a tax loophole that allowed anyone with UK assets registered abroad to pay 25% capital gains tax instead of 40%. This was estimated to cost the taxpayer £10 billion a year.

The 1990s recession caused several donors and companies to stop or reduce the amount they gave to the Tory Party. Construction companies Taylor Woodrow and Newarthill, as well as United Biscuits, drastically reduced their donations. Following a 'mini-budget' in 1994 that raised alcohol duties, brewers and whisky producers reduced their contributions.

Between 2001 and 2010, £72 million came from 50 'donor groups', this constituting half of the Tory Party's reported donations. Donor groups are a technique that Tory donors use to avoid one wealthy person giving a large amount of money that will get press attention. Instead, the money is spread between the donor, their husband or wife, family members, companies and business partners. And £45.5 million came from 15 donor groups, which is just under a third of Tory Party donations during this period. Significant funders include Michael Ashcroft, £2 million, and £4 million from the Bamford family, who own the JCB company.[10]

In 2010-2011, the Tories received £12.3 million in donations; half came from the financial sector.[11] In 2013, the Tory Party had an income of £25.4 million, with only £749,000 coming from membership fees.[12] The Labour Party identified that 27 of the 59 wealthiest fund managers donated more than £19 million to the Tory Party.[13] Between 2007 and 2017, the Tories received £430,000 from Wates Groups and £8.1 million from JCB.[14]

Between 2010-2019, the Tory Party received £130 million in donations from the members of the 'Leaders Club', which is made up of rich individuals with links to Russia, the fossil fuel industry and climate change denial, and those in finance in the City of London and hedge fund managers. Most of this group feature on the Sunday Times rich list.[15] Individuals and companies in the property sector have given £60 million to the Tories between 2010 and 2020. Of all donations to political parties from the property sector, 80% went to the Tory party.[16]

In the first week of the 2019 general election, donations from the Leaders Club comprised 80% of Tory Party donations of £4.4 million. In the same week, the Labour Party raised £220,000.[17] It was reported that in 2019, of the 151 billionaires in the UK, 48 had donated to the Tory Party, totalling £52 million.[18]

In 2019, the Tories received donations of £68 million compared to the Labour Party's £57 million.[19] Between July 2019 and August 2021, the Tory Party received £38.6 million in individual donations. £10 million of this was from 10 super-rich supporters from the finance and property sectors.[20] It was revealed in 2021 that the Tories have been offering House of Lords peerages to wealthy benefactors as a "reward" for large donations of over £3 million. Sixteen Tory Party Treasures and twenty-two Tory donors have been given seats in the House of Lords since 2010.[21] In December 2021, twelve Tory Party donors gave £10 million between them and were given peerages, knighthoods or senior positions in the party.[22]

In 2022, it was reported that 6 Russian oligarchs gave £2 million to the Tory Party since Johnson became leader in July 2019. 34 Tory MPs have been named as taking Russian donations. For the 2019 general election campaign the Tory Party received £600,000 from Ehud Sheleg's Russian bank account.[23] Johnson gave the major party donor Michael Hintze a peerage in 2022. The hedge fund billionaire is a climate sceptic and co-founded the climate denial think tank Global Warming Policy Foundation (GWPF) in 2009.[24]

PART 3:

HOW THE TORIES GOVERN TO ENSURE THEY WIN THE NEXT ELECTION

When the Tories are in government, they take full advantage to win the next election and stay in power. There are several aspects of being in government most of the time that assist the Tories' continued dominance that I will describe in the next 5 chapters. Some are intentional, and some are accidental. First, Tory dominance means they can present themselves as the natural party of government. Second, the Tories strongly identify the party with the UK nation, the nation-state and are proudly patriotic, which is appealing to millions of voters. Third, the Tories excel at 'statecraft,' which is effective party management in government, winning elections, government competence and winning the political argument. Fourth, the Tories project government and economic competence. Fifth, the Tories work very hard in government to introduce policies to manufacture and build future Tory voters. Sixth, to cover up for their failure to govern, the Tories distract, invent enemies, use dirty tricks and crush opponents.

The Tories benefit from being in office most of the time; this is known as the 'incumbency advantage'. One benefit is name recognition. Prime Ministers and parties in government are constantly in the media, whereas opposition parties find it hard to punch through to voters most of the time. It has also been found that incumbent MPs enjoy an extra 2% of the vote simply for being in office. Very helpful in a tight election. A second advantage for the UK Prime Minister is that since the Fixed Term Parliament Act was scrapped, the Tory Prime Minister can call a general election when it suits them electorally.[1]

9

THE TORY PARTY PRESENTS ITSELF AS THE NATURAL PARTY OF GOVERNMENT

The Tories' electoral dominance has been self-reinforcing; it has come to be seen as the 'natural' party of government, leading to a greater likelihood that it will be voted in. Tory governments are generally seen as the norm, with other parties seen as different and substandard. This ensures the party's ongoing significance as a political force and is the basis of its ability to bounce back from defeat.

The Tory Party has historically been a 'mass party' in terms of its ability to appeal to broad and varied groups of British society and to mobilise many volunteers that work to make the party an election-winning force. This meant that the Tory Party turned the extension of voting in 1867, 1884 and 1918 (to include the working class and women) into an opportunity against pessimistic expectations. The party also adapted to the decline of fixed social class differences and deference since the early twentieth century. The Tories developed an identity during the 20th century, so many voters did not see the party to be fixed to specific issues or special interests. By the second half of the twentieth century, it was accepted that the party had broad popular support, and this was a key part of how the party presented itself to the public.[1]

The mass-based politics the Tories developed during the 20th century was presented through the 'one nation' tradition of paternalism and benevolence. Following the extension of voting rights, Conservatives were concerned about 'trusting the people' but gradually accepted the role of a mass party as a counterweight to the rise of class-based politics from the Labour Party. Both the Labour Party and the Tory Party were attracting voters from more than one class, with the Tories getting the support of large numbers of work-class voters. The Tories found this a popular and unifying position by appealing to the centre ground, where most of the general public was. From the 1920s, the Tories understood how to keep the support of the masses and desired the general public's support and the legitimacy that this gave. The party designed the party organisation, campaigning, propaganda and policies to build a mass movement.[2] Baldwin, Churchill (1951-1955), Macmillan, Thatcher, Cameron and Johnson all broaden the appeal of the Tory Party to new voters.

The Tories reference 'common sense' but without explaining what this is. They claim it for themselves, a clever cultural tactic and something that the Tories have done very successfully. When Tories are trying to win support for their policies, they claim that these policies are endorsed by 'hard-working families'. The Tories argue that their policies are practical, reasonable and measured because they are aligned with public opinion. They say things like 'what everyone knows' or 'takes-for-granted and agrees with' so the policies gain general legitimacy. They are so good at claiming their policies agree with popular opinion when in fact, the Tories are constantly moulding and influencing public perception so they can channel public opinion to their advantage. They claim that the general public already supports the policy in the hope that this will result in that outcome. It is a circular strategy to get their desired outcome.

Examples of the Tories using common sense rhetoric include Thatcher claiming she was speaking for the 'common sense' of the British people when moving the party and then the country in a right-wing direction.[3] Tory leader William Hague in 2001 referenced the 'common sense revolution'. Cameron stated in 2011, '...and let this be our message - common sense for the common good'. Johnson claimed that common sense was Britain's 'single greatest weapon' against the Covid pandemic. Tory backbench MPs formed the 'Common Sense Group' in parliament in 2020 and announced that "84% of the public agreed with the statement: 'We need to restore some common sense in this country'". Truss was described as the Tories' Common Sense Champion. During the summer 2022 Tory leadership election, Rishi Sunak called his economic approach 'common sense Thatcherism'.[4]

The Conservative Party is the only political party in Britain that has forced other political parties to remake themselves in the Tories' image. Thatcher achieved this during the 1980s. It transformed the Labour Party and the Liberal Democrats. Labour leaders Neil Kinnock, John Smith and Tony Blair all copied the style, policies, strategy, and organisation of the Tory Party under Thatcher. Changes to policies include dropping policies around nationalisation, accepting the selling off of council houses, avoiding taxing the wealthy and a move from collectivism and strong trade union culture to individual rights and opportunities.[5] In 2002, Thatcher was asked what she saw as her greatest achievement, and she replied, "Tony Blair and New Labour. We forced our opponents to change their minds."

Stability, Continuity, Tradition

Part of the Tories' historical offer is that they will ensure everything stays the same. This is a key part of conservatism ideology. The Tories present themselves as the party of continuity. This can be linked to the fact that Britain has never been invaded and has had a continuous monarchy and aristocracy for thousands of years.[6]

Throughout most of the twentieth century, the Tory party also presented themselves as governing through gradual change, limited reform, security, moderation and in a responsible way. They regularly appeal to the 'common interest' and 'national unity', with many voters seeing the Tories as the natural option when there is a national crisis or instability, such as during economic crises and wars. Tory leaders such as Salisbury, Baldwin, Churchill or Macmillan excelled at projecting reassurance.[7] Thatcher had a mixed offer of social conservatism around traditional family values, law and order, and radical economic libertarianism. Johnson introduced a very hard Brexit, which couldn't be called conservatism; they adapted to win and stay in power.

The Tory Party is a great defender of British tradition and its 'proud' history. The party constantly defines the past and remodels the understanding of tradition in line with its contemporary needs. The party protects a specific image of the past. Johnson claimed that those that took down the statue of the slave trader Colston in Bristol in 2020 were trying to rewrite history without acknowledging that every statue is an attempt to write the establishment version of history. The Conservative Party promotes a positive view of Britain's past and constantly paints its opponents as attacking Britain. It maintains that holding Britain to account for its history is running Britain down. There is a conflation of the history that is told of Britain compared with Britain as it is today. This is a powerful basis for the Tories to campaign on; the country and the people are the same. The Tories also claim that a patriotic party and a national party are the same. The Tories then claim they represent the country and its people and are Britain's patriotic and national political party. Therefore, if you attack the Tory Party, you are attacking Britain. This is very powerful propaganda.[8]

The Tories Position Themselves As The Defenders of Popular British Institutions

The key institutions of the British establishment over the last 123 years are the Empire, military, monarchy, police and courts. Related to this are key issues important to the general public, such as patriotism, governing and economic competence, and ensuring stability, security, national defence, and law and order.

The decline of the Liberal Party in the early twentieth century gave the Tories an increased and undisputed amount of legitimacy. The party became associated with British society's dominant institutions and values.[2] There is a long history of the British governing class creating or reinventing institutions and techniques of government without having to destroy them. For example, the unrest, challenges and threats during the 19th century from industrialisation and a new urban society were successfully contained by new institutions such as the constitutional monarchy, a modern Civil Service, political parties and by reforming the Church of England.

The Tories are robust defenders of these institutions because these structures make up mainstream values and principles of British society. Many in Britain do not consider these institutions ideological, so they are not part of party politics. These institutions are also an effective way to channel and dampen radical demand for reform. The British establishment and its institutions are conservative in nature, and the Tory Party has been networking and influencing through these institutions for centuries to their advantage.

The important nature of the monarchy meant that republican Labour Prime Ministers showed loyalty and deference to the crown. The monarchy and the Tories worked hard to project the royal family's public duty and service ethic. During the twentieth century, the Church of England was considered the Tory Party at prayer. Until after the Second World War, Tory parliamentary candidates had to state their religion on application forms to the Central Office. Catholics or Jews did not stand much chance of getting through. Senior members of the Church of England had similar privileged backgrounds as the Tory Party. Both groups were also very traditional in their worldview.

There are very close links between the Tory Party and the press. The wealthy have set up and bought newspapers, and these individuals normally back the party. During the twentieth century, the party secretly channelled funds to struggling newspapers to keep them going in return for backing the party. In 1927, the party supported 230 different papers. In the early twentieth century, the British press might question institutions but would never challenge them. An example is the abdication of Edward VIII in 1936. There was a complete news blackout by the newspaper owners and editors, so the public did not know about it. The war machine absorbed the press during both world wars to support the nation and war effort. The Tories also took control of the BBC during the 1926 general strike. In the 1980s, Thatcher eased restrictions on Rupert Murdoch's cross-media holdings, and in return, his many UK newspapers backed the Tories, ensuring they won general elections in the 1980s and 1992.

Thatcher took more control of British institutions. The Civil Service was made to operate with a more commercial ethic and contract out more work. Multiple government bodies were created to manage government operations and public services, which people appointed by the Thatcher government managed. Thatcher was always a staunch defender of the armed forces.[10]

There has always been a close relationship between the government and the police. Liberal and Tory governments in the early twentieth century relied on the police to deal with the 1919 unrest and the 1926 general strike. In the 1970s, senior police officers were politicised as law and order became politically important. Senior police officers and the Police Federation publicly supported the Tories' law and order agenda, which helped Thatcher get elected in 1979.[11] Thatcher reorganised and strengthened the police into a politicised force to deal with the 1984-5 miners' strike, the Wapping News International printers strike, and the poll tax protests in London in 1990. The police under Johnson also became more politicised and aggressive against the 'kill the bill' protests in response to the 2022 Police, Crime, Sentencing and Courts Bill. The Metropolitan police in London were also very slow to investigate the reported parties at Downing Street during the Covid lockdown and finally issued Johnson one fine because public attention was so focused on the scandal. At the time, it was clear that the police were giving Johnson an easy ride.[12]

Tory Party Identifies Itself With The British Nation, Nation-State And Patriotism

The Tories' strong identification with the UK nation (England, Scotland, Wales and Northern Ireland) and the nation-state (government, civil service, Bank of England, courts, police, military) is a key part of the party's image. The party has benefited by gaining the support of average voters by presenting itself as the true patriotic party that defended the Constitution, the Union and the Empire during the 19th and the first half of the 20th century. The Tories' politics of nationhood is based on three components. The first is a consistent vision of the nation and conservative patriotism. The second is the effective use of patriotic ideas and language to present the Tories as a national party that represents the whole population, to promote this vision of the nation and constantly question the patriotic beliefs of its opponents. Third, the importance of the nation-state and national identity and the need to protect them is central to Tory political strategy.[13]

Many patriotic older people and swing voters in English marginal seats think the Empire is good and supports the monarchy and the military. These represent Anglo-British Nationalism, and the Tories are seen as the party of Anglo-British Nationalism, so they will always benefit electorally from this. This relates to the calls to 'make Britain great again' that led to popular Tory policies such as Brexit and the renewal of the Trident nuclear weapon system.[14] A softer version of English Nationalism was Baldwin's version of conservatism in the 1920s. It focused on the calm and safe feelings related to English society, such as village life, local church, royal events, national sporting events, pageantry and customs.[15]

For the Tories, a persistent tension exists between viewing the nation as 'English' and 'British.' The Tories very clearly identify with the English nation, but the British nation is less clear for them. The Tories have always been strongest in England, especially now. Globalisation and joining the EU have also weakened our relationship with that nation-state and 'Britishness'.[16] Following the 2016 Brexit referendum, the Tory party adapted again to keep winning and has become, in effect, an 'English nationalist party'. Many in the Tory Party believe that the break-up of the UK would be an acceptable price for getting Brexit done. Brexit has caused significant damage to the union and the idea of Britishness, fueling nationalism in Scotland, Wales and Northern Ireland.[17]

The full name of the Tory Party is the 'Conservative and Unionist Party'. Over the last 123 years, there have been changing opinions on the UK's relationship with the smaller nations. The party was forced into Irish Independence in 1922 following the Irish War of Independence, creating the Irish Free State. This turned out to be an electoral advantage to the Tories in Westminster, as many anti-Tory MPs in the new Irish Free State left the UK parliament, and those that remained in Northern Ireland supported the Tories. Tory leaders through the twentieth century considered Scottish devolution or Independence, including Churchill, Heath and Thatcher. Due to Labour's domination in Scotland, this was seen as a way to weaken the Labour Party.[18] Recently there has been pressure on the Tory government to allow a second referendum on Scottish Independence, which the Tories are resisting.

Throughout the 20th century, the Tories defended the Commonwealth, Empire and Ireland to the bitter end. Once it became clear that the Empire and Ireland countries demanded independence, the Tories changed their position and made the best of the new arrangements. Following the Second World War, the Tories submitted to the pressure for decolonisation throughout the British Empire. The 1956 Suez crisis saw the Suez Canal nationalised by Egyptian dictator Nasser. In response, Britain, France and Israel invaded to reclaim it but had to pull out early in the face of US and international opposition. This caused the Tories to adapt and switch their identification with the Empire to European unity.[19]

From this point, patriotism lost its imperial identity and shifted to being about national defence against foreign powers, such as Communist countries or the 1982 Falklands War.[20] The Labour Party's policy favouring unilateral nuclear disarmament in the early

1980s made it vulnerable to attacks from the Tories over national defence during the Cold War. The next general election in 1983 saw the Tories win one of their largest parliamentary majorities since the war.[21] Many swing voters are doubtful that Labour would do enough to defend the country, which has persisted to the present day. Labour leader Jeremy Corbyn had a big problem maintaining a credible position that national security would be handled well due to his anti-nuclear weapons position and campaigning.

The Tories' image as a patriotic party has benefited from all the wars and conflicts over the last 123 years. They were part of coalition governments during World War One and World War Two. During the 1980s, Thatcher made a big show of taking on the USSR during the Cold War. The Falklands War of 1982 helped them win the 1983 election. Although, this war is generally now viewed as a pointless military exercise in post-imperial nationalism. But before this conflict, Thatcher and the Tories were struggling in the polls, and the Falklands War turned that around. Thatcher's popularity in Britain soared after she reacted quickly to the invasion of the British-controlled island, and the 74-day war ended with the Argentinians surrendering.[22] In the 2000s, the Tories backed the Iraq and Afghanistan invasions to the hilt, with popular support following the 9/11 terrorist attack on the US. And in 2022, no one can miss how Johnson, Truss and Suank have all made a big show of supporting the Ukrainians against the Russian invasion, as there is a lot of public support for the Ukrainians.

10

TORY STATECRAFT

The statecraft concept has several components. It is a cycle that starts with a party in opposition that wins a general election, forms a government and ends with the party winning a second election while in office. There are five components: effective party management, a strategy to win the next election, winning the political argument, governing competence, and winning the next election.[1] I discussed the Tories' effective party management in Chapter 7. Chapter 11 will look at the Tories' perceived governing and economic competence. In Part 4, I will look at how the Tories win elections. This chapter will broadly describe Tory statecraft theory and how it works in practice.

Effective Tory statecraft operates within the limitations constraining governing political parties due to the changing political environment. When in government, the Tories work hard to insulate the party from domestic and foreign challenges by using parliament as a talking shop and intermediary to defuse problematic issues and channel low-priority issues to state institutions away from government.

Statecraft is a form of governing that places your party's core values into the mainstream arena of ideas and forces your opponent's core values out of this space. Politicians compete so their party's interests win the day. This creates its own dynamics, which can never be fully controlled. This 'mobilising of bias' aims to benefit your party's interests to ensure that your policies are the only ones viewed as legitimate. This is done most effectively when a party's policies reflect the interests of the broad community or 'national interest', with your opponent's policies perceived to serve the interests of small sections of society.[2]

The aim of Tory statecraft is always to maintain dominance of economics, politics and ideology in state institutions and civil society. They achieve this by using the Tory Party to identify their operating conditions, building support and negotiating power dynamics among political actors and interest groups by winning the debate of ideas and describing and implementing a credible economic strategy.[3]

Over the last 123 years, Tory statecraft has had two broad traditions; examples are in the section below. The first tradition is the early and mid-20th century 'one-nation' approach of opportunism, delay and making concessions as appropriate. Ideally, effective statecraft means that the government does not need to make concessions.

The second style was implemented by Thatcher, involving recovering the state's authority and making no concessions or compromise with those deemed the enemy, such as the trade unions. For Thatcher, this resulted in the following: centralisation of power, conflict with British institutions such as the trade unions and local government, and society becoming polarised between rich versus poor, south versus north, and unemployed versus employed. This 'Thatcherite offensive' resulted in the alienation of the Conservative Party from many of society's institutions and a polarisation of British society with clear winners and losers.[4]

These two traditions can also be described further; the one-nation Tories as 'positional conservatism' and Thatcher's politics as 'doctrinal.' Doctrinal conservatism becomes dominant during times of social and political instability. This values loyalty, conviction and commitment rather than compromise. It looks for victories over enemies it identifies. Whereas positional conservatism is focused on managing the current order, it avoids fixed ideas and instead develops the skills of the ruling class to ensure a stable society. Policy decisions are based on carefully assessing factors instead of implementing theoretical principles. Flexibility is valued. The opposition between these two approaches is always there, with the one that dominates being decided by the political context and balance of forces in the Tory Party, which means which political faction is dominant. British conservatives have generally favoured the positional tradition. Many Tories thought Thatcher broke with conservative tradition and the key principles of conservative one-nation statecraft because it implemented radical and destabilising change, only represented certain interests and was fixed to set ideas and doctrine.[5]

Thatcherism can be seen as a different approach to statecraft from the one-nation Tories. Instead of Tory statecraft involving opportunism, flexibility and conceding principles to new demands and interests, Thatcher's political project prioritised restoring the Tory Party's dominant role in British politics regarding electoral politics, ideas and economics. A key focus was rebuilding the British state's domestic and international authority and 'fixing' Britain's declining economy.[6]

The one-nation Tories believe that there is no set level of government intervention. Tory statecraft prioritises policies that are politically advantageous to the Tory Party over what is politically and economically beneficial to Britain and the population. These Tories claim that policies are selected not based on economic or political theory but to ensure the continuation of capitalist society so that British institutions receive respect and allegiance and society has minimal social tensions and injustice. In the 1950s, government intervention was seen to be needed to reduce abuses and ensure the population's consent. It absorbs new ideas and political actors into the governing system by making concessions to ensure the government's legitimacy, authority and stability. A key factor in policy decisions for Tories is if they will result in increased or reduced loyalty to the state, to increase loyalty.[7]

Another aspect of Tory statecraft is the importance of maintaining a stable governing class. Originally this was based on property ownership and the landed aristocracies, and during the twentieth century was expanded to the middle classes forming a new political class. This political class are expected to approach governing as a highly skilled activity, with an expectation of applying an ethic of public service combined with the privileges that come with it.[8]

Describing Tory Statecraft In Practice

At the start of the 20th century, Tory leader Lord Salisbury worked to defend the established institutions and the state to delay democracy and collectivism for as long as possible. He accepted the need to adapt to the new democratic political system and worked to position the Tories in the best position to defend the existing social order. [9]

After 1918 the Tories maintained their dominance by effectively focusing on returning to power. The Tories' statecraft had three elements: winning power on the centre ground; pragmatically appealing to a broad range of voters; and once in office, they worked to separate the government from domestic and external pressures. The aim was to give the government autonomy in how it governed.[10]

The domination of Tory politics and statecraft can be seen in the 1920s when the Labour Party was accepted into legitimate politics on the basis that it conformed to the established institutional politics and principles. This included that the state should not intervene on the side of social justice, ensuring the Tory Party remained the dominant political force in the interwar years. During this period, the Tories strengthened their public appeal by pushing a negative perception of the labour movement, that it was against the interests of ordinary working people. The party also linked the labour movement with the Labour Party, claiming both had sectional interests and that the Tory Party pursued the national interest. Baldwin also promoted a positive image of decent, hard-working men and women and encouraged patriotic trade unionism. He also advocated democracy and fairness.[11]

The absorption of the Labour Party and the labour movement into the government and war effort in 1940 meant that the negative Tory attacks on these institutions of the left ended. One-nation conservatism was an adaptation to this change, with the labour movement now part of the state. The 1945-51 Labour government enlarged the state in economic and social terms with nationalisations of industry and the creation of new public services. The state's established conservative ideas and institutions were left unchanged, meaning the rules of British politics remained mostly the same. The post-war Tory Party adapted well to Keynesianism and built on it to stay popular. The Tories' reputation also benefited from being in power during an economic boom of the 1950s and 1960s.[12]

The first half of the 1970s saw the failure of Heath's statecraft, with the Tories losing four general elections and two embarrassing defeats to the miners. At this point, the Labour Party was more credible as the natural government of Britain. This resulted in the Tory Party moving away from the interventionist one-nation approach towards a traditional free market Tory statecraft from the 19th century.[13]

Thatcher was elected leader of the Tories in opposition in 1975 and was determined to rebuild the party's governing and economic competence with voters. She also needed to effectively manage the party, win the political argument and recover the party's election-winning abilities. To do this, she adopted an economic strategy of 'monetarism', where the government limits the supply of money in circulation to control prices and inflation. She ensured that trade unions could not control the price of goods. She wanted to avoid her government having to negotiate with unions to agree on worker income levels. Thatcher saw this as a return to Tory statecraft before interventionist policies became dominant. The rest of the party united behind this, mainly because her opponents in the party didn't have an alternative strategy. Thatcher was determined to win the political argument, so she included other issues, such as immigration and the need to reduce the size of the state. Until winning the 1979 general election, the Tory Party under Thatcher was quite divided, although they hid it well. Thatcher managed the party carefully and inclusively until she established her authority. Thatcher was also lucky; the Winter of Discontent in 1978-9, characterised by major trade union strikes, heavily damaged the Labour Party's reputation with the unions and the public due to the general sense of chaos and government incompetence; to the advantage of the Tories.[14]

Seven areas of Thatcher's statecraft can be identified.

1. Thatcher and the media successfully portrayed the Labour Party and the labour movement as favouring sectional interests rather than national ones;
2. These sectional interests were depicted as breaking the British economy with an out-of-date production strategy, strikes and a failure to modernise. The Tories argued instead that consumers' needs must be at the centre of the economic strategy;
3. Thatcher created 'enemies of the people': the welfare state was presented as being operated in the interests of an unaccountable professional section of society, public sector workers, instead of the public's interests;
4. These professional middle-class public sector workers were labelled as not running things in the national interest, meaning that a new group - business-minded middle class was needed to replace them;
5. The grassroots of the Labour Party were labelled as a sectional interest attempting to force the Parliamentary Labour Party to operate unconstitutionally, which went against the national interest;
6. Thatcher's statecraft restructured the institutions of the state to the Tories' advantage by centralising power and weakening local government. It also brought in anti-trade union laws to weaken the unions;
7. Thatcher employed populism around issues of public concern, such as morality, the British nation, law and order, and against those identified as working against the national interest, such as supporters of social democracy, the welfare state and the labour movement. She blamed these social groups for causing all the chaos of the 1970s and holding Britain and its economy back.[15]

If we look at Bulpitt's five elements of effective Tory statecraft for the Thatcher years, firstly, Thatcher did manage her party effectively until the end, when the party forced her out. But the Tory Party's problems in the 1990s and 2000s originated during Thatcher's leadership. Thatcher was successful at winning elections, and then some of this can be put down to other factors such as a divided opposition splitting the vote, luck (such as the Falkland War boosting her popularity) and using the advantage of being in office to call general elections at the time which looked best for the Tories. She wasn't successful in winning the political argument and battle of ideas. The opposition parties received above 50% of the vote combined, and it is unclear if she won the political argument within her cabinet. Regarding governing competence, Thatcher's record does not stand up well, with unrest, unemployment, scandals, questionable economic competence and finally, the Poll Tax disaster that finished her off.[16]

Other weaknesses of Thatcherism include its failure to appeal to the centre ground. The Tories also failed to combine the interests of its natural allies, taxation and public spending cuts with the general demands of a well-funded welfare state of healthcare, education, public transport, benefits and a social safety net. This could only be achieved with a genuine national economic strategy to increase economic growth and prosperity across all parts of Britain. Although Thatcher did increase Britain's economic growth, this mostly benefited the South of England, and it came at a high cost of deindustrialisation and high unemployment. This national economic strategy to help all parts of the country was beyond Thatcher's Tory Party, which instead preferred a small-state strategy to undermine social democracy.[17]

Major continued with Thatcherite policies such as privatisation. He did not have strong convictions and operated in a more conciliatory way to keep the party united. He wasn't Thatcherite enough for the party's rightwing, which caused him problems. The failure of Tory statecraft from 1992 resulted in the party losing the 1997 general election. Factors include sleaze, division over the EU, a revitalised Labour Party, unpopular public services policies, and loss of reputation for economic competence. After the 1992 election, the Tories' election-winning statecraft strategy failed to convincingly portray the Labour Party as representing sectional interests such as the labour movement. Tory sleaze meant the party looked compromised by wealthy sectional interests. The social and economic problems of the 1990s were viewed as caused by government management failure. The Tory free market approach had not produced economic stability or adequately funded the NHS. The Tories had not increased the size of the welfare state since 1979, and the Labour Party were viewed as better stewards of public services.[18]

Tory statecraft was missing between 1997 to 2005 as the party attempted to come to terms with defeat and was divided over Europe. In 2005, with the election of Cameron as leader, the party recovered its statecraft abilities, and the party moved back to the centre ground. Regarding party management, Cameron modernised the party by prioritising non-white and women parliamentary candidates. He also effectively handled the 2009 MPs' expenses scandal to minimise the damage to the party and take advantage of the issue when canvassing by focusing on the Labour Party's failure to deal with the crisis. But Cameron's party management struggled with disunity over his socially liberal policies and support for the EU, with the fallout from the EU referendum vote nearly splitting the Tory party. To win the political agreement, Cameron worked to give Thatcherism a human face, recognising the importance of tackling environmental and social issues. Cameron already had governing experience, having worked for the Tory Chancellor during the economic crisis of the 1990s. Fortunately for Cameron, the public never became aware of this, and the Tories were helped in the 2010 general election by Labour's perceived economic incompetence over the 2008 financial crisis. Cameron's statecraft abilities at winning elections were the best since Thatcher, with the Tories winning the largest number of seats in 2010 and then a majority in 2015.[19]

In 2019, the Brexit vote allowed Johnson to recreate British politics, so the Tories were again politically dominant. It was the most effective statecraft strategy since Thatcher. The core of Johnson's statecraft was Brexit, with leaving the EU framed as a demand to rebuild Britain's national community based on a narrow English understanding of the Union of the UK. This focus on national identity politics meant that the party worked to link the dominant narratives of British politics with the Tory Party. The Tories under Johnson were able to effectively reposition the party to take advantage of the new electoral terrain and recruit the support of leave voters under the 2019 general election slogan of 'Get Brexit Done'. The Labour Party were unable to build a coalition of Remain voters. Johnson's early party management saw him remove all MPs that did not commit to a hard Brexit. However, Partygate and other scandals resulted in party disunity and his removal after three years. Johnson effectively portrayed himself and the Tory party as the defender of the 'the people' and the Brexit vote against parliament and the EU to protect the national interest. This proved very successful. The other part of Johnson's offer was 'levelling up' to tackle the UK regional economic inequalities, framed as 'one nation' politics. This policy has been an important part of Tory statecraft strategy to attempt to hold onto new Tory voters in previous Labour 'red wall' constituencies in the Midlands and North of England.[20]

11

PROJECT GOVERNING AND ECONOMIC COMPETENCE

Through the last 123 years, the Tory Party have successfully managed to project an image of governing competence, certainly more so than the Labour Party. This is a key factor in governments winning reelection. It requires a credible leader, being on top of events and crises, party unity and economic competence, as discussed below. The Tories also benefit from a supportive press and media that cover for mistakes and help the Tories deflect blame as much as possible.

Governing competence is the perceived ability of a party in power to administer state affairs effectively. It also relates to voters' perceived competence of the opposition party to run the government. Governments generally lose elections rather than opposition parties winning them. And this is based on how governments perform, especially regarding economic competence. Other governing competence factors include policy success, having a clear agenda, a united and effective leadership team, and which party is perceived to provide the highest quality public services.

Following the Labour government's perceived incompetence during the 1970s, many skilled workers voted for Thatcher in 1979. Many kept voting Tory and then switched to Labour in 1997, following Major's poor government management during the 1990s. Many kept voting for Labour through the 2000s and switched to the Tories in 2010 following the 2008 financial crisis, which damaged

Labour's reputation for economic competence.[1]

During the run-up to the 2015 general election, the Tories compared the competence of Cameron's government with the possible chaos of Labour winning under Miliband. For the 2017 election, May's campaign tried to present her as 'strong and stable' versus a radical Labour Party under Corbyn. Johnson also employed this approach against Corbyn for the 2019 general election, with more success.[2]

Examples of Tory governments being viewed as incompetent and out of touch have heavily influenced their defeats, including in 1929, 1964, 1974 and 1997. These governments also struggled with disunity and scandals.[3] The current Tories have been in government for 13 years, with five leaders, and there is a general sense of incompetence about them. Cameron managed to project competence, but May, Johnson and especially Truss came across as incompetent. Sunak (so far) is perceived as relatively competent but based on Johnson and Truss's low bar.

Importance Of Economic Competence To Keep Winning

In the last 30 years, whichever party has led on the economy in opinion polls during a general election campaign has won and formed the next government. This applies to the Tories in 1992 and 2010 onwards and for Labour from 1997 to 2005. In 2023, Labour is now leading the Tories on managing the economy.[4]

Voters' opinions about the economy and who to vote for are based on three thought processes. First, voters assess the economy and if there is any reason to be optimistic about its future. Second, they identify current and future individual financial well-being. Third, an assessment of the economic competence of the party in government.[5] If these are positive and voters are optimistic about the future, the governing party will likely be reelected.

This helps explain why voters keep electing Tory governments, which generally have unpopular policies but are perceived to manage the economy well. Key factors that help a government's credibility are increasing wages and disposable income, lower unemployment levels, lower public sector borrowing, and low inflation and interest rates. Taxation is interesting because the conventional wisdom is that voters want lower taxes, but it's not that simple. A majority of the public would prefer to pay slightly higher taxes than see cuts to public services, and there is public support for tax increases for the wealthy.[6] This means that Tory governments have to be careful to make sure they are seen as investing in public services just enough and not reducing taxes too much, especially on the wealthy.

British governments were not considered responsible for the economy until 1914, but if the economy did well before this, the government normally benefited in elections.[7] Baldwin, Macmillan and Thatcher presented themselves as having governing and electoral competence by appealing to the British public's 'safety first' preference and labelling potential Labour governments as a risk to national economic security. Thatcher used the analogy of the housewife managing the household budget to argue for reducing public spending. During the 20th century, the public generally understood that the Tories were the party of balancing the books and effective government, whilst Labour governments implemented redistributive policies based on higher taxation and spending. This was unfortunately fueled by Labour governments being in office during several crises, followed by negative economic fallout and losing subsequent general elections. Prominent examples of this trend which span the last century, include the Wall Street Crash in 1929, a sterling crisis in 1947, the Winter of Discontent in the late 1970s, and the 2008 financial crisis.[8] However, when the Tories were in government during political and economic crises, they lost the next election, such as crises in the 1920s, 1930s, 1960s, 1970s and 1990s.[9] All this shows what an important factor it is for winning general elections in Britain.

Another important factor that helps the Tories regarding government competence is that if there is a choice between a perceived cruel and competent government versus a caring but incompetent one, voters will go with competence and cruelty. They would prefer caring and competent, but if that is not on offer, then competent always wins.[10]

The Tory Party presents itself as more focused on wealth creation than wealth distribution. Of course, the Tories do a lot of wealth distribution from ordinary people to the wealthy. The party projects its superior ability to generate economic growth, which it argues will benefit everyone. The Tories support people running businesses or owning property because it gives people a stake in the system, making them less likely to challenge it and also vote Tory. The Tories claim their close links to business, industry, and the City of London mean they are best placed to ensure Britain has a strong economy. [11]

The Tories' Poor Economic Record

Ironically, the Tories are seen as more competent at managing the economy than Labour because the facts show the opposite. The two Labour governments with working majorities, where the party had enough MPs to govern effectively, were in 1951 and 1970, and they left office with the economy in relevantly good shape.

Examples of Tory economic failures in the postwar period are as follows. In the 1950s, Macmillan's high government spending resulted in inflation and the resignation of his treasury team in 1958. In 1972, the 'Barber Boom' was set in motion by Chancellor Barber, which was intended to deal with periods of low growth and high inflation by delivering economic growth of 10% over 2 years. However, this resulted in hyperinflation, forcing anti-inflationary policies to control wages and prices. This led to the Heath government leaving office in 1974 with record-high inflation, budget deficits and balance of payments deficits. During Thatcher's rule in the 1980s, there were two long periods of recession, and following Thatcher, Major presided over another recession, as well as the economic disaster of Britain leaving the Exchange Rate Mechanism (ERM) in 1992. Finally, Cameron, May and Johnson have kept productivity and wages low, which can't be blamed on the Labour Party and the 2008 financial crisis.[12] And finally, we are all aware of how Truss crashed the British economy with her disastrous mini-budget of unfunded tax cuts.

Tory Economic Myths That Help Them Look Competent And Keep Winning

A recent clever Tory trick since Thatcher is how they've convinced the public that government debt is like credit card or household debt, which needs to be paid off urgently. This has been used to justify the Tories' austerity policies since 2010. It means Labour always have to promise to 'balance the books', even though this is not how a government deficit works, but the public believes it, so that's what matters. Government borrowing (by selling government bonds to international financial institutions) can be used for state capital investment and services to improve the country, help the economy grow, and raise more taxes as the economy grows. None of this applies to a household budget. The other difference is that those in a household will, at some point, retire, so their income will drop, as it is only supported by a fixed pension income. They will, therefore, not want any debt. This does not apply to a country, a national economy expects to keep growing, and it doesn't retire, so as long as it can make debt payments, it is not an issue. If economic growth is high, it's good to clear national debts so the country can borrow when the next economic crisis arrives. The Tories and their media have conned the public to believe a financial analogy that isn't true, but we all have to play along as voters believe it's true. Also, Labour must always go further than the Tories regarding fiscal (tax and spend) restraint, or they won't win elections. The Tories can get away with being less restrained because the right-wing media cover for them, an advantage Labour is lacking.[13]

Even though the Tories and the right-wing media repeatedly insist that British governments must 'balance the books' like a household, data shows that the Tories have failed to do this, compared to Labour. Since the Second World War, on average, the Tories have borrowed more than Labour, repaid less and are the party of greater deficit spending, which is spending above the amount raised through taxation. Labour repay government debts more of the time when in government and pay greater amounts. Since 1945, no government has cut spending to reduce the national debt. During this period, national debt repayments averaged about 4% of total borrowing, a small amount.[14]

12

MANUFACTURE TORY VOTERS

An advantage of being in power most of the time means the Tories can bring in policies to improve their chances of winning future elections. This includes supporting popular social policies around the welfare state and tackling poverty, even if the Tories don't try that hard on these areas once in government. Thatcher effectively widened asset ownership (houses and shares) during the 1980s to help her voter support base and build new support. The Tories use economic policy to help win elections: increasing government spending in marginal seats, reducing taxes just before an election, maintaining the triple-lock pension arrangements, and minimising the impacts of recent austerity cuts in Tory MP's seats. The Tories work hard to tilt the electoral playing field to help them keep winning elections. They practise 'gerrymandering', changing parliamentary seat boundaries to their advantage. Recently the Tories have borrowed voter suppression tactics from the US, such as introducing ID cards when voting.

Social Reform

Many Tories face a dilemma over social reform. Some might feel compassion for the low standard of living of millions of poor women and men in Britain, and they are also fully committed to the present social, political and economic system. They believe that the system has problems, but it is the best on offer to maintain stability, protect the nation and improve people's living standards in a gradual and measured way. But on the other hand, they think radical reform would end in disaster.

But to keep winning elections, the Tory Party must be seen to be concerned about the welfare of all parts of British society, especially the poorest and most disadvantaged. The party must also be perceived to represent all sections of the nation because if large numbers of voters realised that the Tories only represent a sectional interest, this would damage their chances of winning the next general election. The Tories will therefore intervene in the market only as far as it is useful and necessary to keep winning. If the proposed legislation is found to threaten any of the party's interests and supporters, then it will also be resisted.

There are varying perspectives within the Tory Party about the amount of welfare the state should provide. Some favour a market-led approach that focuses on wealth creation and economic growth. They believe private welfare services are more effective and efficient than public services. Other Tories believe that the state needs to intervene in the market to reduce inequality and that social reform is morally correct and a better alternative to socialism.

In the first half of the twentieth century, the Tories introduced minimal social reforms. These reforms did just enough for the Tories to remain popular but did not attempt to change the core arrangements of the system. During this period, the Tories favoured a voluntarist approach, believing it was best for individuals to arrange their private welfare provisions.

Another consideration for the Tories is the need for a well-fed, healthy and educated workforce for commercial purposes. Failure to ensure an available workforce would result in businesses struggling to operate effectively. This commercial self-interest argument to ensure Britain has a strong national economy became popular with Tories through the twentieth century. However, it is not something that 21st-century Tory governments have prioritised.

The Second World War highlighted the gaps in social provision at the time, and the war shifted the population to the left, with a general expectation that after the war, the state would resolve these problems. However, it was clear to all that private services could not provide what was needed and demanded. Therefore, after the 1945 Tory defeat, the party worked on presenting itself as more compassionate and interventionist.

The 1950s saw cross-party support for social justice and the welfare state, with Macmillan being a determined social reformer. An example of a specific social reform driven by electoral factors was a decision in 1955 that female civil servants were to be paid the same as their male colleagues. Labour had announced a campaign on the issue, and the Tories were concerned that this might make them vulnerable at the next election. Also, during the 1950s, the Tories held back on introducing immigration controls to project a progressive image and, again, not give Labour something to exploit.

From the 1970s, Heath moved back towards the market from intervention via the welfare state. Thatcher then took this further, with her reform being focused on increasing government centralisation and reducing 'bureaucracy' in public services by introducing commercial principles and privatisation. By the 1990s, poverty had increased, taxes had increased on low-wage workers, and the living standards of the poorest 10% hadn't increased in twenty years. These facts were hard for those not affected to relate to, but there was a noticeable increase in burglaries, muggings, car theft, beggars and homelessness. The 1980s and 1990s saw Britain become visibly more unequal, undermining the Tories' claim to represent the whole country.[1]

Between 2005 and 2010, Cameron led the Tories in opposition, and the party strongly promoted the idea of 'compassionate conservatism'. This was part of the modernisation process of the party to show it had changed and make it electable again after years in opposition. The party stressed the importance of tackling social issues such as poverty, inequality, social mobility, family structure and maintaining public services spending. Once in government, and following the 2008 financial crisis, this agenda became less of a priority than managing the Coalition government, austerity and disagreements over EU membership. 'Compassionate conservative' policies from this period included Marriage (Same Sex Couples) Act in 2013, protecting NHS spending, protecting the pension triple lock, an increase the UK's international aid to 0.7% of GDP, increasing income tax personal allowance and the introduction of the Pupil Premium for schools. But most of these policies were brought in to win and hold on to power for the party.[2]

Theresa May based her 2016 leadership campaign for the Tory Party and Prime Minister on 'one-nation' principles of uniting the country and radical social reform. She vaguely said this would include 'reforming capitalism', helping the 'left behind' and 'just about managing'. But this all came to nothing as Brexit consumed her. Johnson and his adviser Dominic Cummings correctly identified that state intervention in the economy is popular. So, 'levelling up' was a key part of the Tory Party's 2019 general election offer to provide government economic investment in the midlands and the north. But, as we all know, this was just a slogan to win the election, and very little levelling up was achieved. Johnson also made a big deal of the Health and Social Care Levy Act 2021 to fund the NHS and the struggling social care system.

Property Owning Democracy

The term 'property-owning democracy' was first used by conservative Noel Skelton in articles for the Tory Spectator magazine in 1923. He believed the increase in the number of property owners would reduce the appeal of socialism to the working class.[3] The Housing Act 1923 was brought in by Chamberlain, which subsidised private businesses for every new house they built. After seven years, over one million houses had been built.[4] Chamberlain stated that "we are building up a whole new class of good citizens," which gave property ownership a sense of civic purpose and moral value normally associated with left policies.[5]

During this period, there were also significant subsidies to local authorities from the Labour government's Wheatley Act of 1924. In 1932, the Tory government cancelled public housing subsidies except for slum clearance. The aim was for all housing to be privately funded, built and owned. During the interwar years, the Tories used the rise of socialism to claim that ordinary people could own their own homes with them in government, but Labour would force everyone to live in council houses. Only one in ten could own their home, which tapped into people's aspirational desires to own their own home.

The Ideal Homes exhibition run by the Daily Mail newspaper was very successful. It was initially held in 1908 and, by the 1930s, had about 700,000 visitors. The newspaper heavily covered it, developing the idea of an individual home with settings, fittings, lifestyle and labour-saving devices. It linked all this to the Tory Party and a vision of an affluent and aspirational society. This was all intentionally framed to appeal to women and to the possibility of transforming the limited role of the housewife in that period.[6]

During the 1930s, Labour was committed to the need for public housing in urban areas. The Tories were not to be outdone, so they invested in large public housing projects such as 40,000 council homes in Birmingham. In addition, Chamberlin supported the creation of the Municipal Savings Bank, with multiple branches in Birmingham, providing a third of the population with mortgages to buy their own homes. Some of these purchases were originally council houses. At the time, Birmingham was seen at the forefront of progressive housing policy.[7]

The Tories were elected in 1951 with a manifesto commitment to build 300,000 houses per year. Macmillan was the housing minister then and realised this target could only be reached through increased public housing projects. Alongside this, the Tories brought in policies encouraging home ownership, such as cheap mortgages, and simplified the process of building private homes. All this resulted in a large increase in homeownership that would continue over the following decade. During the 1950s and 1960s, council housing tenants were allowed to purchase their homes. Macmillan removed the obstacles to the sale of council housing, and during this period, Tory councils sold thousands of public houses to tenants. Due to this popularity, it became of interest nationally and was broadly supported by the Tory Party.[8]

In the 1980s, Thatcher promoted individualism to create new voters and undermine the collectivism of working-class voters. She wanted people to think of themselves as consumers and make choices to benefit themselves. Individualism first took hold in middle-class corporate culture and spread to the working class. Many voters were convinced by the aspirational lifestyle based on material goods funded by disposable income or credit. This provided a solid base of support for the Tories under Thatcher.

A key part of Thatcher's strategy to increase individualism was to increase homeownership. Tax cuts achieved this, increased shared ownership schemes, cuts to public services to keep interest rates low and therefore support mortgage holders, the selling off of council housing to tenants at a reduced rate of 50% (right to buy) and deregulating the private rental sector to the benefit of landlords and disadvantage of renters. Increased home ownership was popular, electorally beneficial and met Thatcher's ideological goals of increasing individualism. Mortgages naturally make people more conservative because they must make monthly payments or lose their homes. They also have an asset that is gaining value and are keen to maximise its value.

Thatcher was keen to get larger companies back into the private rental sector, having been driven out by rent controls. By 1983, there were 1 million extra homeowners, and the Tories could accuse Labour of wanting to reverse the right to buy scheme. The 1983 Tory Party election manifesto offered increased right to buy discounts, increased access to mortgages and supported house building to rent out. Council tenants were given the right to repair their homes and reclaim the money from local authorities. The 1987 Tory election manifesto had little homeownership specifics except the aspiration to extend it. The party proudly claimed that two-thirds of homes were owner-occupied.

By the late 1980s, there was a shortage of private rental properties, so Thatcher introduced several policies to increase flexibility and bring empty properties back onto the market. Council tenants were given more choices about how to manage their properties. This caused council and social housing tenants to have a more individualistic outlook. In the private rental sector, the landlord's rights were increased, with renters becoming legally powerless. Rent rates were to be set by the market. This has encouraged many homeowners to become landlords, strengthening the Tory voting base.[9] Thatcher also deregulated the mortgage industry, resulting in commercial banks entering the market. Credit availability in the housing market increased, leading to a house price boom, which encouraged more people to take out large mortgages, further fueling the boom.[10]

Between 1979 and 1995, 2.1 million homes were bought by their occupants. In 2019, 2 million publicly owned houses were left, a big decrease from 6.5 million in 1980. Thatcher manufactured new Tory voters who were upwardly socially mobile, homeowners, and car owners and felt they were sharing the benefits of a growing economy. Thatcher presented a clear and credible political offer to build a strong economy, increase living standards, and renew national pride. Thatcher convincingly presented her party as having moved on from the post-war narrative of Britain in decline and made an aspirational offer to voters.[11] The huge increase in homeownership has increased people's investment in private property and the national economy. The Tories understand that aspiration, homeownership and voting preferences are closely linked, and they work hard so this benefits their electoral prospects.[12]

The Cameron and Osborne years saw several housing-related policies intended to help get young people onto the housing ladder and ensure house prices continued to increase to look after the Tories' property-owning coalition of voters. These policies included part-rent part-mortgage deals, Help to Buy schemes, and a new right to buy offer for those in housing association properties. They had little effect and were mainly to help with the 2015 general election campaign. Cameron's governments restricted councils from building more public houses to maintain property prices. They also allowed private property developers to miss their targets on building social housing.[13]

Privatisation And Public Share Sell Offs

Thatcher's privatisation program aimed to roll back state intervention, reduce government spending and borrowing, ensure low-interest rates, and force nationalised service providers to become competitive and customer-focused. Most public sectors faced some form of privatisation. Two of the largest nationalised monopolies the Tories privatised were British Telecom and British Gas Corporation. The monopolies were broken up by selling shares to employees and the public.

In 1984, the Tory government sold half of its shares in BT. Trade unions opposed the denationalisation, so the Tories sweetened the deal by offering BT employees free shares, which most workers claimed. They also offered £3 million in shares to the public, hoping to appeal to small and new investors. It raised £3.9 billion, and the share offer was highly oversubscribed. The British Gas share sell-off in 1986 was bigger than BT's, raising £9 billion from 1.5 million shareholders from an effective marketing campaign. The Tories went on to comfortably win the 1987 general election. The number of individual shareholders nationally increased from 7% in 1979 to 25% in 1991, a total of 12.5 million people.[14]

Using Economic Policy For Political Gain

The Tories have used economic policies for electoral gain for a long time, specifically fiscal policy, which relates to government taxation and spending. This has been used to maintain the support of the Tory voter base and appeal to floating or swing voters in marginal parliamentary constituencies instead of applying economic policies for the long-term benefit of the British economy. They are more interested in ensuring the British economy's electoral cycle and economic health are in sync to help them win.

Given a choice, the Tories will go for short-term policies so that voters relate the 'feel good' factor to the Tory government in the months before a general election. For example, this happened before, and after the elections in 1955, 1964, 1983, 1987, 1992, 2015, 2017 and 2019 This approach unites the party, and the Tories won each of those elections, except in 1964. Post-election, the Tories must reduce public spending or increase taxes to balance the books.

A key part of the Tory Party's con is to raise taxes in the early part of a parliament and then drop taxes a bit as the next election approaches. However, overall taxes are still higher than they were before the initial increase, but they still call this slight drop in taxes a tax cut. The right-wing media back them up, and millions of voters believe them.[15]

The Tories get away with this due to the public's lack of understanding and interest in how government economic policy works. They have successfully framed how people think about the economy concerning taxation. It has become a simple question of if people want to pay more or less in taxes, and of course, the Tories always argue they will keep taxes low. The Tories have taken advantage of this since the 1980s, distracting voters from general tax increases by increasing indirect taxes and making a big show of decreasing income tax. Sneaky increases in indirect taxes in the 1980s and 1990s were the doubling of VAT, freezing personal allowance tax and increasing National Insurance contributions.[16] Osborne tried to do this with inheritance tax in the 2010s.

In the 1970s, the amount of money pensioners got was linked to average earnings, price and inflation to ensure pensioners had enough to live on. Thatcher scrapped the link between pensions and average earnings and kept the prices/inflation link. Pension payments went up but at a lower rate. Inflation was low during the late 1990s and early 2000s, and Labour under Blair introduced a change to increase pensions by at least 2.5% even if inflation were low. Labour committed to adding the earnings link at a later date. The Coalition government added the earnings link in 2012, creating the 'triple lock pension'. Since then, pensions have increased by whichever gives the higher pension amount, based on either inflation, average wage increases or a 2.5% pension rise. The government pension bill is 4.8% of the UK's GDP (about £121 billion) and will only increase due to the UK's ageing population.[17]

Pensioners are much more likely to vote in elections and also much more likely to vote Tory than those under 65. Therefore, the pension triple lock was a key part of Tory manifestos throughout the 2010s. Cameron focused on winning the vote of the retired by protecting the pension triple lock and providing incentives for this age group to buy second and third homes to rent out privately, further binding this group to the Tories.[18] Since 2012 the May, Johnson, and Sunak governments have considered changing the pension triple lock to reduce public spending on pensions, and all three have backed off following an outcry from pensioners and the right-wing media coming to their defence.

Suppose we look at the Coalition government's austerity program. Councils most severely affected by the cuts in public spending are in poorer areas represented by Labour MPs, and Councils in Tory MPs seats were less affected. Recent Tory governments have been protecting areas with Tory MPs from the worst effects of austerity to help them win elections.[19]

The Johnson government used the levelling up agenda to funnel public money to wealthy areas with Tory MPs, so the party kept winning these seats. Of the government's £4.8 billion levelling up regional deprivation fund, there were 31 priority English regions, and 26 are only represented by Tory MPs. Of the other 5, one is a Tory-Labour marginal seat.[20] Sunak was caught on camera during the 2022 leadership election claiming that he reallocated public money from 'deprived urban areas' to wealthy areas when he was chancellor.[21]

Another Tory trick to win general elections is to spend public money in seats with Tory MPs to help them win again. In the months before the 2019 general election, Johnson directed levelling up funds to schools in Tory seats.[22] He also used the £3.6 billion Towns Fund, which is meant to help struggling communities, to help Tory MPs in marginal seats. Labour MPs represent 85% of England's most deprived urban areas but over half of this funding went to seats with

Tory MPs.

The Tories Tilt The Electoral Playing Field To Help Them Keep Winning Elections

There was a lot of resistance from the Tories to public demands to extend the franchise in the 19th century, so all could vote. These reforms were introduced in stages, starting in the 1860s, and weren't complete until 1928. These reforms were carried out by Liberal governments or moderate Tory Prime Ministers seeking to appeal to the centre ground, against the wishes of many in the party.

The Tories have long practised gerrymandering to improve their chances of winning elections. This is changing the geography of boundaries of parliamentary constituencies to strengthen marginal seats with a Tory MP or dilute the vote of opposition parties in marginal seats without a Tory MP.

Boundary changes and the introduction of postal voting brought in during the 1951-64 period of rule helped the Tories. There were boundary changes in 1974 and 1983, each of which was believed to have resulted in Labour losing thirty seats. Seats decreased in the north and increased in southern counties and suburban areas.[24] The Johnson government has brought in boundary changes that will come in 2023 and could mean that the Tories gain 5-10 extra seats. Scotland is expected to have 2 fewer seats and Wales 8 fewer seats, with England gaining 10, where the Tories are most dominant.[25]

Over the last 13 years of this Tory government, they have also been working on changes to voter registration to disenfranchise voters. They claim it was to stop voter fraud, but this is not a credible reason based on the very low levels of voting fraud in the UK. In the mid-2010s, the electoral register switched from households being able to register to everyone having to register individually. This sounds rational enough, but about 2 million people were estimated to be removed from the electoral register. The Tories did this to reduce voter turnout, which helps them in elections, as explained in Chapter 1.[26]

In 2016, the Tories also reduced 'Short money'. These are the payments that opposition parties receive from Parliament to be able to function. The Labour Party lost more than £1 million annually. Also, in 2016, the Tories introduced the Trade Union Act, which was legislation intended to disadvantage both unions and the Labour Party. The act forces unions to ask all members to 'opt-in' to politically funding the Labour Party. This is intended to reduce the ability of the unions to campaign politically and significantly reduces trade union funding for the Labour Party. Hypocritically, there is no similar legislation to force companies to ballot their shareholders about donating to the Tories.[27]

The recent Elections Act 2022 has brought in legislation that, from 2023, voters need to show photo identification when casting their vote. This is from the US 'Voter Suppression Playbook' of 'protecting voter integrity' when voter fraud is almost non-existent in Britain. The Tories hope this will benefit them because older voters are more likely to carry identification, and people of colour and young people are less likely to have it, which are groups that typically vote Labour. The Elections Act has also given the Tory government direct control of the Electoral Commission, so it is no longer independent. This means that the Tories can change who can campaign, the types of activities they can perform, and spending limits. One change relates to campaigning groups and organisations and how these activities are now linked to political parties' spending limits. This directly affects trade unions, with the spending any campaigning a union does for the Labour Party now having to be allocated to the Labour Party's spending limits. This will result in an overall reduction in campaigning for Tory opposition parties.[28]

13

DISTRACT, INVENT ENEMIES, DIRTY TRICKS, CRUSH OPPONENTS

The Tories are skilled in explaining away and normalising their failure to govern and the negative impacts on the most vulnerable. They distract, blame others, or claim that things are bad but would be much worse if Labour were in government. They invent domestic and foreign enemies that they claim only the Tory Party can save the nation from. The Tories also take action to crush their opponents, either inventing enemies that they don't see as a threat but are good scapegoats or opponents that they do see as a potential threat or obstacle to their aims, such as the Labour Party and trade unions. Finally, this chapter will cover how the Tories use dirty tricks and illegal methods to keep winning.

Distract, Blame Others, Invent Enemies

The Tories work hard to dissociate their poor ability to govern by avoiding responsibility for any problems while in government, thus shifting the blame elsewhere. Instead, they invent problems, enemies, and threats to the nation and demonise 'other' social groups that do not vote for them in elections, such as the poor, the vulnerable and the young. The Tories claim that only they can save us from these threats.

The Tories and the press first employed this tactic in the interwar years by trying to link the Labour Party to the British Communist Party and the USSR. This 'red menace' method effectively attracted votes.[1] The tactic was repeated with Labour leader Michel Foot in the 1980s and Jeremy Corbyn in the 2010s.

Thatcher invented a lot of enemies during her 11 years in power. These included the unemployed, even though she caused mass unemployment with her economic policies. She accused the unemployed of being scrounger welfare dependents cheating the system. However, only one in three thousand welfare claimants were found to claim benefits without needing them, and 1.3 million out of 3 million unemployed did not claim any benefits they were entitled to at all.[2] Other enemies that Thatcher invented include the miners, gay people, Greenham Common women peace campaigners, black people in urban areas, new age travellers, far left/far-right groups, and football hooligans. Thatcher labelled these invented enemies as the 'enemy within'.[3]

Thatcher presented herself as against the establishment and the institutions of the British state, which included the civil service, local government, the Church, universities and the BBC. Before Thatcher, the Tories defended these institutions, but she saw them as feeding an anti-business culture that blocked her vision for a 'free economy'.[4] The Tories during the 1980s attacked what they saw as the BBC's bias and lack of patriotism over the Falklands War. Thatcher also attacked commercial television by bringing in a franchise system, with auctions for the highest bidder. [5]

When John Major replaced Thatcher as Prime Minister in 1990, he invented new enemies; single mothers and teachers replaced the trade unions. The attack on single mothers was part of moral panic during the 1990s related to the Tories' 'Back to Basic' campaign. This campaign was an attempt to promote the social conservatism of the traditional family. Several Tories condemned young women for having babies without stable relationships and for having babies to get state welfare benefits.[6]

For Cameron, there were several invented enemies. There was an ongoing attack on benefit claimants as a 'lifestyle choice' and that they should be working. His government 'reformed' the benefits system to make claiming benefits more difficult. In opposition, Cameron said he wanted to reduce poverty in Britain, but his austerity and benefit-cutting policies in government did the opposite. Cameron also attacked migrants for coming to Britain and claiming benefits, so he brought in policies to reduce their access to unemployment benefits, housing benefits and the NHS.[7]

Cameron used the 2008 financial crisis to create a narrative of 'always cleaning up Labour's messes' to bring in austerity and 'balance the books'. Although austerity was accepted during the 2010s, it is now seen to have damaged the British economy, combined with serious social and health impacts on the population.[8]

The Tories under Johnson managed to present themselves as challengers of the establishment (known as populism) and also defenders of the nation against the threat of the Labour Party. Tory rule since 2010 has resulted in declining wages and living standards and created the Brexit crisis. But at the 2019 general election, they presented themselves as the only party that could solve Britain's problems. We have now had five Tory Prime Ministers in seven years, and May, Johnson, Truss, and Sunak have each claimed that their government is a clean slate and a new beginning, even though the new Prime Minister and cabinet were part of the last administration. This ability to disassociate is enabled by Britain's right-wing media, an unsuspecting public and a weak Labour Party that generally plays along.[9]

Johnson's invented threats for his 'culture wars' have included the judges, the EU, the liberal elite, universities, the BBC, and 'wokeness', which is a negative use of the term to undermine racial and social justice. All this maintains the Tory coalition and ensures that any debates regarding patriotism and social issues are done on right-wing terms.[10]

During the Covid pandemic, Johnson and the Tories blamed anyone else to distract from the thousands of unnecessary deaths due to the Tory government's mishandling of the crisis. The Tories tried to blame the public, migrants, Black Lives Matter protesters, young people having a night out and the use of the racist euphemism 'communities with large households'. The Tories also blamed local councils, city mayors, the care home sector (especially temporary care workers), new public health bodies, the NHS, and the scientific establishment.

Johnson and Sunak have put a lot of effort into blaming any problems on external factors and claiming that there is little that the government can do about it. For example, they absolve themselves of responsibility for the pandemic by identifying it as an international crisis. They also blamed the war on Ukraine as being the cause of Britain's economic problems, energy crisis, rising inflation and cost of living. In addition, Johnson tried to blame the last Labour government for recent economic problems, despite Labour being out of government for the last 13 years.[11] Johnson and his Transport Secretary attempt to blame Labour for the strikes in 2022 and 2023, presumably trying to connect the current wave of strikes to the 1970s and 1980s strikes.[12] And in the last few months of Johnson's government, the Tories tried to blame the Bank of England for the economic crisis.[13]

In 2021 there was the 'Beergate' controversy. Labour leader Starmer was videoed drinking beer during a Covid pandemic lockdown at a Labour campaign meeting in Durham for the local elections. Labour and Starmer explained that he was complying with the lockdown rules as it was during a break from a work event. The police investigated and cleared all those present. The event was covered in the press but got little attention. Following Johnson's Partygate allegations and Starmer's calls for Johnson to resign, the Tories and the right-wing media ran ongoing press stories stating Starmer broke lockdown rules and was a hypocrite. This was an attempt to distract the public from the Johnson scandal. After Johnson was fined for breaking his own Covid lockdown rules, Starmer again said he should resign. The Press and Tories made a big fuss just before the 2022 local elections and said the Labour Durham event should be investigated again, even though Starmer had been clearer. Durham police were under pressure, so did open a new investigation. Starmer said he would resign if found to have broken lockdown rules. The police cleared Starmer in July 2022, and by that time, Johnson's government was in crisis, and he was about to resign as Prime Minister.

The 2022 Tory leadership election saw the candidates invent multiple enemies, including LGBT+ people, immigrants, and human rights being 'forced' on the UK by 'foreign courts', the EU and the Northern Ireland Protocol.[14] Truss tried to use trade union strikes as part of the culture wars to blame them for the economic crisis, even though voters normally blame the government for economic problems.[15] Truss's government tried to blame the Labour Party and the Bank of England for the economic crisis following her disastrous Mini-Budget in September 2022. In late 2022, Sunak's Home Secretary Suella Braverman escalated the racist scapegoating by describing refugees and asylum seekers arriving in England from Europe as an 'invasion'.

The Dead Cat Strategy

Over the last 13 years, the Tories have introduced the 'dead cat strategy'. This communication technique uses a shocking announcement to distract attention from a failure, scandal or crisis and redirect it elsewhere. It is associated with the Australian political strategist Lynton Crosby.[16]

Here are some examples. In 2013, Miliband, the Labour Party leader of the time, pushed the cost of living crisis to dominate the political agenda. The Tories and right-wing media successfully distracted from this by making a fuss over an investigation into the Falkirk local Labour Party candidate selection process. The trade union, Unite, was accused of attempting to recruit Labour Party members to ensure their preferred candidate was successful. The police investigated the issue, and no laws or party rules were found to have been broken.[17]

In 2016, Cameron used a shocking line about immigration to distract from a government failure to tax the tech giant Google.[18] In 2018, following an embarrassing debate in Parliament for Theresa May over her Brexit deal, Labour leader Corbyn was accused of calling Teresa May a 'stupid woman'. It's unlikely that Corbyn said this, but it was enough to distract from May's political failings.[19]

Johnson was the master of the dead cat strategy. In 2019, the Tories needed to distract from a scandal over the Brexit bus claim that winning the Brexit referendum would mean £350 million extra would go to the NHS per week. So an ingenious distraction story was made up about Johnson making model buses from wine crates, so this story is what comes up on internet searches related to Johnson and buses.[20] In 2020, the Tories used Johnson catching and nearly dying from Covid to distract from bad headlines.[21] In 2021, it's likely that Johnson brought in new Covid measures for the public to distract from the Downing Street parties during Covid lockdowns, known as the Partygate scandal.[22] In April 2021, Johnson was caught up in lobbying scandals with James Dyson and the Saudi Crown Prince. Attention was deflected by claiming the leaks came from Dominic Cummings, Johnson's former advisor, who had left on bad terms, which cast doubt on the whole story.[23] In February 2022, to avoid attention from the Partygate scandal, Johnson accused Labour leader Starmer of helping Jimmy Savile, a child sex offender, to avoid prosecution when Starmer was director of public prosecutions. This was truly shocking at the time, and one of Johnson's top aides resigned, stating this was the reason.[24] It also looks like Johnson tried to use the plan to deport asylum seekers to Rwanda to distract from his Partygate fine.[25]

Crush Domestic Enemies

Tories bring in policies and use state forces to crush two main domestic groups in Britain. The first is 'invented enemies;' these are no threat to the status quo but fuel their populist politics—examples include immigrants, people with low incomes or benefit claimants.

The Tories can get away with attacking these groups as they are small social groups that either don't vote or don't vote for the Tories. The second group are those the Tories do see as a potential real threat, with the trade unions being the main example.

During periods of unrest in the last 123 years, the Tories have implemented subtle and discreet strategies that are unnoticed by most voters. Of the big strikes we saw in the 20th century, few trade unionists wanted to bring down the government. Therefore, governments could keep control during each period of unrest. Tory governments have broken the law over the years. Still, the draconian power available from the Emergency Powers Act of 1920 has given governments plenty to work with to keep control. The British state has never seriously been threatened with insurrection or revolutionary overthrow. How they responded to serious challenges, such as the Chartists in the 1840s and unrest before and after the First World War, indicate how seriously the establishment will defend the system.[26]

Britain saw a lot of unrest from 1910-14 and the years after the First World War from 1918-26. Mostly this was disputes between workers and employers that escalated, and the Liberal coalition government (including the Tories) had to step in. The Suffragette movement was also using militant tactics in their struggles for the vote for women. 1919 saw strikes and unrest in Glasgow, Belfast and Liverpool. The coalition government called the army into each city to restore control. In Glasgow, tanks were driven through the city, and warships were anchored in the Mersey, next to Liverpool, as a show of strength.

In response, the coalition government set up the Supply and Transport Committee (STC) in 1919 to deal with any future unrest. The army did not want to get involved in civil matters unless there was no other choice, so the government needed to find its own way of maintaining control. The STC stockpiled rifles and machine guns at army bases to be available to 'loyal' civilians in an emergency, and an emergency communication system was created. The STC was improved and expanded during the 1920s and maintained by the first Labour government from 1923-4, to the Tories' surprise.

The General Strike of 1926 lasted for nine days in May. It was called by the Trade Union Congress (TUC) to force the government to prevent wage reduction and worsening conditions for 1.2 million coal miners. 1.7 million workers went on strike: miners, transport and dockers, printers, ironworkers and steelworkers. The government was well prepared for the strike. This was the first test of the STC, and it proved itself. Transport systems and the electricity grid continued to function with the help of volunteers. The army marched through London, and highly visible military camps were set up in London's parks. The strike was defeated as the TUC was not committed and looking for any excuse to end the strikes.[27]

The next period of serious unrest was the 1970s. Tory Prime Minister Heath was elected in 1970 and aimed to take on the unions. He brought in legislation to arbitrate disputes between unions and employers. The labour movement refused to recognise the legitimacy of the new arbitration process, resulting in strikes and protests. In 1971 a recession caused miners' strikes over wages, and Heath was forced to back down. That year, Heath set up the Civil Contingencies Unit (CCU) in secret to deal with potential disorder. In 1973, The CCU identified 16 vulnerable industries and their potential for disruption. It described how the army could be used during strikes. Strikes continued from 1972-4, resulting in the three-day week and power cuts.[28]

Thatcher's 1979 election manifesto stated that the most serious threat to Britain's freedom and security was the increasing disrespect for the rule of law. The Labour Party and labour movement were blamed for undermining law and order. This gave Thatcher the legitimacy to take on the miners in 1984-5.[29] Thatcher implemented a 'two-nation' strategy. She labelled some groups as domestic enemies, such as black people, the labour movement, the anti-nuclear movement, anti-Cruise-missile feminists, New Age Travelers, homosexuals and rebellious local councils. Thatcher believed that these groups needed to be disciplined because they were 'holding Britain back' and 'working against the national interest' to limit hard-working peoples 'freedom of choice' about how they live their lives.

This polarised many voters to support her against these 'public enemies,' combined with the strategic introduction of social and economic policies to shore up her support.[30]

During the 1970s, a moral panic developed around muggings by black people. It was completely unfounded, as there was no actual increase in violent assaults. Once elected, Thatcher, in response to this, gave the police more power to stop and search, resulting in racist discrimination against black people and tensions with the police. There was also increasing inner-city unemployment and deprivation. Tension built up, leading to riots in several cities and towns in England in 1981, with violent clashes between police and protesters.

In opposition, Thatcher and her advisors developed strategies to privatise nationalised industries slowly and methodically. They took on the trade unions in non-vulnerable industries where the Tory government could win. Following two years in office, the Tories backed down to the miners' demands in 1981, as they were not ready for the confrontation at that point. However, following their 1983 general election victory, Thatcher was ready to take the miners on, leading to the 1984-5 miners' strike. In preparation for the conflict, the government built up coal stocks, ensured new anti-union laws were in place, centralised the command of the police force and trained thousands of extra riot police. The Tories won, and the miners had to back down and go back to work without their demands being met. The conflict cost the taxpayer £3.75 billion, and the Tories went on to close over 100 coal pits. Over 100,000 miners were made redundant, destroying hundreds of mining villages.

The Tories during the 1980s attacked the BBC for not being sufficiently patriotic and supportive of the government during the Falklands War. The BBC Radio 4 Today programme was seen to damage relations with the government over perceived bias. Rupert Murdoch's newspapers, such as the Sun, also attacked the BBC and aimed to end the BBC's licence fee funding model and the BBC's independence. Thatcher also went after the commercial television stations, awarding new franchises to the highest bidder. The new franchise system allocated more advertising revenue to the government, leaving less for making programmes.[31]

In addition, Thatcher went after local Labour government administrations in urban areas that opposed her policies. In 1985, Thatcher restricted local council spending. Fifteen councils refused to set budgets, to force the government to intervene and provide local services or back down. Liverpool and Lambeth held out the longest but backed down in the end, in what is known as the 'rate-capping rebellion'.[32] The Greater London Council (GLC) had been created by previous Tory Prime Minister Macmillan in 1963 but became a thorn in Thatcher's side during the 1980s. It was led by Ken Livingston and the Labour Party and implemented progressive policies across London, much to Thatcher's annoyance. So in 1986, Thatcher simply abolished the GLC, along with other metropolitan councils.[33]

Thatcher attempted to change how local government was funded by introducing The Community Charge, known as the 'poll tax', in 1989. This was very unpopular; it shifted the tax burden from the rich to the poor based on the number of people living in a house instead of an estimate of the property's market value. It resulted in protests, a large nonpayment campaign, and riots, contributing to Thatcher's resignation as Prime Minister. Major replaced it with Council Tax in 1991.[34]

Thatcher also took on the civil service. She saw the state as a drag on economic activity and despised the civil service's ethic of neutral 'non-political' professionalism. Thatcher had a blacklist of militant civil service workers. She brought in a business leader to advise on 'waste' in the civil service. In 1980, the Tories got into a 20-week pay dispute strike with the civil service union. The union lost. Thatcher then brought all civil service management departments under her control in the Cabinet Office and Treasury. She also ended national collective bargaining for the civil service to weaken union power. She introduced business management practices to the civil service, such as pay increases based on performance. Between 1979 and 1986, the civil service lost a fifth of its staff.[35]

Over the last 35 years, the Tories have brought in four pieces of 'public order' legislation. The 1986 Public Order Act was in response to the unrest in the 1980s. It imposed limits on public assembly and protests, which, if ignored, allowed the police to make arrests. The Criminal Justice and Public Order Act 1994 was brought in to give police preemptive powers to stop unlicensed outdoor raves/free party events and the itinerant communities associated with them that the police were struggling to control.

More recently, the Tories brought in the Police, Crime, Sentencing and Courts Act 2022, which updates the two previous Acts to give the police more powers to stop 'disruptive protests' and tackle unlawful trespass and 'unauthorised encampments'.[36] This Act didn't go far enough for the Tories, who introduced the Public Order Act in 2023 to target 'guerilla' protest tactics by groups such as Extinction Rebellion, Just Stop Oil, and Insulate Britain. New offences relate to 'locking on', disrupting transport and infrastructure and 'Serious Disruption Prevention Orders' to limit the freedoms of repeat offenders. Police will also get increased stop and search power to 'prevent' disruptive protests.[37]

Dirty Tricks

The Tory Party is comfortable using dirty and sometimes illegal methods to keep winning. To avoid being accused of sharing conspiracy theories, this section is based on Establishment sources, which can be checked. Some may find it hard to believe that the Tories would behave like this because we are meant to live in a 'decent and fair' country. But millions of people in Britain know exactly what the Tories are and how they operate, although the Tories ignore these people. The Tories only need to con the correct number of voters in a certain number of marginal seats to keep governing.

An interesting example can be found following the First World War when Philip Cambray joined the Tory Party Central Office, where he supervised mass letter writing to the press in secret. Multiple Tory letter writers would send dozens of letters to newsletters under different pseudonyms, promoting Tory ideas or criticising the ideas of the opposition. Cambray also set up a 'front' organisation called the Industrial Press Service, which inserted Tory propaganda in non-conservative newspapers.[38]

Another example is the publication of the Zinoviev letter during the October 1924 general election campaign. The letter turned out to be a fake. It claimed to be instructions from Zinoviev, the head of the Communist International in Moscow, encouraging the Communist Party of Great Britain (CPGB) to influence the Labour government to normalise its relationship with the Soviet Union. The fake letter claimed this would radicalise the British working class, so the CPGB was in a good position to conduct a Bolshevik-style revolution. The Labour government was in office then, advocating a policy of better diplomatic relations and increasing trade with the Soviet Union, which gave the letter credibility. The Conservative Party paid for a copy of the letter and gave it to the Daily Mail newspaper to distribute for maximum effect. The newspaper made it a front-page story three days before the election, and it is believed to have convinced many Liberal voters to vote for the Tories out of fear, resulting in a large majority for the Tories at the election.[39]

Also during this period, one of Baldwin's advisors wrote in their memoirs that the Tory Central Office had an agent in the Labour Party Headquarters. The Tories were given Labour Party reports on the British public's political opinions and preferences. The Tory Central Office also had a relationship with the Labour Party's printers, so Tories got copies of Labour's leaflets and pamphlets. This meant that the Tories could produce a response to these publications immediately. [40]

Labour leaders and politicians were targeted throughout the twentieth century. Ramsay MacDonald, for example, was critical of how the First World War was conducted, after which his birth certificate was made public in the press, which showed that he was an illegitimate child. Stone-throwing mobs disrupted his public meetings, and the government kept him under surveillance. When MacDonald became Prime Minister in 1923, the Daily Mail ran a campaign claiming that the private car and driver were a bribe from Sir Alexander Grant, Chairman of McVitie, for a knighthood. The

Daily Mail conveniently forgot that the previous Tory Prime Minister gave Grant the knighthood.

During the Second World War, Aneurin Bevan was under surveillance by MI5. One agent worked his way into Bevan's home until Bevan caught him in a lie and got a confession out of him. During the 1960s, Wilson was seen as a threat to the City of London and other establishment interests. He also supported parliamentary oversight of the intelligence services. The homes and offices of Wilson and his advisors were regularly broken into, with no valuables taken. The front pages of newspapers regularly had smears against Labour Party politicians and their supporters. Peter Wright confirmed in his memoir 'Spycatcher' that during the 1960s, the intelligence services were bugging and burgling Labour Party politicians' homes and offices. At the same time, senior civil servants looked the other way.

In the 1970s, the Tory Party looked to be involved in a campaign against Tony Benn. His telephone was tapped, his house bugged, and he received death threats. In 1981, Benn was also attacked in the press. The Daily Mail compared him to Hitler, and the Sun had a front page asking, 'Mr Benn – Is He Mad or a Killer?'

In 1994, a leaked Tory Party strategy document by the party's deputy chairman showed proposals to have Labour leader Blair roughed up by Tory backbench MPs. Other reports in the press said that the Tory Party Central Office was looking to leak personal and financial information about Blair to try to discredit him.[41]

More recently, after the Tories nearly lost the 2017 general election, Labour leader Corbyn came to be seen as more of the threat. The right-wing press went on the attack against him and weaponised issues in the Labour Party around anti-semitism to discredit Corbyn. This was combined with linking Corbyn to terrorists, his lack of British patriotism, his anti-nuclear weapons position and his vague position on Brexit to give the Tories a landslide victory in the 2019 general election.

PART 4:

HOW THE TORIES WIN MORE GENERAL ELECTIONS

14

APPEALING ELECTORAL PROGRAMMES AND MANIFESTOS

Traditionally the Tories have avoided making specific commitments and pledges in their election manifestos. They prefer to give general indications instead of details. The Labour Party tends to do the opposite, with specific pledges and promises and a policy on everything. Many voters can find this unrealistic and alarming, with the 2019 election manifesto being a good example.

There are consistent themes in Tory election propaganda, such as patriotism, tax cuts, economic competence, family, defence, and law and order. The party appeals to its record and will run the country better than Labour at a lower cost. This electoral offer is hard for many of us to understand as appealing, but it does convince millions of voters.[1]

Since the 1950s, the Tories have used opinion polling on an ongoing basis to understand what voters want, especially swing voters in marginal seats. This allows them to tailor their election offer to appeal to these voters by offering moderate policies around public services spending and committing to strong economic growth.

Most voters do not read party election manifestos and rely on the media and parties to summarise them through campaign slogans and rhetoric. Parties need a few effective slogans that connect and appeal to voters. So the Tories use opinion polling and focus groups (in-depth conversations with voters) to test them. These slogans then frame the campaign narrative and make it easy for voters to understand what the Tories stand for and what the voter thinks they will get if they elect the Tories into government. Good election slogans are ambiguous and mean different things to different people, so they appeal to a broad range of people.

Effective Tory slogans from the past:
1. The 1979 elections were 'Labour Isn't Working' and 'Don't just hope for a better life, vote for one'. Against a weak one from Labour, 'The Labour Way is the Better Way';
2. In 2010 the slogan was 'Vote for Change', focusing on the economy. Again against a weak slogan from Labour, 'A future fair for all';
3. In 2015 the Tories' slogan was 'Strong Leadership, A Clear Economic Plan And A Brighter, More Secure Future'. Labour's were better with 'Britain can be better' and 'A better plan, a better future';
4. Tory slogans for the 2017 election didn't work with their weak leader, 'Forward, Together' and 'Strong and Stable'. Labour had a powerful slogan that year 'For the Many, not the Few';
5. The Tories' 2019 slogans were very effective: 'Get Brexit Done' and 'Levelling Up'.

The Tories Lie And Make Election Promises They Have No Intention Of Keeping

The Tories know that if they were honest with voters about the policies they want to introduce, they would lose every election, so they have to lie. Opposition parties produce manifestos that they genuinely intend to deliver if elected. At every election, the Tories include multiple pledges they do not intend to implement. They are purely included to win the election and are then forgotten. Examples include reducing poverty, protecting and funding public services, and helping the vulnerable.[2]

The Tories also lie to hide the damage they do to the country.

Since returning to power in 2010, the Tories have been determined to reduce state intervention and the size of the welfare state. Cameron and Osborne justified austerity – cutting public spending – to 'balance the books' by claiming that Labour had caused the 2008 financial crisis and that the UK was on the brink of bankruptcy. To hide the Tories' destructive policies, Cameron lied by claiming his government had reduced public debt; increased funding to the NHS when they had cut funding, and claimed there was a reduction in the average waiting time in Accident & Emergency when the opposite was true. Tory ministers in Cameron's government lied and misrepresented benefit numbers, violent crime statistics and investment in infrastructure. The Tories also claimed schools were failing to justify Tory privatisation reforms.[3]

Another Tory trick is to claim that the solution to the current problems is just around the corner. They claim to have a brilliant plan to deal with the current problems, and it will all be fine if you stick with them for another election, but if Labour wins the next election, it will be a disaster. Cameron and Osborne always talked about the 'green shoots' of recovery. Johnson was particularly good at a baseless form of optimism. Brexit was meant to bring in a new golden age for global Britain.[4] But after 13 years of Tory misrule, what do the Tories have to show for it that benefits ordinary voters?

Over the last 13 years, the Tories have changed their approach to their manifestos. They now make promises they intend to break, requiring constant lying. They know that voters will vote for the party that offers appealing policies with no downsides, even if unrealistic. Tories break their big manifesto promise, and many voters forget about this by the time the next election comes around. The Tories are helped by the media's failure to report or hold the Tories accountable for these failures. Labour has to make moderate manifesto promises that are fully costed but still struggle to convince many voters due to the hostile media environment.[5]

For Cameron, he made several promises that he broke. He promised to get immigration down to the tens of thousands; by 2015, it was over 300,000. He promised no third runway at Heathrow, and the government agreed. He rebranded the Tory Party to be environmentally friendly. Then he removed onshore wind subsidies, cut energy efficiency funding and dropped a programme to require all new homes to be carbon neutral. The 2010 manifesto committed to not raising VAT and did it in the first budget. Cameron made an election promise not to change child benefits and then did by removing it from a million higher-rate taxpayers. Before the 2010 election, he promised that there would not be any top-down restructuring of the NHS, and then in 2012, the Tories brought in the biggest reorganisation of the NHS in its history. A big part of the Tories' 2010 election offer was a long-term economic plan to deal with the government debt and deficit. But Cameron's government consistently missed the target to achieve this.[6] Following the 2015 election Cameron broke promises not to cut child benefits and child tax credits. He cancelled plans to invest in rail electrification around the country. The Tories completely failed to build 200,000 affordable homes as promised. The Tories also delayed plans to introduce tax-free childcare and to cap social care costs.[7]

For the 2019 election, the Tories quietly released a short manifesto with few details and costings on a Saturday to avoid media attention. Beyond Getting Brexit Done and Levelling Up, it made dubious claims to building 40 new hospitals, recruiting 50,000 more nurses and 20,000 more police officers. The Tory campaign repeated all of these promises, and it went down well with voters sick of endless Brexit negotiations and desperate for government investment in tackling regional inequalities and struggling public services.[8]

By the time Johnson resigned in the summer of 2022, he had broken most of his promises. Johnson did get Brexit done, for all the good it is doing us but failed with levelling up. There were 13,000 new police officers, 23,000 new nurses, and 0 new hospitals. Johnson has also committed to build 300,000 new homes annually; 216,000 were built in 2020-1. He promised not to raise income tax, National Insurance (NI) or VAT and then increased NI in 2021. This increase was meant to help fix social care, another manifesto promise. A cap has been placed on social care of £86,000 since 2021, but nothing has been done to deal with the large shortage of workers. Johnson promised to keep 0.7% of GDP going to international aid and reduced it to 0.5 %.[9]

15

EFFECTIVE ELECTIONEERING TECHNIQUES

The Tories are very good at running strategic, dirty, disciplined election campaigns. There are several aspects of the Tories' effectiveness at running elections. The Tories practice message discipline during campaigns and create a lot of fear about the Labour Party and its leaders. They are skilled at using the press to their advantage. They are better at adapting to new technology. They are experienced at using polling and focus groups to understand the electorate and carefully tailor their election offer to give them what they want. At every election, the Tories strategically target swing voters in marginals so they win lots of seats with an efficient spread of votes. They lie and repeat the lies until they stick. They use events and crises to shift blame from the Tories' failure to govern. Finally, the Tories are very good at firing up their supporters to make sure they go out and vote, which is something parties on the centre-left struggle with.

On the question of if election campaigns make a difference, they clearly do, or political parties would not spend so much money on them. An effective election campaign can increase voter support by 2-3%, which can be very important in a tight general election or a marginal seat. That said, campaigns rarely affect the outcome of elections; the party ahead in opinion polls at the start of the election is normally ahead at the end.[1]

The Tories Create A Lot Of Fear About The Labour Party

The Tories are very effective at creating a lot of fear about their opposition during their election campaigns; the right-wing media then amplify this. In the early 20th century, the Tories created the narrative that the other parties were financially incompetent and dangerous. That the socialist Labour Party would take people's savings and houses away from them. In 1923 the Tories spread rumours that socialists would introduce 'compulsory free love'; sounds nice. The fake Zinoviev letter was used to undermine the Labour Party in 1924 by linking it to Soviet Russia. The 1931 election was dominated by claims that the Labour Party would take people's post office savings if they won.

A core weapon of post-war Tory election campaigns is negative attacks on the Labour leader. These include that Labour is incompetent, will put up taxes and is a threat to national security. The Tory poster for the 1959 election stated: "Life's better with the Conservatives. Don't let Labour ruin it." For the 1983, 1987 and 1992 elections, the Tories labelled Labour as extremist and dangerous with 'loony left' local authorities and 'tax double whammies' slogans.[2]

For the 2015, 2017 and 2019 elections, the Tories created a lot of fear around a possible hung parliament, potentially leading to a Labour-SNP coalition government which they claim would be followed by economic chaos and Scotland leaving the UK. The Tories have effectively presented themselves as the only party preventing Labour leaders Miliband and then Corbyn, who would threaten national security and economic stability.[3] During the 2019 campaign, Johnson compared Corbyn to the Russian dictator Stalin over Labour's planned tax increases on the wealthy. Johnson's pitch regarding Labour was that even if you think things are bad under the Tories, then it will be even worse with a Labour government.[4]

Strategic Lying

The last 13 years of Tory government have seen the evolution of 'strategic lying', especially since the 2016 Brexit referendum. In the past, if a politician were caught lying, they would have felt obligated to resign, but this is no longer the case. Strategic lying involves the Tories telling a controversial lie that they know will be immediately identified as a lie, but this does not matter. The purpose of the lie is to have an impact and not communicate a message. Because of the impact of these untrue statements, they are shared online via social media and then re-posted thousands of times. This is all repeated with the rebuttals. The second function of Strategic lying is to keep the issue at the top of the news agenda. The third function is more general; it aims to confuse voters so they are less receptive to responses from the opposition parties that might correct the misleading narrative.

An example of strategic lying from the 2019 campaign included an edited video of Starmer that was edited so it looked as if he could not answer a question on Labour's Brexit position. The clip went viral and was played again when being responded to by Labour. It achieved its goal of being widely shared and reinforced the idea that Labour's Brexit policy was unclear. Another example was Johnson's claims that there would not be border checks between Britain and Northern Ireland when other parts of the government were saying the opposite. A third example is the false claim that Labour's manifesto would cost £1.2 trillion. The Tories kept this going for days, ensuring that the narrative that Labour overspends was kept in the headlines.

There are three reasons why strategic lying is so effective. First, correcting misinformation might convince the uncommitted, but those that believed the original lie would likely reject the correction. This may cause them to increase their belief in the original lie if the correction comes from those seen as political opponents. Second, for those neutral about the original lie, remembering the correction fades quickly but the original message sticks in their memory. Third, the power of repetition means that if a lie is repeated enough, audiences find it easier to process and start to believe it as the truth compared to any related corrections.[5]

Better At Communicating With Voters

The Tories consistently adapted effectively to new communication and campaigning technology such as radio, cinema vans, television, use of computers, direct mail, and, more recently, the internet, especially social media. In addition, due to their funding advantage over Labour, the Tories have taken full advantage of specialist expertise in advertising agencies, opinion polling, mass communication professionals, expensive election-winning experts and strategists.

The next section is divided up into four sections to describe how the Tories have operated to communicate so well to keep winning elections. First, there is the early 20th-century development of propaganda; the post-war adaptation to television; Thatcher's use of American-style campaigning techniques; and the 21st-century use of big data and digital campaigning.

<u>The early 20th-century development of propaganda</u>
The Tories were early adopters of the power of image manipulation through stage-managed events to attempt to produce an effect greater than the event alone. In the early 20th century, Chamberlain arranged his arrival at railway stations to be carefully stage-managed for maximum effect. Sometimes, he would be followed by musicians and entertainers from the station to the community hall. During this period, the Tories also sent out vans with magic lanterns with speakers giving lectures. The Labour Party preferred a traditional public meeting and a leaflet.

Newspapers became more sophisticated after 1900, and the Tories developed an effective news dissemination system to supportive editors and journalists. The Tory Press Bureau was set up in 1911 with several teams. The Lobby Press Service provided regular news to hundreds of weekly and daily local papers. These supportive local papers would 'top-and-tail' the articles and give them a local context to disguise them. The General Press Service met the demands of the national press and met political correspondents twice a day with updates.

The 1920s saw the Tories send out cinema vans nationwide that set up screens in town squares and halls that showed heavily propagandist films. In villages, the cinema vans were large crowd-pullers, and most locals would attend. For the 1931 election, the Tories had eleven cinema vans, reaching voters that would never attend a meeting. They started with cartoons, documentaries, travel or sports films. This was followed by a build-up film, such as a section from the popular film 'Disraeli' (1929), to appeal to patriotism and love of country. The propaganda films and speeches were next, and it finished with a feature film that was what most people came for. For the 1935 election, the Tories had twenty-two cinema vans in operation, reaching over 1.5 million people. The Conservative Central Office (CCO) had its film unit provide footage for the newsreels. The Tories produced 520 newsreels in 1930. They were seen as an effective way to reach new working-class voters in cinemas.

Labour and Tory Party leaders first used radio to address the public for the 1924 election. Tory leader Baldwin understood that this required a different approach than a public meeting, so he prepared and recorded his speech in advance. Labour leader MacDonald did a live broadcast from City Hall in Glasgow, but he kept stepping away from the microphone, so those listening could not hear much of what he said. MacDonald improved his technique for the 1929 election, but the Tory leader gave a more effective radio address. By the 1931 election, one in three families had a radio, and Baldwin continued to give more powerful radio performances. Baldwin was projected as the face of 'new Conservatism'. He was very focused on connecting with voters and understanding his radio audience. It was made up of working-class and middle-class listeners. He had a friendly, personal style that went down well. Baldwin built on his radio performances by being filmed for newsreels and photo opportunities.

The Tories lost the 1929 election and then joined the Labour

National Government in 1931 and 1935, which gained large majorities, so it's easy to discount the impact of Baldwin and the Tories' adaptation to the new technology. The Tories used an external advertising agency to help produce posters and leaflets for each election. In addition, the party ran courses in public speaking for Tory activists and created a fleet of loudspeaker vans. This shows that the Tories' desire to win elections meant it took the Tory offer and represented it to the new and complex electorate; their superior abilities with these new radio and television technologies assisted with the Tories' dominance in the inter-war years.

During the 1930s, the Tories established a secretive electioneering agency called the National Publicity Bureau. It pioneered new campaigning techniques, such as targeting 330 key parliamentary seats and sending direct mail to specific voters. For the 1935 election, the bureau spent £300,000, which would be £25 million today. In addition, it organised national large-scale poster campaigns and produced millions of broadsheets (propaganda newspapers) that looked like ordinary newspapers. The National Publicity Bureau was active for the 1945 election but on a reduced budget to run poster and broadsheet campaigns. As a result, it was closed down in 1946.

The post-war adaptation to television

The 1945 election was the last before television became important. From the 1950s, the Tories quickly adapted to the new medium. Instead of reading from a script, Tory leaders and ministers would spend hours rehearsing so that they could film what looked to be a 'spontaneous' question-and-answer session. Macmillan honed his abilities, so he came across with polished performances. The Tory publicity department understood the importance of television, so it set up an area with television equipment so MPs and potential MPs could practise and improve. Training was also provided. By the end of the 1950s, the question-and-answer format looked tired, so the Tories asked several young independent producers for a new option. This led to a switch to unrehearsed interviews that became popular in the

1960s.

The Tories used an advertising agency from 1950 to 1964 to produce election posters and newspaper adverts that used accessible language and connected with voters emotionally. The 1959 campaign used modern marketing and research methods to target key working-class voters essential to winning the election. Tory Central Office recognised the importance of these techniques, so a Psephology Group (analysis of elections) was set up. This conducted regular opinion polls and consulted with external experts.

The Public Opinion Research Department was established in 1947, advising on strategy. During the 1950s, polling helped the party focus on the centre ground, ex-labour voters, floating voters, young men, manual workers with families, homeowners and disposable income to buy consumer items. Polling helped the Tories understand two by-election defeats in 1958 due to losing the support of lower-middle-class and skilled working-class voters due to their dissatisfaction with the government. Polling also showed the party how voters' support improved through each campaign. Although many voters were unhappy with the Tory government at the start of the campaign, by the end, they decided to stick with the Tories based on perceived competence and doubts about Labour.

Labour improved its media professionalism in the 1960s under Wilson. Wilson's quick political skills helped this, focused on modernisation and technological revolution. For the 1964 election, the Tory Prime Minister Douglas-Home preferred to hold open-air meetings. So when he attended a television election event, he was unprepared. This changed when Heath took over, with a more professional approach to polling, advertising, broadcasting and evidence-based policy-making. Heath understood the importance of strong media performances. During the 1970 election, Heath had an advertising team, a portable studio set and introduced television-style press conferences. This meant he out-competed Wilson with the new communication medium.

The Tories' publicity department was less effective in the early and mid-1960s, but this also changed under Heath. Outside professionals were brought in-house through the 1970s and 1980s. They focused on television and advertising. These external professionals were brought in to create high-quality Party Political Broadcasts. Some of these attempted to show the human side of Heath with some success. Market research was used to identify target voters to improve the party's advertising reach. For the 1970 election, they focused on increasing prices to attract the wives of skilled workers that voted Labour. However, following the Tories winning the 1970 election, Heath neglected these external advisors, so when he called on them for the 1974 election, it was too late to devise an effective campaign strategy.

Thatcher's use of American-style campaigning techniques

Thatcher introduced American-style campaigning techniques, including an aggressive advertising agency (Saatchi and Saatchi) employed full-time to do all the Tories' publicity, press and poster advertising, television and voter research. They were kept on a retainer between elections to ensure that a campaign strategy was designed well before elections to avoid the mistakes in the 1970s. Thatcher wanted all the help she could get from them regarding her personal presentation on television and how to present the party in the media best. The agency helped Thatcher change her voice and appearance to present more professionally and also advised her to appeal on 'popular' television programs to broaden her appeal. Saatchi and Saatchi came up with the highly effective 'Labour isn't working' poster, with a long queue of unemployed people. Saatchi and Saatchi were kept on for the 1979, 1983, 1987 and 1992 elections.

The Tories also got outside help to redesign the party's 1979 election rallies to have more impact, like US-style election rallies. It made them more impressive and sophisticated for the following two elections. The party conferences were also made into staged events for television. The election campaign tours were improved to ensure that Thatcher's message was as easy as possible for the media to receive and share.

Marketing professionals were also brought in-house to improve the party's brand. This saw the introduction of direct mail, telephone canvassing, and a 6-month plan before an election. There was an increased use of detailed opinion polling. There was a focus on 'unpaid media', normal television and newspaper news that most voters saw. This was done through 'sound bites' and 'photo opportunities'. New research techniques were developed, such as the 'Fast Feed Back System', which had 150 people around the country that had contact with a broad range of the public to phone in their views by 6 pm so a report could be produced for the morning strategy meeting. This was seen as so effective that President Reagan employed these marketing professionals for his 1984 campaign.

The 1983 election saw a big contrast between the Tories and Labour election campaign operations. The Tories used word processors, computers and direct mail advertising to 2 million voters. They focused the party's resources on 100 target marginal seats and set up a 24-hour monitoring team that could react immediately to press stories. The Tories had over 400 hundred election agents. Tickets were needed for public events with Thatcher to minimise disruption. An audio-vision 'sincerity' device was introduced so Tory politicians could read from notes but look at the audience or camera. Tory campaign staff organised multi-photo opportunities for journalists and photographers, with coaches provided to follow Thatcher. In contrast, Labour's campaign was run by party members or supporters with little professional help. Labour had one faulty computer and no facilities for journalists: opinion polling only started three months before the election, and disagreements over how the advertising agency presented the party. Nevertheless, the Tories spent £3.7 million on their campaign, nearly double that of Labour and went on to win a large majority.[6]

The Tories introduced news management techniques to control how the media reported on their campaigns. The Labour Party professionalised their 1987 and 1992 campaigns to be seen as an equal standard. Many Tories thought they had lost the 1987 election in the days before the vote. The Tories outspent Labour nationally and in local constituencies. For the 1987 election, Labour spent £4.7

million nationally, and the Tories spent £9 million.

Major's 1992 campaign extensively used 'knocking copy', negative attacks on Labour leader Kinnock. This was another US election campaign import. The party used an effective poster, 'Labour's double whammy', with one being more taxes and two being higher prices. The 1990s saw a sophistication and professionalisation of campaign techniques such as direct mail and opinion poll research.[7]

21st-century use of big data and digital campaigning

The Tories' 2010 election campaign was among the best prepared, funded and technically advanced campaigns ever. Funds were spent on significant amounts of advertising, and plenty of staff were hired. It linked opinion research, canvassing and demographic information from private credit referencing agencies. The Tories started with one advertising agency (Euro RSCG) that produced several positive posters but switched to tried-and-tested M&C Saatchi, which produced more negative posters against Labour Prime Minister Brown. The highly successful elections consultant Lynton Crosby was also part of the campaign and brought a high level of discipline, although there were some issues over who was in charge.[8]

At the 2015 election, the Tories employed Lynton Crosby again, and the general election campaign was planned from 2012. It was a highly disciplined campaign. Crosby conducted detailed polling of 80 non-Tory marginal seats. The campaign had three key messages: Labour had 'crashed the economy', the Tories 'long-term economic plan', and on leadership, Miliband was not a credible Prime Minister. The Tories relentlessly attacked Labour leader Miliband throughout the whole campaign.

The Tories and Labour employed experts from the 2012 US President Obama campaign, and both parties used similar techniques to target specific voters. They used party voter identification and commercially available information, known as 'big data'. The Tories created a target voters list, breaking them into 10 categories. Each category had a specific message delivered by phone, direct mail, social media or on the doorstep. The Tories developed a 50-50 strategy focusing on 50 Tory seats to defend and 50 seats to take from Labour and the Liberal Democrats. In these 100 target seats, each voter got eight personalised messages. In addition, the Tories micro-targeted undecided voters in marginal seats using opinion polling and social media. The Tories had 100,000 volunteers helping constituency activists in the 100 target seats.

Labour won the 'ground war' for the 2015 election by knocking on more doors and speaking to more voters, but the Tories won the 'digital war'; they spent £100,000 a month on Facebook advertising to collect email addresses. Labour spent about £10,000 a month on Facebook adverts and instead relied on supporters sharing content for free, which was untargeted and severely limited its effectiveness. Labour focused on direct mail over digital due to a lack of funds. The Tories had more funding available than Labour. The Tories spent over £100,000 on social media advertising to voters in some constituencies, but this was counted as 'national' spending instead of local spending, getting around election local spending limits.

Labour suffered as many voters preferred Cameron to Miliband and Tory policies to Labours. On election day, the Tories had a far more effective 'Get Out the Vote' drive. The Tories had a more efficient distribution of voters than in the past, with the party's share of the vote dropping by 2% in their safe seats and increasing by the same amount in marginal constituencies.[2]

The 2017 general election was called at short notice. May's leadership team were keen to make the election about radical social and economic reform. The Tories again used the election adviser, Crosby, who disagreed with this approach because Brexit had created a lot of uncertainty, so voters were looking for stability. The Tories had not planned to use May much in the campaign, and Crosby thought the opposite as she was seen as an asset at this point. Crosby framed the election around 'strong and stable' leadership from May and weak leadership from Corbyn.

The Tories were unprepared for the election, with Labour being better prepared in terms of fundraising and logistics around the country. The Tories used canvassing scripts with attitudinal questions to help them identify how voters would vote instead of asking them directly. The Tories lacked activists, and Labour had more than in 2015, so they made more voter contact. Labour was also helped by a significant number of external groups and campaigns that spread the campaign messages online. Labour used Corbyn to front mass rallies that effectively built support and was featured on local news. By 2017, traditional forms of electioneering, such as the daily press conference, posters and billboards, had declined significantly. Most poster launches we run to generate publicity rather than the poster being seen by anyone.

The Tories again used political and commercial data to target voters that might switch to the Tories in marginals. But there were multiple cases of canvassers being sent to what they thought were possibly Tory voters, but it turned out the residents were anti-Tory. The Tories' target voters were repeatedly contacted with direct mail, on social media and on phone calls. In 2015, the Tories targeted Liberal Democrat voters in the south. In this election, they targeted Labour Leave voters and previous UKIP supporters. The Tories outspent Labour during the campaign, £18.6 million to Labour's £11 million. By the end of the campaign, the Tories and Labour were putting out material in about 200 target seats each.

The Tories ran a poor campaign. It lacked leadership, and its digital campaign was poor compared to Labour. There were a lot of negative stories about Corbyn in the press, but little of this was shared on social media. The printed press and social media were like different worlds, and Corybn's popularity increased through the campaign, even with the press onslaught. Newspapers were less important in this election. The Tories spent £2.3 million on Facebook ads, with Labour spending £500,000.

Labour had an ambiguous Brexit position, and instead of the economy being the most important factor, many voters were more concerned with the cost of living, austerity and increasing pay for better public services. This was to Corbyn's advantage. The Tories lost many weak Tory voters, put off by the Tories' Brexit position.

Labour won the ground and digital wars, even if they ultimately lost the election. But the Tories felt like they lost as they felt on track to increase their majority and instead had to form a minority government with the DUP.[10]

Johnson called a much-predicted general election for December 2019. The Tories learnt the lessons from the disastrous 2017 campaign, that one person needed to be in charge and that the public needed to be convinced that the election was necessary. The Tories hired Isaac Levido, a Crosby acolyte, to run the campaign. The deadlock over Brexit during the Autumn of 2019 meant that most voters understood the election was necessary. The Tories were also well prepared for the election by overhauling party organisation, fundraising, and communications with a united leadership team. Labour had also been preparing through 2019 but was deeply divided over campaign strategy, and its infrastructure was weak. There was much more support from Tories CCHQ for candidates.

The Tories ran a consultancy-led campaign based on slogans, with Labour following a movement-led campaign that was policy-heavy. Johnson was a good campaigner who remained disciplined, and the Tories kept focused on their key message, 'Get Brexit Done'. The Tories also made the election about leadership on dealing with Brexit; Johnson would resolve the crisis, compared to ambivalence from Corbyn. Labour attempted to shift attention to domestic issues such as the NHS. The Tories mostly neutralised this with a safety-first manifesto with modest spending commitments that signalled an end to austerity. The Labour Manifesto had big policy commitments that the Tories then claimed weren't credible and would cost £1.2 trillion. This was a dubious figure, but it got the desired headlines. The Tories refused to be drawn into policy rows that would have played to Labour's strengths over popular policies, much to the frustration of the Labour campaign.

There were multiple leaders' debates and television interviews. Johnson did well in those he attended, and the party's ruthless approach to message control restricted Johnson's media appearances, so he did not attend some debates and interviews, but this did not impact his popularity. Corbyn struggled in some of the television appearances.

The Tories' digital campaign was more successful. Their simple 'Get Brexit Done' message helped, combined with repeating it to the widest possible online audience. This included two full-day 'takeovers' of YouTube so everyone using the site would have seen something from the Tories. The Tories used targeted advertising based on target parliamentary seats. Labour and the Liberal Democrats did much more focused digital advertising based on creating audience profiles. The Tories' campaign aggressively shared disinformation online. It ran 167 advertisements on Facebook and Google that were removed due to a breach of the platform's advertising policies or had misleading or inaccurate claims. Labour was also found to have run inaccurate adverts online, but the Tories' false online advertising was seven times that of Labour.

During the election campaign, it was found that 88% of the Tories' sponsored Facebook adverts were lies, mainly focused on the cost of Labour policies and claims that individual tax bills will increase by £2,400, which was completely untrue. Also, a Tory Party 'front group' organised a large illegal national propaganda campaign that targeted polling stations and high streets in marginal constituencies. It involved cardboard posters on lampposts and sign vans with digital billboards. The posters had an image of Corbyn in red and black stripes, and the message stated: "Would you trust this man with your children, he steals their inheritance, he dictates their education, he defends terrorists. Jeremy Corbyn is a threat to our security and democracy. Don't let this extremist win."

The claims were lies; there was no change to inheritances under £425,000 for most people. Labour policies were to increase funding in education after Tory cuts and end student loans. The terrorist claims are ridiculous, with Corbyn being punished for not having a simplistic position on the struggles against oppression in Ireland and Palestine. Corbyn is a democratic socialist, and the Labour platform was a return to post-war social democracy, hardly an extremist position.[11]

The Tories started the election ahead in the polls and kept this lead to the end, unlike the 2017 election. The Tories took a majority of leave voters, spread efficiently across multiple seats, resulting in an 80-seat majority. The Labour campaign wasn't effective, with the remain vote being split between Labour, Liberal Democrats and Greens.[12]

16

HOW THE RIGHT-WING MEDIA HELPS THE TORIES WIN ELECTIONS

The media plays a significant role in general election campaigns. Three groups of political players operate in the media environment during elections: political parties, news media and the public. The public are both voters and media users. The media and political parties use the media environment in five ways. First, to provide information and commentary to voters. Second, political leaders use the media as a platform to communicate their messages to voters. Third, most of the press takes an active role in supporting political parties. Fourth, political parties and the media interact to construct the campaign agenda. Fifth, political parties and the media contribute to the mobilisation of voters.[1]

Forms Of Media In Britain

Newspapers and commercial broadcasters' core business is to sell products and services to audiences and sell audiences to advertisers. The initial cost of production of the first product, a newspaper or television programme, is high due to the high capital costs, but after that, costs drop dramatically. These media producers are protected by copyright so that these companies can charge customers more than the production cost.[2]

Britain has three broad forms of media: newspaper (the press), broadcasting (television and radio), and social media and online media. Newspapers are considered the most influential form of media, but television is the main source of news information, with 75% of adults stating they rely on it to catch up on the news.[3] Ofcom regulates broadcasting, but the press is effectively unregulated, so it gets away with lying and manipulating its readers.

Newspapers

The start of the twentieth century saw the establishment of mass-circulation newspapers such as The Times, The Telegraph, the (Manchester) Guardian, the Daily Mail, the Daily Express and Daily Mirror to provide news on current affairs to those recently given the right to vote. The Daily Mail was launched in 1896 at a very low price, gaining a circulation of 1 million by 1900.

There are three types of newspapers. First, there are 'quality,' that used to be called broadsheets due to the literal size of the newspaper. These included The Times, The Telegraph, The Guardian, the Financial Times and the Independent, plus their Sunday editions. Second, are the 'mid-tabloids' such as the Daily Mail and Daily Express. Third, are the 'red-top' tabloids, also known as the popular press that include The Sun, Daily Mirror and Daily Star. In theory, each type of newspaper is aimed at a demographic group: professional middle class, lower middle class and working class, respectively.

There has been a decline in newspaper sales since the end of the twentieth century. Daily papers went from 15 million in 1990 to 13 million in 1998 to 6.7 million in 2020. Sunday papers declined from 17 million in 1990 to 15 million in 1998 to 4 million in 2020. This decline is due less young people reading newspapers and many reading news online. There is also much more competition with other pastimes and increasing newspaper prices. As a result, most papers have been losing readers at 2-3% a year.

The declining newspaper market results in high levels of competition between the tabloids. Papers report on what they think sells, political 'sleaze', controversy, and celebrity gossip. Political parties pay close attention to the tabloids, especially the Daily Mail and the Sun, as millions read them. Party leadership teams follow and write articles for these papers' editorial positions.[4]

Broadcasting
This includes radio and television. Radio was important during the first half of the twentieth century following the founding of the BBC in 1926. Television became the most important form of media in general elections after the Second World War, with BBC1 and BBC2 established in 1964. The first commercial television was ITV which started broadcasting in 1955. Commercial radio was opened up in 1973. Channel 4 started broadcasting in 1982, Sky Television in 1989, and then Channel 5 in 1997. SkyNews and the BBC's 24-hour news channels provide around-the-clock news updates. Recently, right-wing broadcasters GB News and TalkTV news have been launched.

The important elements of broadcasting during general elections are news updates, current affairs programmes, interviews with leaders and senior politicians from parties and Party Political Broadcasts. Recently, parties have employed professional media managers (spin doctors), speech writers, pollsters, advertising agencies and filmmakers to communicate well on radio and television. Generally, political meetings have declined, and events are planned to get the best media coverage, including stage-managed rallies. There is a focus on 'sound bites', which serve news editors' demands for short, easily packaged messages that can be repeatedly played on that day's news updates. There have been ongoing demands by broadcasters for political party leaders' debates, and since the 2010 election, these have started taking place.

Surveys of the public identify that television and the recent leadership debates have been many voters' main sources of information about the election, and parties and have influenced their views.[5] Unlike newspapers, broadcasters are meant to be impartial and balanced in reporting. This means giving the political parties time and coverage based on each party's support in the country. The regulator Ofcom monitors all broadcasters during general elections for fairness and balance.

Many on both sides of the political spectrum see the BBC as biased. It is argued that if both the Tories and Labour have accused the BBC of bias, it is effectively steering a middle way. Research has found a generational divide, with many over 50 thinking the BBC is biased in favour of left views and younger people thinking the opposite. The BBC is limited by its news content being based on national press reports, which have a right-wing bias. This right-wing media agenda is then reflected in the BBC's broadcast and online content. The BBC's online readership in March 2021 was 1.5 billion views.[6]

Social media and online media
Social media is now a big part of everyone's lives. In 2016, 22.5 million households (86%) had internet access, an increase from 57% in 2006. The Internet was accessed by 39.3 million adults daily (78%) in 2016 compared with 16.2 million (35%) in 2006. There is a generational difference; 96% of 16-24-year-olds access the Internet on mobile devices, compared to 29% of those over 65. Social media is used by 61% of adults, with 79% of those accessing it every day.[7] Social media was a significant factor in the 2017 and 2019 general elections. The parties have heavily used platforms such as Facebook and Twitter. The Labour Party was seen to be more successful with social media in 2017, and the Tories dominated it in 2019, see Chapter 15 for more details.

There are multiple new online media publications on the right and the left that challenge established news outlets. But these are currently dwarfed by traditional news websites such as the MailOnline, the Guardian and Sun Online, which have monthly visits in the hundreds of millions. Social media also gives these big newspaper websites an advantage, with more than 22 million people in the UK using Facebook to find and read the news regularly. It is estimated that the content from mainstream news publications contributes to about half of the news that ends up on social media feeds. Companies like Meta (Facebook and Instagram), Alphabet (Google and YouTube), and Apple have significant power over what news users see, and these companies are unregulated and unaccountable.[8]

Does The Media Influence Elections?

There has been significant research into the impact of the media on general elections and voters. Some academics argue that the media has a limited effect. The media is more likely to impact people's views over the long term or to reinforce views that people already have. The media are important in setting the agenda of debate of elections, with the BBC news broadcast programmes and online content driven by newspaper articles. The political parties attempt to set the political agenda in an election, but the media are not always compliant.[9]

There is a 'chicken and egg' question regarding readers and their newspaper of choice. Do people choose their paper because of its political position, or do people select a newspaper for non-political reasons such as its sports coverage or supplements, and are they then politically influenced without realising it? It is likely both play a part, with research showing that many media users are unaware of the political affiliations of the media publications they follow.[10]

Most voters' electoral preferences are fixed before general elections begin, so the media can never dramatically impact the result. During the 2005 election, 60% had decided before the election started, and 25% decided in the later stages of the campaign.[11] Research shows that Tory-supporting newspapers help the Tories and that in a close election, this is especially important in helping them win.[12] In several close elections, the opinion polls have incorrectly predicted that it is a close election and Labour might win, such as in 1992 and 2015. This incorrect prediction has been reported in the media and likely encouraged apathetic Tory voters to get out and vote Conservative.[13]

Social media played a big role in recent elections. The Tories mostly benefited from this due to their deep pockets. They consistently spend over £1 million on Facebook adverts, specifically targeting marginal seats with tailored messages. However, the popularity of Corbyn during the 2017 election did see Labour win the digital war due to organic peer-to-peer sharing, out-competing the Tories, even though they spent more.

The Tories press advantage

The Tories consistently have had more support from British newspapers and much higher numbers of people reading Tory-supporting papers than Labour. The Tory-dominated newspapers set election agendas with the public and heavily influence broadcasting and online news reporting by the BBC and others. Research shows that the Tory press plays a crucial role in close elections. And there is likely to be a strong connection between the Tories' success at winning elections and staying in power for long periods and the right-wing media bias in favour of the Tories.

In the early 20th century, the Tories had a clear press advantage with high levels of integration and collusion between the Tory Party and the press barons. From the 1940s to 1970s, when Labour and the Tories more evenly shared power, press support for the parties was more even. In 1945, the Tory papers had 6.7 million readers, with 4.4 million readers of Labour papers. The Labour-supporting papers were the Daily Mirror and Daily Herald.

In the 1960s, the Daily Herald was rebranded and called the Sun, which Murdoch bought in 1969. The Sun supported Labour in the 1960s and switched to the Tories in the 1970s, so the only Labour-supporting paper was the Daily Mirror.

During the 1980s, Thatcher's Tories had the support for most papers, with only the Daily Mirror consistently supporting Labour. The Tories had the support of 5 large newspapers (Daily Express, Daily Mail, the Sun, Daily Telegraph, Financial Times) with a combined circulation of 10 million. Labour only had the Daily Mirror with a circulation of 3.7 million. It is estimated that this press support was worth an extra £16 million in campaign spending for the Tories, compared to £5 million for the Labour Party. During the 1987 election, the largest swing to the Tories was from the regular readers of the pro-Tory tabloids.[14]

By the 1992 election, the Tories had the support of 9.7 million daily and Sunday newspapers to 3.3 million for Labour. The 1992 election was the closest in decades, with some polls showing the Labour Party were ahead of the Tories. In the week before the campaign, the editors of the Tory tabloids coordinated their attacks on Labour and its leader. The Tories got a surprise win, and the Sun claimed that the paper had helped the Tories win the election with its front page, 'The Sun wot won it'.[15] This was a close election where the Tories' press support likely played a disproportionate role in helping the Tories win.[16]

The Sun switched from backing the Tories to Labour and Blair in 1995 and continued supporting Labour until switching back to the Tories in 2010. Blair's communications director, Alastair Campbell, stated that the Sun's support was a big factor in Labour's 1997 landslide win. It could be argued that this shows that the press isn't biased toward one party. Another perspective is that the Sun is a commercial paper and, with its mixed readership, does not want to be seen supporting an unpopular government when a popular opposition looks likely to win. Murdoch could see which way the wind was blowing in public opinion and had assurances from Blair regarding political access. There was no threat of media reform from Labour.

The 2010 election saw the Tory-supporting press make up 74% of daily circulation. There was a much greater swing in support for the Tories for Sun readers than the national average.[17] The 2015 election was very dirty, following years of right-wing press attacks on Labour leader Miliband. Due to Miliband's commitments to media reform, Murdoch was highly motivated to stop the Labour Party from winning. The broadcasters acted as uncritical megaphones for the Tory campaign, taking their lead from the Tory press. There was a distinct lack of impartiality and objectivity from senior journalists.[18]

The Tories had the normally pro-Tory papers backing for the

2017 election. However, the Times and Financial Times were unimpressed with the party's 'hard' Brexit position. There were fierce attacks on Labour leader Corbyn, but his popularity rose through the campaign due to successful digital and ground-game campaigning. The Tory press drastically increased its attacks on Corbyn for the 2019 election and took him much more seriously than in 2017. The Tory papers had also tested anti-Labour attack lines since the 2017 election and settled on highly damaging attacks around anti-Semitism. The papers gave Johnson and his vague slogans an easy ride.

In 2021, there were 11 major newspapers, with six supporting the Tories: The Times, the Daily Telegraph, the Daily Mail, the Sun, the Daily Express and the Evening Standard. Labour only had the Daily Mirror. There is also the Guardian, I, the Daily Star and the Financial Times, which changed their support between elections and sometimes supported the Liberal Democrats. The Tory press's daily circulation was 6.8 million, more than seven times that of the Guardian and the Daily Mirror. The Tory press's online monthly views are 131 million compared to 61 million for the two Labour papers websites.[19] News UK, which publishes the Times, Sunday Times and the Sun, have claimed that their papers reach 72% of UK adults at least once a month. This is a significant influence with no accountability.[20]

Agenda setting
The right-wing press use their dominance of the newspaper market to set the agenda during elections and between them. Agenda setting involves influencing the understanding of the relative importance of issues. It is a metaphor that describes the cognitive process of how people think about current important issues. Instead of 'changing people's minds', agenda setting increases or decreases voters' assessment of the importance of an issue or problem. Repeated headlines on a topic will move that issue higher in people's priorities. It is unclear exactly how much influence the media has in telling people what to think, but it is very successful at telling people what to think about. An example is the decades of anti-immigration headlines

by the Tory press that have resulted in millions of people thinking immigration is a much more serious problem than it is. This agenda-setting process also shifts what is more important in broader society. Many may not be concerned about the issues the Tory press focus on. Because the media constantly focus on these issues, this leads people to believe that the issue is important to society in general.[21]

One agenda-setting process influencing public opinion and attitudes is 'priming', which identifies some issues as important and ignores others. So, for example, during an election campaign, the Tory press generally focuses on the importance of the economy and how the Tories are better at managing the economy than, say, struggling public services. So as people are thinking about who to vote for during the campaign and in the polling booth, this focus by the media on the economy will influence what the voter deems important and, therefore, who to vote for.

A second agenda-setting process is 'framing', which is how a news story is communicated. Framing is how the news story is presented to influence how those receiving it judge the topic or issue. There are two forms of frames: episodic and thematic. News stories framed episodically present the issue in question in concrete terms through examples such as interviewing poor people about poverty. This can also be event focused, such as terrorist attacks.

Thematic frames present the issue in a more abstract context that includes general evidence, such as parliamentary debates on public service cuts or expert analysis of an economic crisis. Research into how the two different forms of frames cause an audience to assign responsibility for the issue is important. For thematic frames, the audience blames the government or relevant public officials. In contrast, episodic frames disperse public judgements of responsibility and accountability from the government or officials. Unsurprisingly, Britain's right-wing media prefer to report the news using episodic frames through controversial examples and dramatic events, which help redirect attention from societal responsibility and protect incumbent politicians from dissatisfaction with how the country is run. It results in people accepting that this is just how things are.[22]

Another concept related to agenda setting is the 'Overton Window', which is the range of acceptable mainstream opinions available for discussion. It is based on people's views and is influenced by society's institutions, such as the media. right-wing and leftwing politics aim to expand this window of what the public believes is acceptable. 'Outriders' can expand what 'reasonable' commentators or those involved in politics can discuss.[23]

If we look at the 2019 election, we can see how the right-wing press set the media agenda. The broadcasting news was dominated by Brexit, the economy and taxation, all beneficial to the Tories. Those issues where Labour are stronger such as health care, public services, and the environment, were of secondary importance.[24]

Media influence beyond elections

There is a lot of focus on the impact of the media on general election results. However, there is conflicting research into the impact of the media on elections, so it is important to consider the impact of the media outside the general election campaign period in influencing people's attitudes, perceptions and agenda. Opinions are formed from a combination of information, predisposition, values and an understanding of the political context. The media are the central player in this process.

We must look at the factors that shape the construction of popular opinion. This includes agenda setting and media frames discussed above and the intensity of the political communications, people's levels of attention to politics, political disposition and factors that impact the importance of an issue. We also need to consider how the media affects people's attitudes to politicians, parties and policies by analysing the content and character of media coverage. An important impact of the media is how it shapes voters' feelings and produces an emotional response instead of rational thought.

Research has found that the increase in watching television has caused a significant amount of 'social disengagement', resulting in less social trust and group membership. In contrast, reading newspapers has the opposite effect. Television is a form of privatised leisure where mistrust increases and feeds narratives about a 'mean world'. This can lead to feelings of fatalism, which reduces people's capacity to behave as citizens leading to civic disengagement.

There is, of course, other research which finds the opposite, and it feels intuitive to me that we have a right-wing dominated media environment that spews out negative and fear-mongering stories because this sells, it will cause some of the audience to feel fatalist and hopeless. These people will then be susceptible to straightforward binary choices that hide complexity and fraudulent promise to fix society's problems. The obvious recent example of this is Brexit.[25]

A key role that the right-wing press plays in Britain is its ability to capture and sustain support for the Tories. It reinforces Tory voters' political allegiance to the party. Research from the 1987 election has confirmed this. Unsurprisingly, the Tory vote was strongest among those reading Tory supporting papers and lowest among those not exposed to pro-Tory messages. But Labour supporters that read right-wing papers were 6% more supportive of the Tories than those that did not read Tory supporting publications.[26]

Why Does The Right-Wing Press Help The Tories?

Why do most newspapers consistently support the Tories in Britain? There is a long history of wealthy businessmen starting or buying newspapers in Britain. The right-wing Tory Party best serves their interests than Labour. There are very close links between the Tory Party and the right-wing press. The wealthy have set up and bought newspapers, and these individuals normally back the party. Many of these press barons have been involved with the Tory Party or Tory governments over the years. As the electoral franchise was extended in the late 19th century, the wealthy started or bought newspapers to steer political opinion in a way that benefited their interests. All this was a rational strategy from their perspective, even if it undermined British democracy for over a century.[27]

Press ownership by the rich

Between 1890 and 1920, newspaper chains were a new development which politicised the relationship between the owner and the newspaper. The three Harmsworths brothers owned a large chunk of the British press. Between them, they owned the Daily Mail, the Times, the Weekly Dispatch, the London Evening News, the Daily Mirror, the Sunday Pictorial, the Daily Record, Sunday Mail and the Glasgow Evening News. They also owned the Amalgamated Press, the largest national magazine group. The total daily circulation of these papers was 6 million. Another rich press baron was Lord Beaverbrook with his Express Group, which included the Daily Express, Sunday Express and Evening Standard, with a daily circulation of 4.1 million in 1937. In 1937, five companies owned 43 % of newspapers in Britain. This concentration of ownership was at a time of growing demand, with daily circulation going from 3.1 million in 1918 to 10.6 million in 1939. These press barons used their power to influence politicians and set the news agenda. As the electoral franchise grew, they saw their power grow.

The Labour-supporting Daily Herald relaunched as the Sun in 1964 and was bought by Rupert Murdoch's News UK in 1969. News UK also bought the News of the World in 1969 and, in 1984, transformed it into a tabloid to become the Sunday paper of The Sun. News UK bought the Times and Sunday Times from the Astor family in 1981. The Daily Mail Group has maintained control of the Daily Mail since it was established, and the 4th Viscount Rothermere is the Chairman of Daily Mail & General Trust (DMGT). DMGT launched the Metro in 1995, providing a free paper Monday to Friday in urban areas in Britain. The Express Group sold the Daily Express and Sunday Express to Richard Desmond in 2000. Desmond has right-wing politics and backed Brexit. He sold these newspapers to the Reach group in 2018, which owns the Daily Mirror. Lord Burnham owned the Daily Telegraph in the late 19th century, then sold it to the Berry family in 1928. The media company Hollinger, run by Conrad Black, took control of the Telegraph in 1986. The Telegraph was bought by the Barclay brothers in 2004. The Russian oligarch Alexey

Lebedev owns The Independent and The Evening Standard. These modern press barons are worth billions.

Newspaper owner editorial control
The owners' political views set the tone for their newspapers, making them 'effective political lobbying machines'. The owners of Britain's right-wing newspaper employ editors that align with their political views. Many editors try to claim that they are just reflecting the views of their readers. But this is nonsense; they print stories that the editor and the owner want.[28]

Most papers push their owner's agenda with varying degrees of editorial control. The obvious place to start is Rupert Murdoch with the Sun, the Times and the Sunday Times. Harold Evans, the former editor of the Times, told a government inquiry that a key part of this job was to do "what Murdoch wants, in political terms'. It doesn't get much clearer than that.[29] In 2007, Murdoch gave evidence to the House of Lords communications committee and stated that he exercised editorial control over the Sun and the News of the World concerning which parties the papers backed in general elections and its position on Europe. During the Leveson Inquiry in 2012, Murdoch stated, "If you want to judge my thinking, look at the Sun". Murdoch claimed he had less power over the Times and Sunday Times but would still ring the editor to ask what they were working on. The editor would likely agree with doing anything Murdoch asked.[30] During the 2015 general election, Murdoch told journalists at the Sun that if Labour won the election, the paper's future would be at risk. He instructed the paper's journalists to increase attacks on Miliband and Labour and write more positive articles about the Tories.[31]

The deputy editor of the Telegraph until 2014, Benedict Brogan, was clear in an interview that newspapers are not public services. They are commercial operations that reflect the views of the owners. The journalist Christopher Hird who writes for the Economist and the Sunday Times, explains in the interview that the rich own newspapers to promote their political views. They expect journalists who write for these right-wing papers to work within the owners' values framework based on unregulated economic markets and private ownership of wealth and assets.[32] At the Daily Mail, Viscount Rothermere has complete control over selecting the paper's editors to ensure the paper follows his political agenda.[33]

Collusion between the right-wing press and Tories

Over the last 123 years, there has been ongoing collusion between the Tories and the newspapers that support the party. During the twentieth century, the party secretly channelled funds to struggling newspapers to keep them going in return for backing the party. In the early 20th century, the founder of the Daily Express worked closely with the Tory Prime Minister Chamberlain to update the parties' techniques to reach the public better, such as the production of gramophone records of his speeches. In 1927, the Tory Party supported 230 different papers with funding. The papers were bought by individuals that could not be linked to the Tories with bank loans backed by the party's capital. All of this was done in secret, as there would have been little point in propping up these papers if the public knew they were front publications for the Tories.[34]

Thatcher had close links with Tory-supporting newspapers and their editors, including the Sun, Daily Mail, and Daily Telegraph. Thatcher's advisors would call these editors weekly to include them in Thatcher's confidence.[35] There are very close links between the Tory Party and Rupert Murdoch. In the 1980s, Thatcher eased restrictions on Rupert Murdoch's purchases of newspapers and broadcasting company British Sky Broadcasting (BSkyB). In return, his many UK newspapers backed the Tories and attacked the Labour Party, assisting with the Tories winning the 1983, 1987 and 1992 general elections. Thatcher also regularly asked the Sun's editor for advice. In return for all this help winning elections, Thatcher gave out multiple honours to her supporters in the press.[36]

Blair managed to get Murdoch and, crucially, the Sun's support from 1995 by giving Murdoch political access to the Labour government, the final say on Labour's policies and a commitment to not bringing in any media reform. All this allowed Murdock to become so powerful that the News of the World developed a corporate culture of hacking people's phones looking for stories. Gordon Brown attempted to win over Murdoch but failed, losing the support of the Sun for the 2010 election.

Following the 2010 election, Prime Minister Cameron hired Andy Coulson as his communication director because he previously worked at the News of the World, and Cameron wanted to keep Murdoch onside. This was despite warnings to Cameron's team that Coulson was involved in phone hacking at the News of the World. Coulson denied involvement but was found guilty of phone hacking in 2014 and forced to resign. Regarding political access, Cameron also met with News UK/International executives twice as often as other media companies and attended social events with senior News UK executives.[37]

There is a revolving door between the media and the Tory Party. Several journalists, such as Michael Gove and Boris Johnson, have become senior Tories. Former Tory chancellor, George Osborne, went the other way by becoming the editor of the Evening Standard. There are also close links between the editors and senior writers of Tory supporting papers and Tory MPs. Several Tory MPs have partners with senior media jobs. Some politicians and journalists go on holiday together. These 'client journalists' are rewarded with access to government sources, favourable policies that directly affect them (such as keeping journalists' income taxes low) and knighthoods and peerages. Johnson recently appointed two editors, two columnists, and a press baron to the House of Lords. Rishi Sunak hired the journalist James Forsyth as his political secretary. This all results in a complete lack of the media holding Tory governments to account.[38]

Specific reasons the right-wing newspaper owners help the Tories
There are at least six reasons that the press barons back the Tories.

1. Influence of media owners on government
The culture of mutual interest between newspaper editors and Tory Party leaders results in them naturally working together to drive the

same right-wing agenda. This gives the press executives dangerous levels of influence and interference with our democracy.[39]

Murdoch and his executives have regular meetings with Tory Prime Ministers and their cabinets to influence government policy and take sides in internal fights within the government. They were also part of the social circle with MPs, top government officials, lobbyists and business leaders. In Cameron's first 15 months in government, he met News UK/International executives 26 times.[40] Between 2018 and 2019, News UK/International staff met government ministers 206 times, which is 2.8 meetings per week from the weeks that parliament was sitting during this period. There is no record of what was discussed at any of these meetings, but we can guess it was to lobby on press regulation and other policy areas. For example, the government has scrapped a public inquiry into alleged corruption between politicians, newspapers and the police. The government also does not tackle the bullying, abusive and unethical behaviour of the press.[41]

2. Maintain an unregulated media environment

The newspaper owners want it both ways: an unregulated media environment with complete press freedom but no responsibility or accountability for what they print. In their view, they are simply providing a service, and the buck stops somewhere else.[42] The Tories have shown no interest in regulating the newspaper industry. In 1986, Labour leader Kinnock proposed legislation to reduce the power of the media if a Labour government were elected. This would restrict the foreign ownership of the media, disqualifying Murdoch from owning British newspapers as he is a US citizen. Murdoch went to war against Kinnock and Labour at the 1987 and 1992 elections.[43]

Following the news of the World phone hacking scandal in 2011, Cameron was forced to set up the Leveson Inquiry and promised to implement its recommendations; he then broke this promise. At the 2015 general election, Labour leader Miliband promised to implement the Leveson recommendations, which the British media owners were against. They saw them as interfering with their freedom of speech. During this election, there was a dirty campaign by the right-wing press against Miliband, even nastier than the attacks on Kinnock.[44]

The Tories' 2019 election manifesto committed to do nothing to improve press accountability or

investigate corruption between the police, politicians and the press. The Labour and the Liberal Democrats manifestos promised to tackle police-press corruption and to implement the Leveson Inquiry recommendation on independent regulation. Unsurprisingly, the right-wing press backed the Tories.[45]

3. The Tories are slowly dismantling the BBC

The right-wing media owners, especially Murdoch, want to see the end of the BBC. Murdoch is against the licence fee funding model and the BBC's independence. Less competition from the BBC would also improve Murdoch's Sky News channel market position.[46]

In the 1980s, Thatcher deregulated the UK television and radio markets resulting in the BBC facing increased competition from the commercial channels. In 2010, the Tory-led Coalition Government froze the licence fee for 5 years and forced the BBC to fully fund the BBC World Service, which the Foreign and Commonwealth Office had funded. In 2011, the government announced a 20% cut to the BBC budget resulting in staff cuts. In 2016, the government announced a free TV licence for over-75 pensioners for £700 million per year, coming out of the BBC's budget. However, drama and sport coverage costs increased, so the BBC had to save £800 million, 23% of the licence fee. In 2020, the BBC was £119 million in debt due to delays to cost reduction plans. Since the 2019 election, there have been ongoing threats to decriminalise non-payment of the licence fee, which the BBC estimates would cost £1 billion over five years.[47]

4. Media owners benefit from the current system

The media owners are all wealthy and benefit from the current system. They are, therefore, against any political and social change. The Tories want to be in office, holding back change but not governing for the population's benefit. The right-wing media owners support the Tories and their shared agenda of maintaining the status quo, especially resisting any media reform from the Labour Party.

5. Ideological
The owners of the Tory press are aligned ideologically with the Tories. They share protecting the interests of the wealthy, private property, a small state, low taxation, privatisation, deregulation, and weak unions. Murdoch's News Group Newspaper, which owns the Sun and Times and their Sunday editions, made a loss of £64.6 million in 2019, up from a loss of £7.7 million in 2017.[48] So clearly, Murdoch isn't running these papers for money. Instead, they are propaganda and lobby machines to push his right-wing agenda.

6. Direct benefits to their media businesses
The press barons seem driven to expand their media empires. You could see this in the early twentieth century with the original press barons and the modern-day equivalents. They are motivated by power and wealth. The Tories help the media moguls buy up disproportionate amounts of the media market. In the 1980s, Thatcher backed a House of Commons vote to allow Murdoch to buy BSkyB without being referred to the regulator. The press owners have benefited from the limited worker rights Thatcher brought in during the 1980s, so their papers are printed without trade union interference compared to the 1970s. The workforce has been more casualised over the last 40 years by successive Tory governments making it easier to fire workers.

The Right-Wing Media Machine

The British national press is unique compared to other large democracies regarding its reach, domination and one-sided support for the Tories. A US Democrat political advisor for Barack Obama, David Axelrod, worked for Labour during the 2015 election and was surprised about the level of press hostility during the campaign. He described how he has worked in aggressive media environments but none as partisan as Britain. He had not seen how a political party and its press supporters worked in lockstep to promote Tory propaganda. During the election, there is little that separates the Tory Party and the right-wing press. They are one unified, coordinated, sophisticated, ruthless machine funded by a few billionaires with multiple newspapers and broadcasting outlets to appeal to a broad range of people. Any disagreements between the Tory press and the party before the election are forgotten as soon as the campaign begins.[49]

There are certain groups of voters that the media play a crucial role in influencing. The media play a propaganda role in maintaining the status quo and the Tories in government. The Tory press lie, manipulate facts and events to present the Tories in a better light and attack and undermine the opposition parties, especially Labour. Significant sections of the population would vote differently if the press gave a truthful and honest reporting of events. The press greatly influences small but strategically important sections of the population: women, swing voters and working-class Tories. The role of the Tory tabloid press is to win over socially conservative working-class voters; who are to the left on economic policy, such as supporting well-funded public services.

The right-wing press targets swing voters that constitute 1-2% of the population, about 500,000 voters spread across 100 marginal seats, enough to decide elections every time. Many of these people are genuinely misled by the press into believing a picture of reality in which crime and migration are much bigger threats to their way of life and security than is actually the case. They are also not aware of the active redistribution of money from the poor and ordinary people to the rich, which has been the key programme of Tory governments since the 1980s and New Labour failed to challenge.[50]

The right-wing media environment in Britain is made up of several newspapers and, recently, two new right-wing news channels. As described above, the Tory-supporting newspapers are The Sun, the Daily Mail, Daily Express, The Times and the Telegraph. Therefore, the papers we should be most concerned about are The Sun and the

Daily Mail.

Since the 1980s, the Sun has publicly backed the winner in every general election. The Sun has always connected with working-class voters open to switching between the Tories and Labour. The Sun's readership historically comprises 80% manual workers, skilled, semi-skilled and unskilled. In the 1992 election, 45% of readers voted Tory and 36% Labour, with the Tories narrowly winning the general election. The 1997 election saw a huge win for Labour, 52% of manual workers voted Labour, and 30% voted Tory.[51] So we can see that there is a core vote for each party in the Sun's readership, and tens of thousands of swing voters switch between the parties. As discussed, in a close election such as 1992 or 2015, the Sun convinces thousands of voters to back the Tories, and this can be enough to clinch the election for them.

An example of the Sun's impact can be seen in Liverpool. The city traditionally had Tory MPs through the twentieth century until the 1980s. There has been an active 'don't buy the Sun' campaign for at least ten years following the Hillsborough disaster in 1989 and The Sun's role in attacking Liverpool fans. There has been a permanent shift in the political culture to the left partly due to the campaign and the difficulty of getting the Sun in the city.[52]

The Daily Mail consistently backs the Tories. Its readers were evenly split between manual workers, managers, and office workers in the mid-20th century. That has slowly shifted, with readers now comprising two-thirds office workers and one-third manual workers. Most of its readers (65% plus) normally vote Tory, but this dropped to 49% in 1997. Many small business owners read it and retired people. Recently the Mail Online website has become very popular. They post large amounts of celebratory gossip clickbait (articles with appealing titles) to pull people in and then feed them extremely right-wing news stories. They target another strategically important part of the electorate, women.

More women voted Tory during most of the twentieth century, including the 1992 election. This changed for the 1997 election with a huge swing to Labour among young women, and this pattern has continued. A key function of David Cameron was his appeal to middle-class women. Many societal pressures drag women leftwards, especially if they have children, due to their interaction with public services, doctors, hospitals, and schools. The Mail Online works to attract women with low levels of education and information about politics to its website and have them read terrifying stories to try to convince them of conservative perspectives on economics, immigration, crime and the left.[53]

Of the other three main Tory papers, the Daily Telegraph and the Times are read by most professionals and office workers. More manual workers read the Express. The last few years have seen two new right-wing News channels launched: GB News and TalkTv. TalkTv is from Murdoch's News UK company. These are seen as trying to introduce a US approach to broadcasting similar to the highly divisive US Fox News and drag all media further rightwards. TalkTv news has three original programmes, one with Pier Morgan, but it has not attracted many viewers.[54] GB News has received a mixed reception, with Nigel Farage, the previous leader of the Brexit Party, being the biggest attraction. Tory MPs such as Jacob Rees-Mogg have recently started presenting their own shows.

Newspapers have come under pressure in the last 20 years from digital news and social media. Traditional media faces declining newspaper circulations threatening their profitability but have become even more influential. They are now 'feeding' news stories to social media, which has increased the influence of press editors to mould perceptions and dominate the news cycle.[55] Controversial right-wing newspaper columnists increase their reach through social media, especially Twitter. This is reinforced by appearing on television panels and political programmes. The left does have media commentators, but the right has many more, who are more aggressive and have greater reach through the right-wing newspapers' online platforms.[56]

How Does The Right-Wing Press Help The Tories

The right-wing press helps the Tories win elections in at least 10 ways.

<u>Lie and distort reality</u>
The right-wing press straight out lies to cover for the Tories. For example, in September 2019, the Telegraph lied about opinion polls to help Johnson shut down parliament.[57] Following the 2021 Tory budget, Chancellor Sunak raised taxes, the Daily Express reported that the Tories were dropping taxes.[58]

Another tactic the Tory press use is to publish stories in which most of the facts are true, but the headline and the claims in the article will be highly misleading. For example, in early 2023, the Irish Prime Minister, Leo Varadkar, expressed regret that the Irish people had no say over the Northern Ireland Protocol because the Tories solely decided it. Several newspapers presented Varadkar's comments as if he expressed personal regret for his role in the affair. The headlines don't match the article, but that's the point; the headline is what is intended to have an impact.[59]

<u>Promote Tory lies</u>
The Tories know they can get away with their lies because the Tory-supporting media either promote these lies or will not challenge them. At the 2019 election, Johnson lied about getting Brexit done, levelling up, 40 new hospitals and other public services commitments. Many of us knew they were lies then, but the Tory press printed them like they were to be trusted. A more blatant example during the 2019 election was when the Tories claimed that the Labour activist assaulted cabinet minister Matt Hancock and the press and the BBC repeated this claim. It turned out to be untrue, many of these outlets apologised, but the damage had been done. During 2022, the Tories have tried to blame the UK's economic problems on the strikes, which the press is happy to repeat.

Repeat lies until people believe them

The Tory press regularly repeats lies, so millions of readers eventually believe them and then adopt them as their own beliefs. The obvious example is that the Tories are better with the economy, this is not true, as explained in chapter 11, but the Tory press has made millions believe it. These lies spread and become ingrained in the nation's understanding of politics, so they are shared by the BBC and other mainstream media publications and into voters' everyday conversations. Our education system does not teach critical thinking skills or economic literacy. Instead, schools encourage rote learning of exam answers. This makes people especially susceptible to repeated lies from cunning right-wing newspapers.[60]

Print Tory propaganda uncritically

The Tory Party feeds the right-wing press stories, which are printed uncritically. During the 1979 election, the Daily Mail printed a front-page story written by Thatcher's communication director.[61]

Cover for Tory misrule and failure

The Tories have been managing the economy since 2010, and it has been much weaker than during the New Labour years, but the media will always claim that the Tories manage the economy better than Labour.[62] Since Brexit, the Tories have become an anti-business party. There is the famous 'fuck business' comment by Johnson in 2018. But they have been given a free pass by the right-wing media. Of course, if a Labour MP said anything like this, it would be on the front page of all the Tory newspapers for days.[63] The Tory press has completely failed to report on the Tories' corrupt Covid PPE 'VIP lane' and the failure of the Tories to chase the missing £10 billion in fraudulent furlough loans.

Following Truss's mini-budget announcement, the Tory press had glowing headlines the next morning. Then when the international markets lost faith in the UK government, causing the country economic problems, the same media did not criticise Truss; instead, they switched coverage to the Royal Family, always a good way to distract.[64] In December 2022, Home Secretary Braverman was caught lying to a Parliament select committee about the nonexistent legal routes for asylum seekers. The press completely ignored this.[65]

The press helps the Tories with a common con trick they use. The Tories and the right-wing media point to a genuine problem and then explain their solution. But they never actually explain how the solution deals with the problem, and many readers will uncritically accept this false logic. The best recent example is Brexit; leaving the EU Customs Union and Single Market was meant to help solve Britain's problems, but it's made them worse.

Identity scapegoats to avoid scrutiny of the Tories and wealthy
The Tories and their media are experts at pointing at groups of people and blaming them for the country's problems. These include the Labour Party, trade unions, benefit claimants, minorities, unpatriotic left, protesters, immigrants, teenage mothers, and Muslims.[66]

The right-wing media work hard with the Tories at the old game of 'divide and conquer' to stop the majority of people who have broadly common interests from coming together and making demands around decent jobs, pay, housing or property-funded public services. Their current tactic of 'culture wars' feeds on bigotry, racism and xenophobia. The scapegoating of groups by the Daily Mail, The Sun and the Daily Express works to redirect anger and scrutiny away from Tories and the wealthy and towards the most marginalised sections of society that happen to not vote much or even have the right to vote.

Media gaslighting
The right-wing news comprises deceptions and distortions that hide the truth about our society and politics and work very hard to maintain the status quo. 'Media gaslighting' is a form of psychological manipulation to create doubt in people's minds so they question reality, their memory and beliefs. The right-wing media use this to control readers' understanding of the world and convince them to think in a right-wing way through repetition. The Tory media is

telling their readers what to think so they 'fit in', and fitting in is a natural human instinct. It goes beyond misinformation to intentionally rewriting the narrative on an issue to control public opinion. It refuses to engage with any information contradicting the narrative being pushed.[67]

A common trick is for the Tory press to say that a problem does not exist and massively play it down, and because of their market dominance, this will convince millions of voters. An example of this is saying that the cost of living crisis did not exist through 2022.

Discredit opposition and promote Tories as better

The Tory press constantly discredits the Labour Party's ability to govern and manage the economy competently. Since the 2008 financial crisis, the Tories have successfully blamed the Labour Party for causing the international banking crisis followed by a recession in the UK economy. The right-wing media were a key part of anti-Labour attacks.[68]

Labour is held to a completely different standard than the Tories. The Tory press will jump on any opportunity to claim Labour are unfit to run the country. During the 2019 election, the Tories claimed the Labour Party manifesto would cost £1.2 trillion. This was a completely made-up inflated figure, but it was happily plastered across all the Tory papers.[69] The press relentlessly attacked Corbyn and the Labour Party for unrealistic spending commitments even though the Labour Party manifesto was fully costed. Of course, the Tories had not costed their manifesto. Also, during that election, the Home Secretary Priti Patel claimed that if Labour won, immigration would drastically increase when the Labour manifesto said nothing of the sort. Again the Tory press was very willing to give this front-page coverage.

Create fear about Labour and Liberal Democrat leaders

The Tory press has viscously attacked Labour leaders since the 1980s, including John Foot, Neil Kinnock, Ed Milliband and Jeremy Corbyn. They are accused of being communists, unpatriotic, and a danger to

Britain's economy and national security. Because the 2017 election was so close, the level of attacks on Corbyn in 2019 was incredible, labelling him a Stalinist, IRA sympathiser and anti-Semitic. It is not just Labour leaders; in 2010, when the Liberal Democrat leader Nick Clegg started doing well in the polls, the Tories and right-wing media aggressively went on the attack.

Maintain right-wing, toxic, unregulated media environment
The Tories and their media benefit from a right-wing, toxic, unregulated media environment, so they work to maintain this by attacking any sign of press reform from the Labour Party and its leaders such as Kinnock, Miliband and Corbyn. They want to be free to spread their hate, propaganda and lies to put off as many decent people from bothering to vote as low turnout benefits the Tories.

17

FACTORS INFLUENCING VOTING BEHAVIOUR

How voters decide which political party to support at elections is based on two factors. The first group are long-term factors such as social class, age, gender, geography and demographic change, home ownership, education, and ethnicity. The second group are short-term factors such as governing competence, the state of the economy, the popularity of the different party leaders, and the election campaign offers. The short-term factors have been covered in previous chapters. This chapter focuses on the long-term factors and includes many statistics and dates. This is useful to help understand how the Tories build voter coalitions, which is covered in the following chapter.

Social Class

There are several ways to consider class in Britain: occupation, income, wealth, culture and identity. In this section, I will describe electoral trends and voting behaviour based on voters' type of occupation, as this information is available from research and surveys. At its most basic, there are manual and non-manual jobs. Since the 1960s, surveys and opinion polling have divided workers into categories A, B, C1, C2, and DE. Of these, A/B are middle-class professionals, C1 is non-manual lower middle class, C2 is skilled manual working class, and D/E are unskilled manual working class.

The first half of the twentieth century saw the working class make up more than three-quarters of the population.[1] These were mostly manual workers and their families including miners, dockers, steelworkers, domestic servants, low-level clerical workers such as typists, secretaries, office assistants and messengers. This also included nurses, technicians and higher-grade clerical workers, who would identify as working class due to their family background and because they worked for a living. They identified more with wage earners than with employers. In the 1900s, employers made up 3% of the workforce.[2] In the early 20th century, a quarter of voters were middle-class or upper-class.[3] The Tory middle class broadly includes farmers, lawyers, doctors, dentists, pharmacists, engineers, shopkeepers, managers, teachers, manufacturers, and business owners.

So based on this, how did the working class vote in the early 20th century? Many believe that Labour was the party of the working class in the 20th century, but this is not the case. Accurate data on how people voted based on social class in the first half of the 20th century is unavailable, so we need to do some extrapolation based on the available data. Let's look at the first general election when all women and men over 21 could vote in 1929. This election saw 21.3 million people vote with 76.3% turnout. This means the total electorate was about 28 million. If the working class comprised 75% of the electorate, this would be about 21 million, with 7 million middle and upper class. In that election, Labour and the Tories got about 8 million voters each, with the Liberals getting 5 million votes. Labour's 8 million votes are 38% of those that voted, well short of the 75% of the electorate seen as working class. So the working class either voted for Labour (8 million) and did not vote (7 million), a total of 15 million votes, but that still left 6 million working-class voters supporting the Tories or Liberals. Does this mean that millions of middle-class voters would have voted for Labour and the Liberals, meaning that millions more working-class voters voted for the Liberals and Tories?

Fortunately, we have much more information in the postwar

period. There is general agreement that in the first half of the 20th century, the Tories had most of the working-class and middle-class support. There is also general agreement that from 1945 to the 1970s, Labour had a small majority of working-class support.[4] But there is some disagreement on what happened in the 1970s. Some claim that the Tories regained a majority of working-class support.[5] But data from the British Election Survey (BES) contradicts this, indicating that Labour had a slim majority of working-class support. This disagreement might be due to how the 'working class' is being defined, with some looking at skilled manual workers (C2) and some looking at manual workers overall C2, DE.

This BES data shows a third of the working class supported the Tories during the 1980s and early 1990s. This dropped to 20% in 1997, which indicates the bottom floor of Tory support in the working class. Tory support among the working class gradually increased after 1997 to over 40% in 2019, ahead of Labour. For Labour, working-class support for Labour from 1979 to 2010 fluctuated between 40 to 60%. It dropped below 40% in the 2015 and 2019 elections. The BES data shows a weakening link between parties and class over the last 40 years.[6]

Regarding middle-class support from the 1960s, the middle and lower middle classes voted in greater numbers for the Tories, with Labour getting between a sixth and a quarter of the middle-class vote. Tory middle-class support was between 50 to 60% in the 1980s and 1992, dropping to below 40% in 1997 and only increasing from 40% in 2010 to about 45% in 2019. Middle-class support for Labour was between 20 to 30% in the 1980s and 1992.[7] Labour's middle-class support increased to 40% in 1997, dropping to just below 30% after the 2010 election. It then increased to nearly 40% in 2017, to drop back down to about 30% in 2019.

There was an important change to voting behaviour in the 1970s, with a weakening of the link between social class and party support; up until that point, occupation class was the most important determining factor in voting choice. This change has multiple causes, including changes to the labour market due to the decline of industry and manufacturing; the increase in female workers; the mass take-up of televisions providing voters with a wider range of views; great affluence and the expansion of higher education.[8]

This period also saw a shift around party loyalty. Up to the 1970s, there had also been strong party loyalty, with voters supporting the same party all their lives. In 1961, 44% of voters were 'strong supporters' of the Tories or Labour; this dropped to 12% by 2010. Voters become more open to different parties and 'shopping around'. Potential causes for this change include economic and political shocks, policy failures and general crises that disrupted people's party allegiances.[9] Labour and Tories got 90% of the vote in the 1960s, and this dropped to 70% in the 1980s. This was caused by the multiparty realignment of British politics with the Liberal-SDP Alliance gaining popularity.[10]

Another important consideration in terms of social class is the changing size of the classes. The number of people in the working class has gradually declined through the last 123 years, with the size of the middle class increasing. The year 2000 has been identified as when there were more middle-class non-manual workers (ABC1) than working-class manual workers (C2DE). By 2015 the middle class had increased to 54.2%.[11]

Age

Data on voting behaviour and age is not available before the 1960s. Looking at elections in 1966, 1970, October 1974 and 1992, we can see that more young have voted for Labour than the old through this period. Tory support is greater for those over 55 in these elections, except in 1974.[12]

Support for the Tories and Labour from 1979 to 2019 can be divided between those under 45 (the young) and 45 and over (the old). We can see broadly similar support for the Tories in 1979 and 1983, with those over 45 marginally supporting the Tories. The 1987 election saw much more support for Labour from the young, with this gap closing again for the 1992 election. For the 1997 election, support for the Tories with the young dropped and increased for Labour, with those over 45 supporting the Tories by a noticeable margin. This margin continued as general support for Labour decreased through the 2000s. Between the five general elections from 1997 and 2015, 42% of those aged 18-24 and 28% of those over 65 voted for Labour. During the same period, 47% over 65 and 23% 18-24 voted Tory.[13]

The gap between the young, middle-aged and old significantly increased in 2015 and became a huge gap in 2017, described as Labour's 'youthquake'. The Tories have made huge gains with older voters, and Labour has done the same with younger voters. In 2019, the Tories got the support of 57% of those over 60s and 67% from over 70s. Johnson's Tories in 2019 appealed to younger people more than in the previous election, with the age of a voter supporting the Tories dropping from 47 in 2017 to 39 in 2019. Even so, the 2010s have seen the biggest conflict between the generations in the last 40 years.[14]

After the 2017 election, there were claims that youth turnout had increased dramatically by 12 to 21%. Later research did not find this to be the case, although this was criticised for a small sample size. The Labour Party estimated that it went up about 10%. But the British Electoral Study argued that even if youth turnout had increased by 10% or more, it would have had a small impact on the result. People aged 18 to 24 comprised 11% of the electorate in 2017, 5.2 million people in total. Labour won 3.5 million more votes in 2017 than in 2015. If turnout among this age group were as high as 72%, then this would have only added 1.2 million young voters. Even if it is assumed that they all voted Labour (unlikely), then this would have only made up a third of the votes gained by Labour in 2017.[15]

Another thing to note is that turnout to vote in elections increases as people age. For those 45 to 65, it is in the 70-80% range; for those over 65, it is around 90%. For those under 45, it is less than 60% and for those under 35 less than 50%. And as we have seen, most older people vote Tory, which gives the Tories a huge advantage.[16]

Gender

Between 1945 and 1979, most women voted Tory, with most men voting Labour. There was a large gap between men and women voting Tory in the 1950s. This gradually decreased during the 1960s and 1970s. In 1966 just over half of men voted for Labour and a third for the Tories. For women, it was 45% for both parties; and both voted 8% Liberal. In 1970, 42% of men voted for the Tories and 47% for Labour, and both voted 7% Liberal. At the same time, half of women voted for the Tories and 41% for Labour. In October 1974, a third of men voted Tory and 43% Labour. Women were close again, 39% Tory, 38% Labour; and around 20% Liberal for both.

By the 1979 election, there was similar support for the Tories between the genders, which continued through the 1980s and the 1990s. In 1979, Thatcher won over more of both sexes, 45% of men and women. Labour got 40% of men and 36% of women, with the Liberals in the teens for both. In 1987, Thatcher got 43% of women and men, and Labour got a third of both. The Liberal Alliance got 23% of both sexes. In 1992, the Tories got 41% of men and 44% of women. Labour got 37% of men and a third of women. Liberals got 18% of both. In 1997, the Tories got 31% of men and 32% of women. Labour got 44% of both, and the Liberal Democrats got 17%. Explanations for the decline in women voting Tory relate to the long-term changes to women's lifestyles. More women are in work; more are joining trade unions, have a university education and have more senior jobs. Also, family sizes have declined, combined with less religious involvement.[17]

At the 2015 election, 37% of women and 38% of men backed the Tories. Labour had the support of a third of women and 30% of men. Johnson and the Tories put young women off in 2019, but Johnson did well with men, achieving a 19% lead over Labour compared to a 6% lead over Labour among women.[18]

Geography And Demographic Change

Each region of the UK has a different political character and electoral history. However, the Tories have consistently dominated in England, especially in the South. About 80% of UK constituencies are in England; this domination in England gives the Tories a big advantage.

In the late 19th century and early 20th century, the Tories expanded their support in Northwest England, London, Birmingham and the West Midlands. Since the Second World War, the Tories have been strongest in the South of England, rural areas, and smaller towns. Labour did better in cities and the North of England, Wales and Scotland.[19] In 1951, the North of England backed the Tories by 47% and the Midlands and South by 50%. However, the divide between the North and South increased through the postwar period, so in the 1980s elections, Labour won few seats in the South apart from in London, and the Tories did badly in the North and Scotland.

Through most of the 20th century, the Tories have had strong support in Scotland and Wales. In the 1955 and 1959 elections, they won a majority of seats in Scotland and held onto 25% of the popular vote and 11 seats in 1992. The Tories won 6 seats in 2019. The Tories also managed to maintain support in Wales up to 1992 in rural areas and those on the border with England. The Tories' support in cities declined through the 20th century. In Birmingham, the Tories won all twelve seats in 1935. In 1945, Labour took all twelve seats. By 1970 Labour and the Tories had six each. Liverpool in 1950 had five Tory MPs, down to two in 1970, and now Liverpool is a no-go area for the Tories.[20]

The Tories dominated the outer London boroughs of London through most of the 20th century, winning more seats than Labour up to the 1992 election. Since 1997, this has been reversed to become a Labour stronghold.[21]

Labour's political support in England has been in London, the North and West Midlands, with a manufacturing and coal mining history. Labour has always had strong electoral support in Scotland and Wales, where there has been industry and mining. Blair and New

Labour won the majority of seats in Scotland and Wales in 1997, which reduced the Tories to a mostly English party with no seats in either region. Then at the 2015 election, Labour lost 40 seats in Scotland, leaving it with only 1. The 2010s have seen Labour become a more English party compared to any point in its history. At the same time, the Tories have expanded their support in Wales and Scotland in the last decade. In Scotland, the Tories are seen as the main Unionist opposition to the SNP.[22] At the 2017 election, the Tories received their highest share of the vote in Wales in a century and were ahead of Labour in Scotland for the first time since 1959.[23]

Until recently, Labour dominated small towns. The Tories' vote in small towns went from 34.5% in 2005 to 48% in 2017, with Labour's support remaining the same. In 2017, Labour had 50% of the vote in ex-industrial towns, with the Tories at 37%, UKIP at 5%, and the Liberal Democrats at 3%. By 2019, polling showed the Tories were still at 37%, Labour at 27%, Brexit Party at 16% and the Liberal Democrats at 14%.[24]

Brexit had a big impact on the 2019 election. The pro-Brexit Tories' vote share increased in leave voting seats and dropped in those that voted to remain. Labour's vote decreased in both remain and leave seats, with more support being lost in leave seats. Liberal Democrat support increased significantly in Tory remain seats. Labour had the worst losses of seats in the northeast and Yorkshire and the Humber. Support for the Tories fell in London and the Southeast and increased in the Northeast and East and West Midlands. In 2010, 31% of Northern voters backed the Tories compared to 43% in the rest of England, and Labour won the majority of Northern seats. Brexit changed this for the 2019 election, resulting in 26 seats switched from Labour to the Tories.[25]

Recent demographic shifts have helped the Tories in Northern seats in the 2017 and 2019 elections. There has been a change to the age profile of the Northern seats. During the 2010s, many young people moved to cities to find jobs and housing. This has resulted in an increase in the proportion of the population over 65, who mostly vote Tory. And the share of the population from 18 to 24, most likely to vote Labour, has declined. This pattern has not been repeated in the South.[26]

Homeownership

Homeownership is the foundation of the Tory support base. Historically, once someone owns a property, they are more likely to vote Tory. Between 1964 and 1992, homeownership went from 48% to 72% nationally. Thatcher's right-to-buy scheme resulted in 2.5 million council houses being purchased by their tenants. Between 1974 and 1992, over half of homeowners voted Tory, and a quarter voted Labour. During this period, 55-65% of council tenants voted Labour. All this mostly helps the Tories.[27]

At the 2019 election, the Tories got support from 57% of owner-occupies (own their house without a mortgage) and 43% of mortgage holders. Labour got 22% of owner-occupies and 33% of those with mortgages. As a result, the Tories won 365 seats in 2019; 315 had a home ownership level above the UK average of 64%, with Labour only having 53 of the 202 seats they won over this level.[28]

Since 2010, the Tories have gained significantly more support from homeowners and landlords than Labour. The 2019 election saw the Tories get 50% support from this group and only 23% for Labour. Due to the crossover between homeownership and older voters, this group votes in greater numbers and is more evenly distributed across the country. This general trend goes against a recent national decrease in property ownership, which has been caused by the Tories' failure to build enough council and affordable homes for the country's growing population. The lack of supply has caused property prices to increase dramatically since the 1990s, which benefits the Tories' older voter base. The young live in private rental properties, and although the Tories had a slight lead over Labour with this group, support has gone in Labour's direction. Many young people are now priced out of the property market in cities. Support for Labour in this group increased during Corbyn's time as he had plans to improve renters' rights and take on exploitative landlords. This has added to the large support for

Labour in cities. The 2019 election saw Labour get 54 % support from private renters.[29]

Another factor in turning seats Tory in Northern and Midlands Labour industrial towns over the last decade is at play. These towns have seen new-build suburbs spring up in the last twenty years, where couples move from urban areas and start a family. As a result, these seats have some of the lowest housing costs in the country and an increasing share of home ownership. This makes a family life of home and car ownership affordable, so many will vote for the Tories as they have an improved standard of living compared to where they moved from.[30]

Education

Between 1979 and 2015, Tory support among university graduates and those without higher qualifications was relatively similar. The 2017 election saw this start to change. The Tories gained support from those without qualifications, and their support with graduates dropped. The gap dramatically widened at the 2019 election, the largest in the last 40 years. In the 20th century, Labour traditionally had more support among those without higher qualifications. This support started to decline in the 2000s and 2010s to narrow the gap between graduate and non-graduate support. Support for Labour with graduates increased in 2017 and stayed consistent with those without qualifications. At the 2019 election, Labour support among those without qualifications dropped significantly.[31]

Ethnicity

In 1974, 17% of non-white voters supported the Tories, and 72% supported Labour. This has not changed much since, in 2010, the Tories won 16% of non-white voters, a total of about 400,000 people. In 2017 about 75% of non-white people voted for Labour, and 20% supported the Tories. The Tories' consistent anti-immigrant rhetoric and policies are a big cause of this.[32]

18

THE TORIES ARE BETTER AT BUILDING VOTER COALITIONS

Winning general elections in the UK is rarely about getting the majority of voters to support a political party. Instead, parties win a large parliamentary majority on a minority of the vote. Parties achieve this by winning over key voter constituencies with particular strategic leverage within marginal seats in the UK's electoral system First Past the Post (FPTP). Parties must extend beyond their core voter bases to win a general election and construct broad voter coalitions to achieve working majorities in parliament. The Tories have shown themselves to be consistently better at this than Labour.

Broadly, the Tories have built voter coalitions of well-off middle-class voters in the South and rural seats, with millions of aspiring working-class voters across the country. Most of the middle and upper class support the Tories, although middle-class support has recently weakened. About a quarter to a third of working-class voters have always supported the Tories, and this has increased since the 1980s. Labour has relied on more working-class voters and a significant minority of middle-class voters. The old have always supported the Tories more than Labour, with a good majority of the young supporting Labour more than the Tories; this has become more pronounced recently. More women supported the Tories and more men Labour in the 20th century, but this has been reversed in the last decade. The Tories have more support in the South, Midlands and rural areas, with Labour's support traditionally being in London, the North, West Midlands, Scotland and Wales. Both parties' support has decreased in Scotland. The Tories started gaining Northern 'red wall' Labour seats in the 2017 and 2019 elections. In the 20th century, the Tories had similar support among graduates and non-graduates, with Labour having more support among those without qualifications. This has been reversed in the last decade, with most university students supporting Labour. Homeownership has always favoured the Tories. Over 70% of non-white voters have supported Labour, with the Tories getting 20% or less.

Early 20th Century

In the early 20th century, the Tories built an electoral alliance of brewing businesses with workers who wanted to enjoy a few pints at the end of the day. The Liberals and Labour were publicly against alcohol on moral grounds and due to its impact on household finances. The Tories effectively aligned themselves with workers' basic freedom to enjoy themselves after work.[1] Following the extension of the vote in 1918 and 1928, the Tories understood that manual workers dominated the electorate. So they needed to gain the support of a significant section of the working class, which they achieved during the interwar years.[2]

The 1920s and 1930s saw the decline of the Liberal Party as the Labour Party replaced it. The Tories gained the vote of millions of middle-class Liberal voters. The Tories had acquired a high degree of legitimacy from their association with the institutions and values of the British state. This gave the party broad appeal across the electorate. Labour had a narrower appeal based on trade unionists, working-class communities and small groups of intellectuals.[3]

Post-War Period

The Tories' post-war domination from 1951 to 1964 was based on a broad appeal to a wide section of the electorate. The party worked hard to be seen as the 'party of the people' and deliver high living standards, lower taxes than Labour, increased home building and ownership, full employment and ensuring peaceful industrial relations with the unions through collective bargaining. This commitment to economic stability domestically was combined with an assertive national security policy abroad. All this created a stable electoral coalition of middle-class voters in the South with aspirational and patriotic working-class voters nationally. High defence spending meant more military manufacturing in the North of England, Scotland and Wales, supporting a growth policy beyond the South of England. Labour struggled to compete due to the memory of the austerity years under Attlee, combined with Labour's resistance to the 'popular affluence society' and the material comforts it brought that the Tories offered. This was electorally catastrophic for Labour, pushing many aspirational working-class voters to the Tories.[4]

The Tory vote during the 1950s was more evenly spread than Labour's, geographically and socially, and about four-fifths of the middle class voted consistently for the Tories, making it about a third of the electorate. The Tories dominated the suburbs of large cities but won the rest of their seats by a small margin. The Tories need a significant section of the working class to keep winning. They secured about a third, and because the working class were such a large social group, this was half of the Tories' electoral support. The Tories' vote was more evenly spread out, so they won seats across the whole country.[5] The Tory Party identified in the late 1950s that to win future elections; they had to attract the support of the lower-middle-class and upper-working-class voters. These voters needed appealing policies to vote for combined with frightening them not to vote for the opposition.[6]

Late 20th Century

In 1979 Thatcher increased her vote by appealing to skilled manual workers and the young. In the previous election in October 1974, these groups had largely voted for Labour, but by 1979, the very young 18-24 were split between Labour and the Tories. Those over 24 were voting for the Tories in greater numbers. In 1974, most skilled manual workers voted for Labour, but by 1979 it was also evenly split. Labour-supporting lower middle class and skilled manual workers were among the main groups that the Tories under Thatcher aimed to attract based on the promise of economic prosperity.[7]

Thatcher built on the Tories' postwar strategy of promoting prosperity and property ownership and pushed it to new limits with the mass sale of council houses and privatisations of national industries, encouraging mass public share ownership. The creation of large numbers of homeowners led to greater support for market solutions to perceived problems with public services.[8] Thatcher promised to smash the unions, privatise public services, restore the traditional family, stop welfare scrounging and restrict immigration. She also promoted xenophobia positions against Europeans.[9] In 1979 and 1983, the Tories' election wins relied on skilled manual workers and the upper working class. This key group of support lived in the South, were homeowners, worked in the private sector and were not union members.[10]

21st Century

In the late 2000s and through the 2010s, Cameron and Osborne effectively constructed a voter coalition using their 'making work pay', 'big society' and austerity programme to cut public services and benefits. It united traditional small-state, low-tax Tory voters with aspiration working class people who supported reducing a perceived culture of welfare dependency.[11]

In addition, the Tories went after working-class voters in small towns by introducing popular income policies for low-paid workers such as the 'National Living Wage'. This was similar to Labour's 'Minimum Wage' but offered a slightly higher amount and was only for those over 23. The Tories also increased the tax-free income tax allowance to £12,500. They claimed to be the 'party of the workers' and labelled Labour as the 'party of the shirkers'. The Tories also emphasised their traditional positions on law and order to appeal to socially conservative voters. They promised to reduce immigration to the 'tens of thousands', which was popular with voters.

Cameron's modernisation of the Tory Party made it more appealing to socially liberal and economically moderate middle-class voters. The party regained Middle England voters that had switched to Labour and the Liberal Democrats since 1997. Once the financial crisis had fully impacted British society in 2008, Cameron was seen by voters as a preferred Prime Minister and more competent to run the country and the economy.[12]

Osborne attempted to broaden the Tories' appeal from the South with the 'Northern Powerhouse' project by directing public money to the North of England as the Tories' first attempts at rebalancing regional inequalities. These policies helped the Tories win a historical gain of 96 seats in 2010, many from Middle England. The Tories introduced several policies to keep over 60s support, including the 'pension triple-lock', universal winter fuel payments, and free bus passes.[13]

In 2015, the Tories increased their vote share and seats to form a majority government, winning over many middle-class Liberal Democrat voters in the suburbs of London and the Southwest of England. The party extended their appeal to working-class and middle-class voters in seats in the north of England, midlands and Wales.[14] At the 2015 election, the Tories did better in seats with above-average levels of household incomes and lower levels of unemployment.[15]

For the 2017 election, May built a voter coalition by reaching out to the 'just about managing' through economic interventionist policy rhetoric, including energy price controls, racial and gender pay audits and giving workers the option to sit on company boards. Although, none of this happened as May was consumed by Brexit negotiations. She moved away from the austerity policies of Cameron and increased spending on the NHS. She reached out to Scottish voters in speeches and visited Scotland to rebuild party support there. May was rewarded for these efforts with a swing in support to the Tories in the North, Midlands, and Wales and won 13 seats in Scotland. The Tories gained 2.4 million votes in 2017, the first time a party has increased its share of the vote for the third election in a row.[16]

May had the support of anti-Labour workers, the petite bourgeoisie, the business and professional managers and the rich. UKIP supporters also backed May, based on her clear position on Brexit. Former Labour voters also supported May for the same reasons, combined with being put off voting for Labour by Corbyn.[17] The 2017 election saw age replace social class as a stronger indicator of voting preference, with the old supporting the Tories and the young preferring Labour. The link between social class and voting was weakened, with an equal amount of middle and working-class voters supporting the parties. The Tories' voter coalition was built around the economy, law and order, security and Brexit.[18]

Following the 2016 EU referendum, the Tories under May and Johnson attracted many working-class voters, and by 2019 they were nearly equal to middle-class support. The Tories' 2019 voter coalition has changed significantly since 2010. It was comprised of old voters with varying affluence levels and spread across the North and Midlands of England, Wales and Scotland.[19] During this election, the Tories had more support than Labour across all social classes. They expanded into seats with lower income levels that were socially and economically deprived and had never voted Conservative.[20] The Tories appealed to Southern middle-class voters with environmental policies and a green industrial strategy, including the building of renewables projects promising thousands of new jobs.[21] Johnson's manifesto was designed to appeal to those that wanted austerity to end, spending on public services to increase and regional inequalities to be tackled through 'levelling up', but it needed to be modest enough not to scare the Tory voting base.[22]

The Tories attracted many that voted remain in the hope that the Tories would resolve the Brexit stalemate so the country could move on. Some traditional Labour voters saw voting for the Tories as a 'one-off' by 'lending' their vote to give the Tories a mandate to follow through on the perceived people's wish to 'get Brexit done 'and end the deadlock in parliament during the autumn of 2019.[23]

After the votes had been counted in England, the Tories won double the number of Labour seats; in Wales, the Tories won 14 seats, the highest in decades; in Scotland, the Tories won 6 seats, losing 7.[24] The Tories had the support of 50% of homeowners, nearly double that of Labour supporters. It is estimated that 1 million Labour voters switched to the Tories in 2019. Many of these votes came from leave-voting towns on the edge of large cities that are poorer than traditional Tory voting seats.[25]

As well as Labour supporters switching their support to the Tories in 2019, there was another important factor. In these former Labour seats that the Tories won, the Liberal Democrat and Green vote went up. Many of these voters had backed Labour in 2017 but were not happy with Labour's Brexit policy, so they went back to supporting their preferred smaller party. This was enough to reduce the majority of the Labour MPs in several seats, so a small increase in Tory support meant the seats switched to the Tories.[26]

Brexit was important in the 2019 election, combined with long-term changes in voter behaviour. Social class has become less important, with cultural values, education and age becoming more significant. The Tories have much more support among the old and those with less education. Labour is favoured by the young, those in urban areas, ethnic minorities and those with university degrees. Values have become more important, those with socially conservative views backing the Tories, those with more socially liberal views backing Labour, the Liberal Democrats, the Greens, the SNP and Plaid Cymru.[27]

19

WHY DO PEOPLE VOTE TORY?

The chapter will consider psychological reasons people back the Tories and then lists six reasons people vote for them. It is a real puzzle why so many millions of people vote for the Tories when it seems plain to many of us how unfit they are to govern and the damage they do to the country's public services and the most vulnerable.

Psychology Of Why People Identify With The Tories

The Tories understand moral psychology better than their opposition. Their slogans, political advertising and speeches appeal to emotions and values. They understand that politics is more like religion than shopping; people are drawn to a moral vision that claims to unite the nation and call it to greatness. Thatcher created the Tories' powerful moral vision in the 1980s based on patriotism, social order, personal responsibility, strong families, and free enterprise instead of government safety nets. These are based on values, not government policies. Generally, Labour and the Liberal Democrats focus more on policies and the benefits they offer voters.[1]

The field of moral psychology helps us understand why people back different political parties. It looks at how researchers understand how children develop their thinking about rules and moral development. Jonathan Haidt has identified several principles related to moral psychology related to why religion and politics divide people. They are:

1. 'Intuitions come first, strategic reasoning second';
2. 'There's more to morality than harm and fairness';
3. 'Morality binds and blinds'.

<u>Intuitions come first, strategic reasoning second</u>
Haidt explains why emotions and intuitions come first and strategic reasons second. He identifies two thought processes, an automatic process of intuition and a controlled process of reasoning. Quick, intuitive thoughts mostly influence political and social judgements. Our physical states can influence moral judgements, such as bad smells and tastes, which can cause thoughts about purity and cleanliness that lead people to be more judgmental. Reason is important, especially between people, and can lead to new intuitions. Intuitions can be influenced by reasoning, particularly when the reasons are received in an accessible way, such as in a friendly conversation or in a novel, film or on the news. When we learn what people do or think, our intuition reacts, and our rational processes try to determine how to justify that response.

Haidt explains that our brains developed like this because humans have evolved to cooperate in social groups beyond our family, and this is a key reason why humans have been so successful as a species. The creation of formal and informal systems of accountability achieves this cooperation. As a result, humans have become experts at holding people accountable for their actions, combined with skilfully navigating through societies where people hold us to account for our behaviour.

He frames moral thinking as similar to a politician chasing voters rather than a scientist looking for truth. This results in people being obsessively focused on how others think about them, with most of it being unconscious, so we are unaware. Our reasoning automatically justifies any intuitive position our brains take. This means we constantly lie and cheat, which our brains cover up so well that we can even convince ourselves. Our reasoning can help us reach almost any conclusion we want to get to. When we want to believe something, our brains ask, 'Can I believe it?' or when we don't want to believe something, our brains ask, 'Must I believe it?'. We also always answer yes to the first questions and no to the second. We are more 'groupish' than selfish on moral and political issues. We apply our reasoning abilities to help our people or team and to display our loyalty to our group.[2]

There's more to morality than harm and fairness
Moving on to Haidt's second principle, "There's more to morality than harm and fairness." He identifies that in Western, educated, industrial, rich and democratic countries, the moral framework is narrower than in other countries. In Western countries, most people prioritise individual autonomy related to concerns about people harming, oppressing or cheating others. In other cultures and for conservative moral frameworks in Western countries, ideas around community and religion are more important. Another factor is that people's moral frameworks tend to blind them to other moral frameworks different from their own. As a result, people struggle to accept that there is more than one valid moral truth for judging others or managing a society.

Haidt's research led him to identify six 'moral foundations' based on innate but flexible and malleable ethical perspectives:

1. The care/harm foundation makes us sensitive to suffering and wants to protect others;
2. The fairness/cheating foundation evolved so that humans could benefit from cooperation and avoid exploitation. It helps people identify if someone might be good or bad to team up with and repay favours. It leads us to reject or punish cheaters. People want to see good or bad team players rewarded or punished in proportion to their behaviour
3. The liberty/oppression foundation is the rejection of tyranny. People reject any sign of domination and come together to stop bullies and dictators. It leads to egalitarianism and anti-authoritarianism on the left and liberty-loving anti-government views of those on the right;

4. The loyalty/betrayal foundation helps us form and maintain groups. It helps us identify when others are team players or not. This leads us to trust and reward some or reject or hurt those that betray the team. Finally, it leads people to stand with their group, family, and nation;
5. The authority/subversion foundation helps us develop relationships within social hierarchies. It alerts us to indications of status and if others are acting appropriately based on their status;
6. The sanctity/degradation foundation causes humans to connect objects with irrational and extreme meanings, positive and negative, which help bring groups together. This especially applies to religions. It can also cause a strong negative reaction to things such as foods or actions seen as disgusting.

Haidt describes that those on the left, most strongly identify with the care/harm and liberty/oppression moral foundations of the six moral foundations. In addition, they relate to principles of social justice, compassion for people experiencing poverty, equality across society and solidarity to challenge oppression by elites. Everyone values care/harm, but those on the left care far more.

Everyone also cares about liberty/oppression, but political affiliations mean people care in different ways. Those on the left care about the rights of vulnerable groups and want the government to defend the weak. Those on the right have a more traditional perspective on liberty and just want to be left alone. They resist liberal or left government programs that reduce their liberties to protect other groups that those on the left care about. For example, many business owners support conservative governments because they dislike being told how to run their businesses based on protecting workers, consumers and the environment. Libertarians go further and care about liberty above all other concerns; they want to be left alone from government interference.

The fairness/cheating foundation relates to proportionality (you should be rewarded or punished in relation to your actions) and karma (you'll get what's coming to you). It prioritises people getting what they deserve and not getting what they don't deserve. Everyone also cares about this and gets angry when people take more than they deserve. Those on the right care much more about this than those on the left. For those on the left, a focus on compassion and challenging oppression results in breaking this principle of karma or proportionality in multiple ways. Conservatives believe it is obvious that those that commit crimes should be punished proportionally. But those on the left struggle with the negative retribution part of karma because retribution causes harm, stimulating their care/harm foundation.

The last three moral foundations of loyalty/betrayal, authority/subversion, and sanctity/degradation show the biggest differences between those on the left and right. Those on the left are ambivalent about these, whereas social conservatives are enthusiastic about them.

In summary, those on the left have a 'three-foundation morality' based on care/harm, liberty/oppression, and fairness/cheating foundations. They will prioritise compassion or the need to challenge oppression over fairness in terms of proportionality. Those on the right value all six moral foundations and are more open than those on the left to sacrifice care that may result in some suffering if it helps the group or society overall.[3]

Morality binds and blinds

Now let's unpack Haidt's third principle: "Morality binds and blinds." He references recent research that shows the importance of the role of groups in how humans evolved, with natural selection operating at multiple levels simultaneously. He explains that it is unknown if human nature was moulded by group selection, but he thinks it would help explain why people can be so selfish and groupish simultaneously. Human nature is mostly formed by natural selection for individuals, but group-level adaptations are also taking place. Haidt argues that we have a dual nature; we are selfish and crave to be part of something bigger and nobler than ourselves.[4]

Haidt describes how we are conditional hive beings. Under the right circumstances, we can transcend self-interest and temporarily become absorbed in something greater than ourselves, feeling joy and happiness. There are specific parts of our brains that bond people to their groups and help us empathise with others, especially those that share a similar moral framework. Instead of humans being able to love everyone, evolution tells us that love within groups is more likely, especially with those with a similar worldview.[5]

Haidt argues that we need to move past seeing religions as beliefs about supernatural beings. Instead, religion is about belonging and an approach to morality. Different religions have been binding our ancestors into groups for thousands of years. Humans can care about things beyond ourselves. We identify the same things to care about with other people, form teams and focus on larger goals. It has also involved blinding people when a group states that a person, book or principle is sacred, which results in followers ceasing to question it. Once groups started to believe in gods and use these ideas to create moral communities, these groups survived better and flourished. These religious communities could cooperate, sacrifice, show commitment to the group, suppress cheating and increase trustworthiness. Haidt describes how it is only communities that can gain commitment and reduce free riding that can succeed. [6]

Haidt looks at political psychology to help explain why people choose political teams. He describes how our genes are a key factor in deciding our politics. Our genes construct our brains that are then edited by lived experiences. This helps explain why people can change their political views when they are adults. For example, people on the left have genes that give people pleasure from new experiences, variety and diversity, combined with less concern for possible threats. These people develop 'life narratives' that lead them to intuitively identify with grand narratives on the left, such as the progress narrative of constant reform towards an equal society; or the liberation narrative, where authority, hierarchy, power and tradition need to be challenged to free its victims.

Those on the right do not get pleasure from new experiences and instead react strongly to signs of threats. These people value loyalty, authority and hierarchy. They identify with grand narratives of the right to protect the nation-state and its traditional values of family and personal responsibility. They identify with aims to conserve and defend against the interference by left governments in society and the economy that lead to hard-earned money going to the 'wrong people', resulting in reduced funding for the military, police and courts.

Haidt explains that once people identify with a political team, it becomes part of their moral framework. They see signs of their grand narrative wherever they look. It is also very hard to persuade them that they are wrong or that there are other ways of looking at things. He suggests that those on the left may find it especially hard to understand conservatives because lefties struggle to understand how the loyalty, authority and sanctity foundation is related to morality.

Those on the left also struggle to see the value of 'moral capital', the resources that maintain moral communities. Most on the left believe that people are inherently good and will succeed and cooperate when restrictions and divisions are removed. But conservatives have a less optimistic view of people, that people are imperfect and will act badly if constraints and accountability are absent. They also think that human reasoning is imperfect, so theories must not be based on reason and must be moderated with intuition and lived experience. They also value institutions that gradually form as respected sites of authority and risk social disorder if undermined. Those on the right believe that people need external structures or restrictions to ensure people act well, cooperate and flourish. People that support this perspective value restrictions such as laws, institutions, customs, traditions, nation-states and religions. They think that if these are undermined, people will free-ride and cheat.

Political parties' policies and voters' values
How important are political parties' policies and manifestos regarding voters' moral framework, emotions and values? Voters do not decide which party to back based purely on rational or instrumental reasons following an objective assessment of how the parties' politics align

with their self-interest. Values and general feelings about a party are important regarding its perceived competence, credible leadership and party unity. Values are voters' desirable beliefs and ideas about society. Policies matter because they reinforce voters' previously formed 'cognitive structures' or frames concerning the parties they support and oppose. Research has also shown that many people vote based on values rather than self-interest. An example is those on low incomes who vote against their economic self-interest by supporting the Tories, which have spent decades underfunding the public services that most depend on. As described above, people use reasoning skills to justify supporting their group. For political parties to be successful, publishing policies is not enough; they also need to calibrate the policies to strategic groups in marginal seats in terms of values, social group identities and cognitive frames to be successful.

The reputation of those sharing the different policy messages is also important; these include a political party, politicians or the media. In the last forty years, Labour and the Tories have had periods in opposition when they were not seen as a credible government in waiting, the 1980s for Labour and the 2000s for the Tories. In the last decade, social media has changed how many receive political messages via a friend, family or associate instead of the media or political parties. Recent research has shown that the values most important to voters are 'family', 'fairness', 'hard work' and 'decency'. Behind them are 'equality' and 'freedom'. Thatcher appealed to the first four with a broad language of 'ordinariness', hard work and family-focused respectability.[7]

How Tories use morals, values, and emotions to win elections

The Tories connect with all six moral foundations, creating a lot of fear about their opponents. They describe the innocent victims of harmful Labour policies to activate the care foundation. On fairness, the Tories point out the unfairness of using tax money from hardworking and careful people and the government giving it to support 'cheaters and lazy, irresponsible fools'. In terms of liberty and oppression, the Tories are constantly talking about 'cutting red tape' to reduce bureaucracy so business owners have more freedom in how they run their businesses. The Tories generally monopolise appeals to loyalty regarding patriotism and supporting the military. For authority, they advocate respect for parents, elders, the police and traditions. The Tories hit the sanctity foundation in two ways. First, they are the party of the Church of England and are consistent in promoting 'family values'. Second, the Tories promote the sacredness of the British nation-state and its uniqueness and glorify the UK's heroes and history.

Labour tends to focus on the care and fairness moral foundations by celebrating diversity and supporting immigration. Based on Haidt's moral foundations, it is clear that this position fails to speak to millions of conservative voters. Haidt advises that those on the left need to stop dismissing conservatism as a pathology caused by overly strict parents; or fear of change, new experiences and complexity, which causes conservatives to hold onto a black-and-white worldview. Instead, he describes how those on the left need to think beyond the care and fairness moral foundations and expand to the Loyalty, Authority and Sanctity foundations. The Labour leader Blair did this successfully, and currently, Starmer is attempting to do it, but many of us on the left find it difficult to support.[8]

I described above how values and emotions are more important in deciding elections than policies or 'the issues'. The emotions give voters a 'gut feeling' that helps them summarise their thoughts and feelings about a political party. In politics, the parties that create emotionally compelling stories about who they are and who their opponents are, win the hearts and minds of voters. The stories that politicians tell about the people they have met are ways to illustrate what they care about so voters can emotionally connect with the speaker.[9]

It has also been found that periods of deep fear, uncertainty, and stress benefit conservatives. Our brain's life-preserving responses to danger kick in. When we're very afraid, strong and decisive leaders, military and clear responses such as war and the death penalty are more appealing to many. And in these circumstances, concerns over issues such as civil liberties are seen as less important.[10]

Why do people vote against their economic interests? Many voters prefer emotional responses to political parties over reasonable arguments. This has allowed the Tories to stir up resentment against enemies that the Tories have created, such as the 'liberal elite', the EU, immigrants, benefit cheats, the Labour Party, trade unions, and protest groups such as Black Lives Matter and XR. These 'enemies' are either do-gooders that assume they know what's best for poor people or are trying to take something from hardworking people. Conveniently for right-wing parties such as the Tories, UKIP and Brexit Party (now Reform UK), they are the only ones that can resolve this problem and become vehicles for channeling this popular anger. This sadly results in many poor and working-class voters becoming emotionally attached to the political party that exists to further the interests of the wealthy. Those that posit themselves as 'authentic politicians' (such as Nigel Farage) are now more trusted by those on lower incomes. These politicians sound like they are speaking from the gut, even if they might be faking this sincerity. In modern politics, those politicians that sound too cerebral or take voters for granted are in trouble.

Broad Reasons Why People Vote For The Tories

Tory politicians and their supporters believe they are the 'good guys', combating the evil left, in the same way that many of us on the left believe the reverse. It is hard for us on the left to understand, but this is true for anyone that believes in an ideology and is part of a social or political group. Below I have identified six broad reasons why people vote for the Tories. These are:
1. fear of the opposition;
2. instrumental or self-interest;
3. ideological;
4. identity group;
5. ignorance and misinformation due to propaganda lies, and the media;
6. working-class conservatism.

Fear of opposition

I have described in previous chapters how the Tories have consistently worked to generate a lot of fear about the Labour Party in terms of being too incompetent to govern the country and manage the economy. The argument is that they would bring in high taxes and public spending. That Labour can't be trusted with national security or would let the trade unions destroy the country again. That the Labour Party are socialist and communist and, if elected, will take away people's freedom, houses, and bank savings.

Those on the right that support the Tories have a lower tolerance to fear than those on the left. Many centrist and centre-right voters are genuinely terrified of the left, whereas those on the left dislike the Tories but are not generally scared of them. So this fear-mongering works; that's why the Tories do it. We can see how Corbyn caused this reaction, resulting in anyone scared of leftwing ideas rushing to vote for the Tories to keep the Labour Party out of power. These anti-leftwing views are widely held across the British electorate, especially with swing voters.[11]

Conservative ideology

Traditional Tory Party ideology was based on the desire to conserve, with suspicion of change. It is characterised by supporting tradition, a belief in human imperfection and maintains the structures of society, hierarchy and authority. Traditional conservatism defends private property, established institutions and values because they safeguard the fragile 'fabric of society', giving those seeking security a sense of stability and rootedness.

The Tories are generally the only party that represents those on the right, so it is a very broad church covering several traditions:

1. Authoritarian conservatism is a tradition that supports authoritarianism – a practice of government 'from above', in which authority is exercised over a population with or without its consent;
2. Paternalistic conservatism is based on the idea that the values important to conservatives – tradition, order, property, authority etc. – will only be maintained if government policy is developed based on practical circumstances and experience instead of theory. This accepts a prudent willingness to 'change in order to conserve'. There are three main traditions of paternalistic conservatism: one-nation conservatism, social conservatism and Christian democracy;
3. Libertarian conservatism advocates the greatest possible economic liberty and the least possible government regulation of social life. They want to reduce the size of the state. Libertarian conservatives are attached to free-market theories because they believe that they ensure social order;
4. Neoliberal economic conservatism or economic liberalism. This is based on classical liberal economics, specifically free market economics, with a critique of 'big' government and economic and social intervention;
5. Conservative new right or 'neoconservatism' This is based on traditional conservatism that defends order, authority and discipline. Therefore, The new right combines economic libertarianism and social authoritarianism.

6. Social conservatism describes moral and social values that prioritise traditional power structures such as duty, traditional values and social institutions such as a traditional family set-up, gender roles, heterosexual sexual relations, the nation-state and patriotism, religion and the church. This tradition resists social change and supports the status quo around social concerns. For example, it is against same-sex marriage and abortion. This ideology naturally supports British institutions such as the military, Royal Family, and the police. It prioritises national security, law and order. It is important to those that value it to encourage acceptable behaviour and personal responsibility;
7. Cultural conservatism refers to protecting the cultural heritage of the nation-state. This relates to collective identity and belonging. It is critical of multiculturalism and supports immigration controls and Brexit. At its most extreme, this includes xenophobia and racism;
8. Reactionary conservatism looks back to a past 'golden age' of supposed economic propriety and moral fortitude.[12]

Most ideological conservatives want a small state with minimum or no regulations. They value self-sufficient and personal choice over the 'nanny state' that interferes with everything. They resent the state telling them how to spend their money or limiting their choices. They see regulations as holding businesses back and wasting money enforcing them. So they want to roll back the state to reduce taxes and public spending. They are ideologically against public services, so they want them to be privatised as they think this would be more efficient and stop 'wasting' their hard-earned money on taxes for the 'undeserving'. Small-state Tories believe that reducing taxes for corporations will encourage business investment and growth. And reducing income tax will encourage aspiration and opportunity.

The ideological Tories with the most extreme views are completely against the redistribution of wealth from the wealthy to the poor and want the removal of all social safety nets, such as state benefits. They believe these benefits hold people back by making them dependent on the state and discouraging aspiration. These Tories would argue that removing benefits incentivises people to find work or start businesses, forcing them to improve their situation. As they see it, all people need is a good work ethic, education, opportunities, help to start a small business, low taxes and investment in transport and education infrastructure. I think these Tories believe this form of 'sink-or-swim' thinking is caring or progressive. This is an incredibly simplistic argument but very appealing to millions of Tory voters. It makes no allowances for those with mental or physical disabilities who cannot do a regular job and need state support to survive.

Many better-off Tory voters (successful working-class people or those with a privileged upbringing) think that poverty and low income are a symptom of laziness and a lack of a good work ethic. These Tory supporters think they could become better off if these poor people worked hard. These Tory voters resent claims by the Labour Party that the poor have no responsibility for their situation and reject Labour's argument that this justifies why the wealthy must be taxed to look after the poor. Instead, these right-wing voters support the Tories' 'make work pay' policies of reducing benefits to the bare minimum to 'incentive' those on benefits into work. They fail to understand that thousands of people who are on benefits are in work, but we have such low wages that they can't get by on their salary alone.

Many British voters are socially and culturally conservative. These voters reject liberal and left positions on free speech, identity politics and woke culture as part of the ongoing 'culture wars'. They find the Tory Party better represents these views.[13]

Instrumental

To vote instrumentally means that people vote for a party to get something they want for personal benefit or self-interest. This is a very broad category. Many voters believe the Tories are the best party to run the country and economy to ensure stability and economic prosperity. They apply a 'least worst option' approach to deciding which party to vote for. They may have concerns or disagree with some Tory policies, but overall, they think the Tories will do a better job running the country. People vote for the Tories because they believe it is the lowest-risk option for the economy, which is the crucial factor for many. They believe the Tories' claims that they will keep taxes and public spending low, reduce the deficit and introduce policies to benefit small businesses. These voters believe that the Tories' economic policies will lead to more jobs, generate a greater amount of wealth shared out to all and more money for public services. The Tories are also considered the safer option regarding national security and law and order. At each election, the Tories claim they are the most sensible and responsible choice.

Some vote Tory because they appreciate the work done by their local Tory MP in the area, where the Tory MP has supported local events and causes that have made a difference; helped get funding for new schools and other facilities in the area. Or simply always reply to letters and emails from constituents. This is helped by Tory governments prioritising public spending in seats held by Tory MPs, as described in Chapter 12.

People vote for the Tories for their anti-immigrant and 'anti-benefit cheat' policies. The Tories have effectively blamed minority groups for the nation's problems, which they claim caused high taxes, failing public services and wasted public spending on those who don't deserve it. This relates to the fairness/cheating moral foundation in the psychology section above. The Tories blame Labour for letting the 'undeserving' live off the state, with hardworking people paying for it.

A key part of the Tories' offer at each election is low taxation, which appeals to millions of voters. Many vote for the Tories because they prioritise their financial self-interest over helping others. The Tories promote the idea that 'a vote for them is a vote you' at the expense of others. This could be described as selfishness or 'greed is good'. For many that are well off enough to only use private schools, healthcare and pensions, they don't see any benefit of state-funded public services. These voters want to pay as little as possible in taxes.

Many long-standing Tory voters in the South of England do not want to pay higher taxes to boost investment in the North through Levelling Up. This would mean either high taxes or taking investments from the South.[14]

Many working-class and middle-class voters support the Tories because of their broad appeal to the aspirations of people to better themselves and their families. The Tories promote the idea of 'a hand up, not a hand out' and popular policies such as increasing property ownership, reducing taxes and encouraging personal responsibility. Not all low-income voters support redistributive economic policies and, instead of envying the rich, want them to succeed and celebrate their success. These conservative voters also believe the achievements of business owners will create economic benefits for all, such as increased employment and investment.[15]

The ownership of property and other assets, such as company shares, causes people to become more conservative as they have something to lose and want to see their assets increase in value. The Tory Party clearly understands this, with Thatcher and Cameron's policies to increase asset ownership, especially housing. Following the 2008 financial crisis, the Bank of England and the Tories kept interest rates very low, which kept mortgages affordable even as house prices increased by 40% between 2010 and 2020. Mortgage payments in 2020 were actually lower than in 2008. At the same time, private rent rose by 30%, helping homeowners and landlords in multiple ways. Their monthly housing outgoings were reduced, the value of their properties increased, and landlords found they could charge more rent and make more profit. The low-interest rates have also resulted in a dramatic increase in car purchases on finance; people pay a small deposit and pay off a low-cost loan over a few years. In the 2000s, less than half of new car purchases were bought this way; by 2019, it was 90%.[16]

Why do older people vote Tory? There are several factors. There is the concept of 'social ageing'. As people get older and get married, and have children, combined with their incomes and property values increasing, this causes people to become more cautiously conservative. The natural psychological process of ageing also makes people more resistant to change. Both factors cause people to be more supportive of the status quo, and the Tories are the party that defends the status quo. For these people, things are good as they are, so why vote Labour and risk things changing or if they might believe the right-wing propaganda that Labour will destroy the economy? These processes also cause people to become more culturally and socially conservative and prioritise immigration controls, Brexit, national security, and law and order. This naturally aligns them more closely with the Tories. The old are generally more economically secure than the young, with assets and state pensions; many have private pensions. Most are homeowners with low outgoings, and some are landlords. The Tories work very hard to protect homeowners and landlords. This means redistributive economic policies are less appealing to these voters. With many being wealthy and Tory tax policies benefiting the wealthy.[17]

Identity Group

Once people identify with a political team, the Tories in this case, then many stick with them for life. Tory tribalism is based on a belief that a Labour government will always be worse than an incompetent Tory government. During the disastrous final days of Truss's short time as Prime Minister, when support for the Tories collapsed, about 20% of people were still backing the Tories. This shows the core of the Tory tribal identity group. Many born into a Tory-supporting family will vote with their family social group. Although, many young people are now starting to break this trend. Aspiring working-class people that do well may identify more with the Tories and join social groups of Tory supporters. Those identifying with the British nation-state, patriotism, military and royal family will naturally be open to voting Tory as the Tories proudly support and romanticise these institutions. There are also strong ties between Christianity (Church of England) and the Tory Party. This connection was very strong at the start of the 20th century and has weakened, but the Tories remain the party of Christianity.

A significant factor in the consistent success of the Tories in rural areas is the strong conservative identity group in these areas that has been maintained for centuries. In the early 20th century, these areas had a strong local culture organised by the upper class and farmers, who would also be active Tory Party members. The local Tory gentry organised regular events to keep the local workers on side, such as visits to country houses and locations of interest around the country and evening social events at pubs and village halls. Due to the close relationship between farmers and farmworkers, workers would be happy to go along with the status quo and vote Tory as they prioritised their income and good working relationship with their employer. Even being seen talking to a Labour Party candidate during this period could risk their job.[18]

Ignorance and misinformation
As described in previous chapters, the Tories and the right-wing media lie, misinform, distract and distort reality to maintain the support of their voters. The low levels of education in economics and critical thinking in Britain make this possible. Millions are in Tory propaganda echo chambers based on their social groups, the right-wing newspapers they read and their social media experiences.

Most people are not interested in politics and just want the country to run well and leave them alone so they can get on with their lives. Most people are not cynical and will give the Tories the benefit of the doubt and believe promises made by a new Tory leader if they haven't given people a reason not to trust them. Labour never gets such an easy ride. This works well for the Tories; they project a reasonable and competent public face, while behind the scenes, they are underfunding public services and redistributing money from ordinary people to the wealthy.

Working Class Conservatism
Most of the reasons that working-class people vote for the Tories have already been listed. Some fear Labour governments will destroy the economy and be much worse than the Tories. They believe that

the Tories will ensure stability and prosperity. They see Labour holding people back with regulations and the over-interfering welfare state. Considering the moral foundations of fairness and cheating, conservative-minded working-class people do not want to see their hard-earned money paid in taxes go to those they see as cheats, lazy, irresponsible and undeserving.

Working-class Tories are hardworking and aspiration and see the Tories as representing those interests. Some run small businesses and see the Tories as the party of business and identity with the Tories over the other parties. Some working-class Tories are supportive of the party for different ideological reasons. They support capitalism and free market economics. They want low taxes and low public spending. Others are socially and culturally conservative. Many working-class Tory voters benefited from Thatcher's right to buy and share sell-offs or have purchased assets separately and have then seen these assets increase in value under the Tories. Consumerism promoted by the Tories since the 1950s has won over many working-class voters.

Moral foundation theory concerns working-class Tories around social identity/groups, loyalty and authority. Many working-class voters support the Tories due to their identity group, family, friends, local community, religious community or workplace. Millions of working-class people are proud of the British nation-state and are deeply patriotic and loyal to the military and the monarchy. The Tories are the natural home for these voters. Working class deference to the upper class and the Tories' authority is significant. These working-class voters see Tory Party leaders as more credible Prime Ministers than many Labour Party leaders. Deference also relates to instrumental self-interest motivations. They think the Tories will run the country better, grow the economy, and this will benefit them personally.

During the 20th century, the Tories convinced large numbers of the working class that 'class struggle' between the workers and the elite was irrelevant and that it was safer to vote Tory.[19]

PART 5:

WEAK AND DIVIDED OPPOSITION

20

THE BRITISH LABOUR PARTY

Chapter 1 described how First Past the Post benefits the Tories as there is only one party on the right but multiple parties on the left, including Labour, SNP, Liberal Democrats, Greens, and Plaid Cymru. This means the Tories can focus their election offer and policies on the centre ground and swing voters in marginal seats. Whereas the parties on the centre-left compete with each other, split the vote, and, in many elections, give the Tories an easy ride.

This chapter focused on the British Labour Party and the factors that caused it to struggle to compete with the Tories. To use a sports analogy, the Labour Party are always playing away against Tory Britain United, with an electoral system tilted against them and a hostile media. Yet, most of the time, Labour's captains and players are not focused enough on winning elections; they are more focused on having the 'correct' ideas and fighting amongst themselves.

Previous chapters show how the British political context is hostile to Tory opposition parties, especially Labour. Key factors include Tory attacks, the right-wing Tory supporting media and the undemocratic electoral system, First Past the Post. The Tories effectively exploit Labour's weaknesses, including linking the Labour Party to Communism and the USSR, relentlessly claiming that Labour will mismanage the economy, and blaming past Labour governments or the current Labour opposition for problems such as strikes. The Tory-supporting press dominates the unregulated newspaper industry setting the media agenda to benefit the Tories. The right-wing media pump out Tory propaganda that is then uncritically distributed through broadcast radio and television news programmes, newspaper and online news websites and social media.

This chapter assesses the Labour Party based on its ability to win elections and form governments. This means playing by the rules of the political game in Britain, which are the electoral system (FPTP) and the right-wing media environment. Sadly, these constraints mean that the most effective strategy for Labour to win general elections is to target swing voters in marginal constituencies, who are ideologically conservative, middle class, and affluent. I don't like these rules, but it's what we're working with. We need to change the voting system for electing MPs if we want authentic progressive parties to succeed. For the Labour Party to win, it needs a leader that swing voters see as electable; the party needs to be visibly united, have an appealing election offer to ordinary voters, and identify with the British state and patriotism. Failure to do these things under FPTP means the party can get large amounts of support around the country, but crucially, it will not be in the locations Labour needs to win elections, marginal seats. This is what happened at the 2017 election.

Labour's History Of Electoral Failure

Over the last 123 years, Labour has won 10 out of 31 elections. It is hard to find any equivalent centre-left parties in democracies that have performed so badly. It is hard to find a comparison of a country that is formally a liberal democracy but has one party, the Tories, that is so successful at consistently winning elections. Japan is the closest, which is an effective one-party state.[1]

The Labour Party and the British labour movement have only been strong enough to overcome Tory political dominance for a sustained period with help from other political parties. The Labour Party was formed in 1900 and initially called the Labour Representation Committee. For the 1906 election, it formed a non-aggression pact with the Liberal Party to win its first seats in parliament. Labour governments in 1924 and 1929 to 1931 were only possible with Liberal support. Churchill needed Labour's help to run the country during the Second World War, so the party joined the national government. Labour commissioned the Beveridge report in 1942 with Liberal support. This was the foundation document for the British welfare state. Labour then spent three years promoting this report and distributing 300,000 copies. Labour based its 1945 election manifesto on it and won a landslide. A unique situation for Labour, never to be repeated.

At the 1951 election, Labour won the popular vote but lost the election, with the Tories winning a small majority of seats. Labour remained in opposition for thirteen years. At the 1964 election, the Tories were in crisis after over a decade in power, and Wilson won a small majority in parliament. In 1966, Wilson called an opportunist election and won a significant majority of seats on 48% of the vote. This election shows that Labour can win a majority on a progressive programme under FPTP, but there are some things to consider. First, Wilson only won his 111-seat majority when Labour was already in government. Second, he could choose the timing of the election at an advantageous point in the economic cycle, a huge advantage. Third, that year post-war social democracy was its most popular, and trade union power was at its strongest, combined with cultural radicalisation and youthful baby-boomer optimism. The best-selling newspaper in the country was the Labour-supporting Daily Mirror. Many in the country were sympathetic to socialism, including some at the BBC and universities. But, again, this period was unique and has not been repeated.

Labour lost the 1970 election and won in 1974 with a small majority. It struggled to manage the economic crisis of the 1970s that the Tories had been lucky to avoid. The crisis was so bad that Labour had to take a bail-out from the International Monetary Fund (IMF) in 1975 but, in exchange, had to cut public spending and start dismantling the post-war welfare state. This seriously damaged voters' trust in Labour to protect public services. Labour lost its majority in 1977 and needed liberal support to govern. Labour lost the 1979 election, and it took 18 years to recover. The 1980s saw the Labour Party struggling with weak leaders, unpopular policies, internal conflict, splits and new parties forming, the crushing of the labour movement and changes to the organisation of industry that undermined Labour's traditional key support areas.

New Labour won in 1997 under Blair, moving to the right of the Liberal Democrats to win the support of aspirational middle-class voters and giving a veto over Labour Party policy to Rupert Murdoch and the City of London. Had Labour leader John Smith not died in 1994, he would have likely won the 1997 election with a smaller majority and implemented a more radical programme than Blair. But it's unlikely he would have had the press onside and would have been attacked from all sides, and likely only managed one term in office.

Under the political and economic constraints of the 1990s and 2000s, it was logical for Labour to do what it needed to keep winning elections in terms of not threatening the status quo, the City of London and keeping the Murdoch press onside. New Labour also improved public services, redistributed wealth and reduced inequality. Blair and the Labour leadership did not see the point in making radical promises that could not be implemented and would likely lose elections. Once Brown took over in 2007, he was hit by the financial crisis. Labour was exhausted, and the Tories weaponised the crisis by accusing Labour of economic incompetence and blaming them for it all. Cameron was a more charismatic and popular leader than Brown, and the Labour leader had lost the support of the Murdoch press. Cameron won many seats but not enough to win a majority and formed a coalition with the Liberal Democrats.[2]

The 2010s saw Labour shift to the left and struggle to win over enough swing voters in marginals. Labour had the Tory media against them, and many voters struggled to see Miliband and Corbyn as up to the job of Prime Minister. In addition, Labour was still struggling with a poor reputation for managing the economy. Then the Brexit referendum radically changed things.

There is a mythology about the 2017 election that Labour under Corbyn was close to forming a government. Sadly this is not what happened. Labour got a good vote share, which is very different from winning a majority or even the largest number of seats. A hung parliament was within reach, where Labour could have formed an extremely weak coalition government with the SNP and Liberal Democrats. This would likely have resulted in 50-odd Labour MPs on the right of the party defecting, and the Labour-led government would have collapsed in crisis. A centre-right Tory-led government would have replaced it.[3]

Labour electoral programmes and Manifestos

Labour Party manifestos are rarely designed to appeal specifically to swing voters. Instead, they tend to be overloaded with specific pledges and promises. As a result, voters find it hard to absorb and understand what is on offer. The 2019 Labour Manifesto is a good example, it was packed with many popular and necessary policies, but swing voters did not find it credible following a decade of Tory austerity. An effective election offer needs 3-5 slogans and policies that will cut through to voters and appeal to them. Unfortunately, Labour regularly fails to achieve this essential component of a competitive election offer.

The Tories and the press attack Labour at most elections, claiming their economic policies will increase taxes and economic instability. Labour is accused of being a tax-and-spend party that will not prioritise 'sound money' and economic growth over public spending. Blair and New Labour overcame this problem by agreeing to the Tories' taxation and spending levels for the first two years of the Labour government.

Labour is at a disadvantage to the Tories as their manifestos must be credible, achievable, and appealing enough to win over target voters. It is a fine balance that Labour rarely manages to find. Whereas the Tories can make all sorts of promises in their manifestos that they have no intention of keeping. The right-wing press promotes these, and millions of Tory supporters and swing voters will believe them. Then when the Tories government fails to follow through on all their commitments, the media cover for them and many voters let them off or forget by the next election.

Labour electioneering
Labour generally runs less effective campaigns compared to the Tories. Labour raises less money and spends less on their campaigns. Many Labour campaigns have been disorganised and lacked message discipline. Labour generally publishes a principled manifesto that sadly does not appeal to the swing voters in seats Labour needs to win. It refuses to engage in the negative campaign attacks on the Tories, which puts them at a disadvantage. Labour prioritises its ideology of Labourism over working with other parties to beat the Tories. Labour insists on standing candidates in every seat in the country, even in seats where they cannot win. These are generally Tory-Liberal Democrat battles, so the Labour candidates split the vote, making it harder for the Liberal Democrat candidate to win.

Labour has historically stuck to their traditional methods of electioneering, while the Tories adapted to new technologies. In the 20th century, Labour was slow to adapt to radio and television, except for Labour leader Wilson. Labour professionalised their election campaigns under Kinnock in the 1980s, bringing in marketing professionals. In the last 20 years, the Tories have employed the best election marketing agencies and election consultants, such as Lynton Crosby, due to their superior fundraising abilities. Labour does employ election professionals but struggles to compete as they have less effective fundraising. Labour was slow to adapt to using social media in the 2010s, again giving the Tories the advantage. Labour was seen to win the 'digital war' in the 2017 election but still ultimately lost the election. The Tories completely dominated social media for the 2019 election.

The Tories consistently raised more money and outspent Labour in general elections between 1910 and 2005, as seen in Table 1 below. In many elections, the Tories have outspent Labour multiple times.

Table 1: Labour Party and Tory Party Central spending on General Elections 1910-2005 in 2007 prices.[4]

Year	Labour Party expenditure (£ millions)	Tory Party expenditure (£ millions)
1910 (December)	0.004	0.136
1929	0.045	0.290
1959	0.239	0.631
1964	0.538	1.233
1970	0.526	0.630
1974 (February)	0.440	0.680
1974 (October)	0.524	0.950
1979	1.566	2.333
1983	2.057	3.700
1987	4.700	9.028
1992	10.200	11.200
1997	26.000	28.300
2001	10.810	11.998
2005	16.864	17.732

The Labour Party Are Not As Committed To Winning Elections As The Tories

The Labour Party has several internal problems that stop it from winning more general elections. The main one is that although it is one of Britain's two main political parties, historically, winning elections is not its main goal. It has been more focused on principles and ideologies such as socialism, public ownership, social justice and equality. These are all important causes but put the party at a disadvantage compared to the Tories' history of doing anything to win.[5]

<u>Unpopular Leaders with swing voters</u>
In the history of the Labour Party over the last 123 years, only three Labour leaders have won a majority and then formed a government: Attlee, Wilson and Blair. As I described in Chapter 1, our undemocratic First Past the Post electoral system means that elections are won and lost in about one hundred marginal seats based on up to 100,000 to 500,000 swing voters. Party members elect Labour leaders, but this is a very different social group to swing voters, who decide general elections. Labour Party members have a history of selecting leaders that do not have broad appeal and are unpopular with swing voters. Suppose the Labour leader has a different political vision from target voters. In that case, even if they get a high number of votes nationally, the party will still lose the election, as happened in 2017. It is unintentional, but Labour members are very good at selecting Labour leaders who will never become Prime Minister.

Labour leaders are also harder to remove than Tory Party leaders, which means there is a history of Labour leaders contesting and losing multiple elections before they stand down. Whereas the Tories are more ruthless, it will remove a Tory Prime Minister that has become unpopular and is unlikely to win the next election. Labour also has a history of electing leaders seen as weak and not Prime Minister material, compared to the Tory leader at the time. Since the 1980s, there have only been John Smith (1992-94), Tony Blair and now Keir Starmer, that are ahead in opinion polls of the Tory Prime Minister at the time. Those that have struggled with being seen as better leaders than their Tory opponents were Michael Foot, Neil Kinnock, Gordon Brown, Ed Miliband and Jeremy Corbyn.

<u>Divided Labour Party</u>
The Tories learnt a painful lesson from the party splits caused by the Corn Laws in the 19th century and, ever since, are very effective at projecting party unity to maintain public support. The Labour Party has never learnt this lesson. There have certainly been periods of relative Labour Party unity, but they are rare and do not last long. This party unity happens when the party is successful and confident, as seen during the Attlee, Wilson and Blair years.

There are two aspects to the Labour Party's divisions: party splits and internal conflict. The party split during the 1930s with several Labour MPs, including the previous leader MacDonald forming National Labour, which then formed a national government with the Tories. In 1981, four Labour MPs on the right of the Labour Party left to form the Social Democratic Party (SDP). At the time, many voters saw Labour and the Tories as extreme, and the SDP and Liberals formed an alliance and significantly split the centre-left vote, hurting Labour.

Internal conflict in the Labour Party has been intense. Labour Party members prioritise ideology, principles and values over loyalty to the party leader unless the leader represents their faction. The Labour Party is composed of several factions that wax and wane in strength and, at certain points, manage to get their leadership candidates elected as party leader. The 1920s saw conflict between the party leadership and communist members, resulting in many radical members being barred from the party.

The right of the Labour Party was dominant from 1955 with the Labour leader Gaitskell until he died in 1963. This faction supported social democracy and some redistribution but didn't favour public ownership. This period saw a civil war between the Labour right and Labour left led by Wilson. Wilson learnt from this period, and once he became leader was focused on keeping the party united, which he managed with some success. Wilson stepped down as leader and Prime Minister in 1976 and was replaced by Jim Callaghan, who was on the party's right. There were intense battles inside the party from 1978 to 1983 between the right and left. The Labour left leader Michael Foot led the party from 1980 to defeat in the 1983 election.

Neil Kinnock was elected leader in 1983 and can be described as 'soft left'. This wing of the party supports socialist policies but is pragmatic about winning elections. Kinnock worked with the right of the party to make it more electable and had an ongoing conflict with the party's far left, especially the Trotsky group 'Militant' (now the Socialist Party). New Labour implemented a moderately redistributive program that was not threatening to the status quo by working inside the Thatcherite economic model and adding socially liberal policies. Blair had complete control of the party until his final days as Prime Minister when Brown and his supporters forced him out. Prime Minister Brown struggled with disunity due to the party's dissatisfaction with his performance. Miliband replaced Brown in 2010 with a soft left program, and he was constantly under attack from the right of the party resulting in a confused and uninspiring 'austerity-lite' 2015 manifesto.

Corbyn was elected leader in 2015, resulting in ongoing divisions in the party. Corbyn is on the Labour left and had the backing of a majority of the membership, with thousands joining the Labour Party to vote for him to become leader and then work to get Labour elected. However, the right of the party resisted Corbyn's leadership, and there were ongoing cabinet resignations and leadership challenges throughout his time. Starmer replaced Corbyn in 2020 and has a soft left program. He has ruthlessly attacked the party's left by banning groups that supported Corbyn. So far, these divisions under Starmer have not cut through to the public, and he is seen as a credible Prime Minister who has reformed the party and is ready for government.

Another important factor in Labour's lack of success and party disunity is that much of the right of the Labour Party do not care if Labour wins elections and forms governments. They are quite happy with the party being mostly in opposition and being MPs or councillors or getting an income from running the party as part of the bureaucracy. They would prefer that the only kind of Labour government to get elected was like New Labour, a centre-right government on economic policy.[6] The right of the Labour Party can be described as the 'loyal opposition'. The left of the party can be described as the 'principled opposition'. They are more concerned about values and principles than strategy and winning elections. The right of the Labour Party does not have a political project or vision beyond stopping the left from occupying the Labour Party and forming a government.[7]

Labourism
The concept of 'Labourism' is another limiting factor. It has several features. First, Labourism is the belief that the Labour Party is the only vehicle for centre-left politics. Trade unions can represent their members in the workplace, but all political campaigning must be left to the party, which is to focus on winning elections. Labour is the only working-class party, and any political movement that does not defer to the party is treated with suspicion. Other parties on the centre-left are seen as opponents. Labourism is also wary of movements and prefers party members and supporters to campaign obediently for the party as directed by the party hierarchy. The concern is that the growth of a political movement around Labour would result in groups that would be hard to discipline, and the party risks losing control of the situation. This ideology has stopped Labour from developing creative political strategies to win elections in a hostile political context, such as working with other centre-left parties to defeat the Tories.[8]

The Labour Party struggles to adapt
The Labour Party and its leaders generally fail at being pragmatic and strategically focusing on winning elections within the constraints of FPTP. Even when leaders do prioritise winning elections, it doesn't always work. Following the 1987 Labour defeat, Labour leader

Kinnock was determined to win the next election, but it wasn't enough. The 1992 election was close, but Labour didn't win until 1997, ten years later.[9]

The Tories are very adaptable both in government; and when they lose an election, so they quickly return to power. The same can not be said for Labour, as seen from the three long stretches in opposition since the Second World War: 1951-64, 1979-1997 and the last 13 years. Following an election defeat, instead of agreeing that they ran a bad campaign, Labour goes into years of soul searching, infighting and introspection, delaying the party's recovery. The party has a much higher tolerance for being in opposition for long periods than the Tories.[10]

Labour is consistently unprepared for predictable lines of attack by the Tories and press, so they fail to have credible arguments and narratives that would deflect them. An example is the 2015 election which was predicted to be a hung parliament. There was a lot of focus on if Labour would form a coalition government with the SNP. Miliband eventually stated he would not work with the SNP. But the damage had been done; the press and Tories created a lot of fear among swing voters that if they voted Labour, it would lead to a chaotic Labour-SNP government.[11] Another example is that following the 2008 financial crisis, the Tories blamed Labour for causing this and the subsequent recession. Both of these are not accurate, the financial crash was a global crisis, and the UK economy was coming out of recession in 2010 before the Tories took over. Again this was a highly predictable attack; the Tories have been saying that Labour can't be trusted with the economy for decades. Labour has failed to challenge this lie over the past 13 years, especially during the early 2010s, so the narrative stuck. The Tories introduced severe austerity and got to blame Labour for it, which millions of Tory voters swallowed.[12]

Party organisation, membership and fundraising
Chapter 8 showed the significant difference between the levels of funding between the Tories and Labour. Labour receives its funding

from membership dues, trade union donations, and individual and corporate donations. In contrast, the Tories can raise much more from the rich, corporations and business owners.

During the 1900s, the Labour Party could not match the individual donations to the Tories and Liberals. The trade union political levy fund was set up early to support the Labour Party based on automatically deducting small sums from members weekly. The courts found this illegal in 1909, which was reversed by the Liberal government in 1913. Trade union members had to actively opt out of giving to the Labour Party political levy fund. Relying on trade union funds had a significant impact on the organisation and policies of the party and the background of MPs. The Labour Party's fundraising suffered during the 1920s, from a recession until 1931, which caused trade union membership to drop from 8 million to below 5 million, drastically impacting the union's political levy funds to the Labour Party. The second problem was that the Tory government introduced the Trade Disputes and Trade Union Act 1927, so union members had to opt into the political levy fund.

From the 1900s to 1930s, most of Labour's funding came from the unions, with local union branches deciding which candidates to fund rather than giving the money to the Labour Party Central Office. Between 1914 and 1927, a third of union funds went to the Labour Party head office; the rest went towards sponsoring parliamentary candidates, maintaining union-sponsored MPs, and funding Constituencies Labour Parties (CLPs). In the 1920s, the party encouraged CLP membership, charging a small fee. Between 1930 and 1945, membership numbers fluctuated between 100,000 to 150,000. At the 1933 Labour Party Conference, party rules were changed to strengthen local parties and their need to increase membership and fundraise for the party.[13]

Following the Second World War, the Attlee government changed the law again over the union political levy fund, so union members had to opt out of the political fund, which boosted Labour Party funding from the unions. Labour failed to raise as much from local branches as the Tories had nearly 3 million members in the 1950s.

Labour had 1 million members in 1952, a big increase from 266,000 in 1944. Labour's local organisation improved in the late 1940s from huge grassroots enthusiasm with the Attlee leadership. However, with Labour out of power in the 1950s, membership numbers declined to 600,000 in 1960 and 300,000 in 1970. Causes for Labour declining local organisation were its years out of power in the 1950s and then during the mid-1960s, disappointment with Wilson's Labour government from 1964-1970. By 1979, there were 250,000 to 300,000 members. This drop in membership numbers resulted in declining funds for the party.

Labour's membership numbers stayed around 250,000 during the 1980s and increased in the mid-1990s to about 300,000 following a recruitment drive. New Labour stepped up fundraising efforts in the 1990s through the 1,000 Club of business individuals that donated at least £1,000, telephone canvassing was increased, and the Co-op bank gave the party £5 for each application for its Visa card.[14]

In 1992, 66% of Labour's income came from the trade unions; this dropped to 40% in 1997 and 33% in 2002. The remainder comes from individual and corporate donations, sponsorship, membership fees, and commercial events. Labour spent £14 million on winning the 2001 election, causing financial problems in 2002. The party saw declining membership numbers, fewer individual donations and reduced donations from trade unions unhappy with the Labour government. Wealthy individuals were put off donating large sums to avoid ending up in the news.[15]

Membership numbers fell from about 250,000 in 2002 to 150,000 in 2010, gradually increasing to 200,000 by 2015. In 2016, the Tories introduced new restrictions on union political funds. This means that new members of unions have to opt-in to paying additional money to the political fund so their money can be donated to the Labour Party.[16]

Following the 2015 election, thousands joined the Labour Party to elect Jeremy Corbyn to take membership to 388,000 in December 2015. By 2018 the Labour Party had 540,000 members. All this meant a large increase in membership fees and donations, so the party was raising more money than the Tories between 2018 and the 2019 election. Membership numbers dropped to 432,213 by the end of 2021.[17]

The Labour Party In Government

There is much about past Labour governments to criticise, and it is important to recognise the important contributions the party has made as well. It is doubtful that there would have been as much progress in Britain without the Labour Party. These include the welfare state, improved educational opportunities, decolonisation and policies to tackle inequality, reduce poverty and redistribute wealth. And even Labour's long years in opposition have acted as a limiting factor, stopping the Tories from being as extreme as they would have liked.

Labour struggles to be seen as the natural party of government

Labour has a mixed record as a defender of British tradition and institutions. This has made it easy for the Tories to label Labour leaders as attacking Britain and its history. Whereas the Tories enthusiastically defend the British Empire, the monarchy, the military and the police, which is in tune with many socially conservative swing voters in marginals.

The Labour Party is associated with class-based politics, the struggle between workers and the labour movement against employers over working conditions, pay, and benefits. The Tories are much better at hiding their sectional interests of protecting the wealthy. As a result, the Labour Party is vulnerable to attacks that it is under the control of 'union bosses' or the leftwing of the party and not working in the interests of ordinary people. During periods of intense union militancy, this has damaged Labour's electoral success, such as from the late 1970s to the early 1990s. These factors mean Labour struggles to convince many voters that the party operates in the 'common interest'.

Labour has always been an urban party, with this getting even more pronounced in the last 20 years. Throughout its history, this has caused it problems claiming to be a 'national' party. In contrast, the

Tories have seats in rural and urban areas. This is complicated because a rural tradition that identifies rural culture with 'Englishness' has evolved. Labour has always been weak in those areas with strong nationalist feelings. This difficulty in connecting to this rural national identity further weakens its claim to be a national party.[18]

Labour Party and the nation, nation-state and patriotism
Labour's relationship with patriotism and national defence has fluctuated. The Attlee government had a leftwing domestic programme, but its foreign policy was consistent with British patriotic and national defence traditions. Attlee's Labour government helped create the Marshall Plan of economic reconstruction of Europe and was a founding member of the North Atlantic Treaty Organisation (NATO) and the United Nations (UN). However, in 1951 Attlee supported increased military spending at the expense of domestic reforms to support the US in the Korean War. This led to divisions in the Labour Party. From the early 1960s to the late 1980s, the party had an ongoing conflict around unilateral nuclear disarmament. This was a problem for Labour in the 1980s when the Tories attacked the party over national defence during the Cold War, contributing to the 1983 and 1987 election losses. Corbyn also struggled to convince many swing voters that he could protect Britain's national security.

Labour Party Statecraft
As described in Chapter 10, statecraft is a process that starts with a party in opposition that wins a general election and forms a government and ends with the party winning a second election while in office. There are five elements: effective party management, a strategy to win the next election, winning the political argument, governing competence, and winning the next election.

Broadly, Labour has struggled with all of these. Labour has been in government for 38 years over the past 123 compared to the Tories' 81. It has had six periods of government during that time. It has shown a fragile grip on power with minority governments, razor-thin majorities, and consistently struggling to win second terms. The main cause of Labour's failure to win second terms is its history of being unable to manage the economy that improves the living standards of most British people. Labour governments have focused more on (important) social policies such as housing, health, education and welfare than economic growth and wealth generation. Labour governments have failed to learn from the mistakes of previous governments and have been too deferential to financial and economic mainstream traditions, such as City of London institutions. Comparing Labour's achievements to centre-left parties in other advanced industrial countries, Labour has delivered less in terms of growth, higher living standards and improved public services.[19]

Labour formed its first (minority) government in January 1924, which only lasted 10 months. This showed that Labour could govern but did not achieve much. Labour won the 1929 election, which it might have been better to lose, and formed a government that struggled with an economic crisis for two years until collapsing. Ramsey MacDonald was Prime Minister for both of these governments. Labour's third time in government was from 1945 to 1951 under Prime Minister Attlee. This was much more successful by following through on most of its manifesto commitments and transforming the country's political priorities for decades. The fourth period was from 1964 to 1970, with Wilson in charge and who struggled under extremely difficult economic and social circumstances. Labour's fifth period was from 1974 to 1979 under Wilson again and then Callaghan. This government was viewed as incompetent and seen as betraying the labour movement over pay. Again this was during difficult economic circumstances. The final period was New Labour from 1997 to 2010 under Blair and Brown. Domestically it is viewed positively with reduced poverty, increased living standards and improved public services. On foreign matters, the Iraq War is seen as a disaster.

Labour is held to a much higher standard than the Tories; they must show much more economic restraint with moderate and fully costed election manifestos. Failure to do this allows the Tories and the right-wing media to scare voters into thinking Labour in government will crash the economy. Voters also generally expect more from Labour than the Tories regarding honesty and responsibility. Labour governments need to show results, follow through on their manifesto promises and make people's lives noticeably better. Without doing this, it is easy for the Tories and right-wing press to claim that Labour is incompetent and damaging the country and economy.[20]

Another key problem for Labour is that to win votes, they need to raise people's expectations that things will improve with them in government. This includes a positive vision for the country and strong economic growth to attract aspirational voters. But raising people's expectations this way has resulted in disappointment when the 'promised land' fails to appear. Attlee, Wilson, Blair and Brown struggled when economic problems caused their governments to lose support.[21] Wilson and New Labour failed to create a new social democratic political agenda and society. New Labour had an ambitious project to transform the country but failed to replace Thatcherism with a new political agenda. It prioritised winning elections over creating a new political system more hospitable to centre-left parties.[22]

The Tories' reputation that they are better at managing the economy, perpetuated by the right-wing press, is based on a history of Labour governments struggling under economic crises. Throughout the 20th century, Labour has had a confused approach to economic strategy between either managing capitalism more effectively than the Tories or trying to create an alternative economic system along socialist lines. Labour governments have rightly been focused on redistributing wealth from the rich to the poor through state intervention but have failed to have a clear strategy for economic growth. All this has meant that when an economic crisis arrives on Labour's watch, they have been forced to cut public spending and increase taxation, disappointing their supporters and leaving the party open to being accused of failing to manage the economy competently.

Labour has to balance keeping their support base happy, who

want radical policies, and convincing swing voters that Labour will do a better job at running the country and economy than the Tories. Finding the balance is one of the most difficult tasks for political parties, and the Tories only get away with their economic incompetence because they lie so effectively and are backed up by the press. The Tories manipulate economic data and blame everyone else for the problems, including Labour, and many voters believe this.

Labour has consistently failed to introduce political and constitutional reform to improve our society and Labour's chances of winning in the future. When they do introduce constitutional reforms, they are far too timid. The party has failed to reverse the over-centralised nature of the British state that concentrates power in the government. In the mid-20th century, reforms such as devolution, House of Lords and Civil Service reform were explored, but little came of it. Labour made no progress on constitutional reform in the post-war period until the late 1990s when Blair introduced limited devolution and House of Lords reform. A key failure of Labour governments is not introducing electoral reform to proportional representation (PR), similar to most Western countries. Had Attlee done this, Labour would likely have won the 1951 election, and Britain would have developed a form of Scandinavian social democracy with all the social benefits that would have brought.[23] New Labour failed to reverse the Thatcher anti-trade union laws and raise union membership numbers. It failed to increase the power of local government or reform our media and support the independent media sector.[24]

Labour has been less effective than the Tories at creating long-term loyal supporters for their party. In the early and mid-20th century, Labour policies on house building, education and the creation of the welfare state created a loyal group of supporters. However, Labour's opposition to Thatcher's council housing right to buy scheme would have alienated some voters. New Labour introduced few policies to manufacture Labour voters as it was limited by the Thatcherite agenda. It won large numbers of instrumental (self-interested) voters but failed to convert many to the party long-term. It improved people's living standards and the quality of public services but had to keep the housing market growing, so it failed to increase house building and deal with the housing crisis. It also improved public pensions, but this social group is difficult for Labour to maintain as most naturally vote for Tory. The one policy New Labour introduced that has created large numbers of Labour voters is the large increase in the number of young people attending university. It is unclear if this was an intentional strategy, but it has resulted in many young people, especially students, backing the party.

Why People Don't Vote Labour

There are several reasons people vote for the Tories (see Chapter 19), which are mostly the same reason why they could not vote for Labour.
1. Some voters fear that socialists and communists run the Labour Party. Many believe that Labour leaders can not competently govern the country, will crash the economy and can't be trusted with national defence;
2. Many do not vote for Labour because they strongly oppose Labour's perceived ideology of a 'big state' with increased taxation and spending on public services and reducing inequality over economic growth and 'sound money';
3. For instrumental reasons, people don't vote for Labour because they don't see any direct benefit to themselves for doing so. Many are comfortably off or wealthy, so they do not need public services or care about reducing inequality, so they see Labour governments as increasing taxation and taking money away from them;
4. Voters' identity is frequently psychologically attached to another party; for many, this will be the Tories, but it could also be the smaller parties;
5. Many are put off Labour because they believe the lies, propaganda and disinformation from the Tories and right-wing media that either discredit Labour or cover for the

Tories and hide the Tories' disastrous history of misrule.

In 2021, the comedian, writer and political commentator Geoff Norcott was interviewed on why Labour keep losing, focusing on the previous 11 years for Tory governments.[25] Norcott grew up in a strong Labour voting household and voted Labour during the New Labour years. In 2010, he then started voting Tory and has kept voting Tory since. Norcott describes how the overall offer of the left is unappealing. This includes the Labour Party and the broader left, including leftwing parts of the party and protest groups. He explains that this broader image of the left is what many people vote for when they vote for Labour. And that many, including himself, are put off voting for Labour because it would be endorsing this broad coalition. On the leadership of the parties, he compares Johnson and Starmer. He thinks Starmer is a reasonable leader but not appealing compared to Johnson for many voters (This interview was before Johnson's many scandals became public knowledge). Norcott described how people want to feel something from a party leader, which Johnson provided.

Norcott criticises Labour's strategy between 2016 to 2021 over Brexit and the Covid pandemic. He saw Labour as not doing much and just standing back and waiting for the Tories to mess up, which he saw as cowardly. His assessment of Labour MPs is that they do not see the world as he does.

Norcott believes that the Tories have grappled with events recently and got results, such as Brexit and tackling the Covid pandemic. He explains how the left has not helped themselves by claiming that Johnson wouldn't achieve results for quite achievable tasks, so when Johnson does achieve them, he gets more credit than he deserves. Examples are the EU withdrawal agreement, a post-Brexit trade deal within a year, winning a general election, and 'turning the Covid pandemic around'. Norcott is critical of how the left goes over the top, saying that everything is terrible and when it doesn't turn out so bad, it is hard to take them seriously. The example here is the dystopian predictions of Brexit by left commentators; also, how Labour went over the top with attacks on Johnson and how they looked fixated on trivial issues such as the Johnson wallpaper scandal.

Norcott describes how Labour seems to be very middle-class and London-focused and does not understand or encounter working-class people that live in towns. There is a very funny bit where he describes how following Labour losing another election, Labour Party people will comment on working-class Tory voters and say something like: 'Why won't these gullible fuckwits vote for us? I mean these stupid people once again committing self-harm; they've been duped'. He comments that if it's easy to dup people, why can't Labour do it? That politics is about propaganda and fluffing an idea, and selling a bigger vision that is positive and hopeful. He gives Levelling Up as an example. For Norcott, it works because it makes people feel good, even if it's unclear how achievable it is. He thinks the Labour Party needs to do this but can't dup anyone at that time (2021). Next, he describes how old certainties about politics and the Tories, in particular, have shifted to benefit the Tories. For example, the furlough scheme has surprised people that the Tories would pay people's wages. Also, Norcott describes how the NHS was prioritised during the pandemic. He states that the Tories are accused of not caring about people, not spending money on them, and destroying the NHS. But they did spend money on people and increased funding of the NHS.

Norcott describes his background and growing up poor on state benefits, clothing grants and free school meals. He was anxious about if state benefits would be stopped and was teased about bad clothes. He didn't like it and wanted more materially. He describes how it is a human reaction to want to do well and improve your situation for yourself, your family and society. He believes this aspirational perspective is generally missing from the Labour Party. The Labour Party can come across viewing people living in towns like Hartlepool as victims. But these people reject this when many are doing well and have a good life with their own home, car, holidays, and socialising a few times a week. Norcott recognises that people in society are struggling, and more resources should be focused on them. He explains that most people don't want the state to provide handouts and free stuff like free internet and that having a job and working for a living is ingrained in people. Many want to take responsibility for their own life, do well and don't want the government taking this control away. Norcott explains that he has to believe that he can make things better for himself. He understands that the government needs to look after the vulnerable; he calls this 'social justice'. Norcott describes how he is generally optimistic and thinks things will be ok. Optimism is something that the Tories do well, especially Johnson, which makes them appealing.

Norcott thinks that the left went over the top with its support for lockdowns during the pandemic, which came across as authoritarianism. He critiques the left's slogan, 'no one is safe until everyone is safe', because this is impossible during any period. That people on the left say it to feel better rather than help people, which he describes as selfish. He critiques how many on the modern left seem to prefer Labour being a principal opposition as more important than being in power, which is narcissistic, and how it's not good for democracy to have such a weak opposition and an effective one-party state in England.

Norcott describes how voters have retreated into identities in recent years. People that voted Tory are more Tory. The radical left has radicalised many people that recently voted for the Tories for the first time by describing Tory voters as selfish and ignorant. He believes that the recent militant protests have helped the Tories gain support because many see the left as being about trying to stop things, which wasn't always the case. In the 1990s, the left was seen as the fun guys; I guess referencing illegal raves and free parties. He explains how lots of people on the left when online don't understand how they come across to a broad range of people. He references the 'free speech' dimension of the culture wars and how leftwing people label those arguing for free speech as 'free speech warriors' as if that's a bad thing, but it sounds quite reasonable to many people. This is a consequence of people on the left burrowing deep into their echo chambers; also how people take online political conflicts too seriously.

Norcott and the interviewers discuss how Labour sees declining voter support but does little to reverse this. Many staunch Labour supporters see politics as a moral issue and that the Tories are immoral. Norcott describes the 'Norcott cycle': the right wins elections, and the left doubles down on culture. The left reacts by producing even more leftwing television shows. These leftwing shows do not represent working-class people's experiences, so they vote Tory again. Labour then loses another election, so the left creates more leftwing television shows. Norcott wants Labour to be more pragmatic, so there is a competitive opposition to hold the Tories to account.

PART 6:

STOPPING THE TORIES

Is Britain a conservative country? It certainly feels that way, and the answer depends on how you think about it. There is certainly an instinctive conservative nature to the British public. The country's conservative institutions include the antiquated House of Commons, the House of Lords, and the monarchy. Britain's culture is also conservative, with period dramas being some of the most popular television shows. The English are also fond of the nation's 'proud history' of the Empire, winning wars and Churchill. There is also the persistent class deference of the aristocratic elite and the wealth that mostly helps the Tories.[1]

When voting is considered, there is a clear non-Tory majority at each general election. In the 2019 election, 16.2 million people voted for centre-left political parties (Labour, Liberal Democrat, Green, SNP, Plaid Cymru), and only 13.9 million voted for parties on the right (Tories, Brexit Party, UKIP). The Tories got an 80-seat majority on 43.6% of the vote. They won a minority of the votes but got 100% of the power to run the country. They only were supported by 29.3% of eligible voters on a turnout of 67.3%. And that is only 20.1% of the total population of the UK. If the Tories' support among eligible voters is considered, this is less than a third. There is no way a party can deliver on the 'will of the people' with so little support.[2]

I'm pleasantly surprised that we don't have a more right-wing and

Tory-supporting electorate than we do, considering the party and right-wing press domination of our politics and culture. A consistent majority of the British public support progressive policies and institutions; the best example is the high levels of support for state-funded public services, especially the NHS.[3] The Tories and the right-wing media must work hard to maintain power. Research has found that the British population have become more socially liberal since the 1980s on immigration, popular culture and gay rights. An increasing sense of 'live and let live' has evolved regarding other people's relationships and lifestyles.[4]

21

HOW TO STOP THE TORIES AT THE NEXT GENERAL ELECTION

The next election must be by January 2025, it could be in late 2023 and is most likely to be in 2024. Although traditionally, general elections are in the Spring, the Tories might prefer Autumn or Winter when turnout will be lower, which will help them. The first obvious step to stop the Tories is the Labour Party winning the next election, even with all the reservations we might have about the Labour Party. To achieve this, those in marginal seats must vote tactically to remove Tory MPs. We must also prepare for the Tories' voter suppression tactic of requiring ID to vote; the simplest way is to apply for a postal vote, or if you wish to vote in person, make sure you have the correct ID.

Some might ask, "What's the point of tactical voting? Labour is going to win anyway." It's likely, but you can never count the Tories out of an election, and the priority at this point is to remove this destructive government. The Tories' general election campaign will reduce Labour's opinion poll lead, and many currently undecided voters will end up voting Tory once their campaign and right-wing press get into gear. The more seats taken from the Tories at the next election, the longer it will take them to sort themselves out and become competitive again. Hopefully it will take them a very long time.

Another factor is that Labour have a tougher job to win a

majority of seats at the next election than in 1997. Labour currently have 197 seats, so to get a majority in 2024, the party would need to win 124 seats. Before the 1997 election, Labour had 273 seats, so Blair only needed 55 seats to get a majority. Labour were 20 points ahead of the Tories through the 1990s and got an extra 146 seats on a 12.5% poll lead on election day, on top of 273, to get a landslide victory. If Labour won 146 seats at the next general election, it would have 343 MPs, with a small majority of 20. This is probably the best it can expect to do, so a hung parliament is still possible. Labour also have a problem in Scotland that Blair did not have. Labour had around 40 seats in Scotland in 1997, which are now held by the Scottish National Party (SNP). The SNP are struggling, so it's likely that Labour will gain 10-20 seats in Scotland and have to find the other seats from England and Wales.

Cooperation Between Parties

Cooperation between parties is one way to stop the Tories at the next election. This has worked in the past. In 1906 the Labour Party (called the Labour Representation Committee at the time) formed a non-aggression pact with the Liberals to get its first MPs in parliament. Electoral pacts between Labour and the Liberal Party kept the Tories out of power in the 1906 and 1910 elections. The early Labour governments of 1924 and 1929 were only formed with the support of the Liberal Party. In the late 1970s, Labour lost its majority in government and was supported by the Liberal Party to form a Lib-Lab pact. In the 1990s, Labour and the Liberal Democrats discussed working together in government in the event of a hung parliament, but this became irrelevant following Labour's landslide victory. Following the 2010 election, the Liberal Democrats and Labour discussed forming a coalition government, but talks broke down, and the Tories formed the Coalition government with the Liberal Democrats. Labour leader Miliband was open to a coalition government with the Liberal Democrats after 2015, but the Tories won a majority.[1]

Starmer has made it clear that there will be no public cooperation between Labour and the Liberal Democrats at the next election. However, Labour and the Liberal Democrats have different target seats, currently all held by the Tories. The one exception is Sheffield Hallam. They have likely privately discussed the seats they are targeting and will not actively campaign in those seats to give both parties the best shot at unseating the Tories. The parties have limited funds, so they have limited target seats. Many progressives advocate 'stand asides' in this situation, to give the progressive party in second place to the Tory MP the best chance of getting all the centre-left votes. This sounds logical, but it is not realistic. The Labour Party has a policy of standing a candidate in every parliamentary seat, and Starmer looks committed to this. There are other arguments against 'stand asides'. One, the media would make a lot of fuss about it being a stitch-up and create fear in voters' minds about Labour-Liberal Democrat chaotic coalition governments. The Tories and the right-wing press have already started doing this following the 2023 local election, so it's strategic for Labour and the Liberal Democrats not to give them any extra ammunition. A second reason is that a Liberal Democrat 'paper candidate' not campaigning but standing in a Labour target seat is very likely to attract 'soft Tory' voters, who would never vote Labour. This helps the cause by allowing these Tory voters to vote but not vote for the Tories.

Tactical Voting

Due to Britain's FPTP voting system, the centre-left vote since the 1970s has been split between multiple parties, and the Tories rarely have any competition on the right. In response, hundreds of thousands of voters at general elections since at least the 1960s and likely before have voted tactically for the candidate most likely to win to remove the Tory MP or keep a Tory candidate from winning. Millions of voters know that FPTP mostly benefits the Tories, so we have to game the system with tactical voting to try to keep the Tories out of government.

Tactical voting works
Here is a brief history of anti-Tory tactical voting in Britain. Tactical voting took place at the 1964 election, in 3 seats with the Liberals in second place, and in 15 other seats with Labour chasing the Tories. This likely decided the outcome of 2-3 seats.[2] Tactical voting mainly helped the Liberals through the 1960s and 1970s.

In the February 1974 election, it is estimated that the Tories lost three safe seats to the Liberals due to tactical voting. This election was close, so Labour supporters voting for Liberals likely helped get a Labour government. The Tories under Heath won 297 seats behind Labour's 301. Heath tried to form a rainbow coalition government with multiple smaller parties but was one seat short, so Labour formed a minority government.[3] At the 1979 election, the only seat that tactical voting is known to have helped is the Liberal seat on the Isle of Wight.[4]

The 1987 election saw active support of tactical voting by publications such as the New Statesman and Today newspapers. The Centre for Electoral Choice published a 'Consumer's Guide to Tactical Voting. A campaign was launched called Tactical Voting 87 (TV87) to encourage voting for Labour or (liberal) Alliance candidates best placed to remove Tory MPs. All this had some limited success, and it is estimated that the Tories' majority would have been 16 seats larger without it.[5]

The 1992 election saw tactical voting become more widespread and significant than in previous elections. In Tory seats with Labour in second place, Labour gained many more votes from the Liberals. And the newly formed Liberal Democrats, previously the Alliance, gained votes from Labour in seats the liberals were second place to the Tories, mostly in the South of England. This informal tactical voting by voters is estimated to have helped Labour win an extra six seats and maybe two more. The Liberal Democrats gained two seats due to tactical voting and possibly one more.[6]

The 1997 election saw the levels of anti-Tory tactical voting increase again. The pattern from previous elections continued with

Labour or Liberal Democrats candidates in second place to the Tories squeezing the other party's vote in third place. This was helped by a behind-the-scenes deal between Labour and Liberal Democrats leaderships to minimise campaigning where the other party was in second place. The Get Rid Of the Tories (GROT) campaign was formed to advise voters on the best candidates to remove Tories in marginals. Anti-Tory tactical voting was also helped by Labour-supporting newspapers giving tactical voting advice just before election day. The Mirror printed a list of 22 seats where if Labour supporters voted Liberal Democrat, they would defeat the Tory MP. The Observer printed a list of 20 seats encouraging voters to vote to unseat Tory MPs tactically. The scale of tactical voting in this election was unprecedented; it is estimated that Labour gained between 15-21 seats and the Liberal Democrats 10-14 seats. The Tories' vote share collapsed, with Liberal Democrat voters more willing to switch to Labour than vice versa.[7]

Anti-Tory tactical voting continued in the 2001 and 2005 elections. The 2010 election saw some tactical voting, but it decreased compared to previous elections. It was expected that tactical voting between Labour and Liberal Democrats would decline for the 2015 election, with the Liberal Democrats in coalition with the Tories. But the election data shows it to be similar to the 2010 election. There was no active tactical voting campaign, but newspapers gave advice similar to previous elections.[8]

In 2017, it was estimated that 6.5 million people (over 20% of voters) voted tactically in the election. Most of these will have been on the centre-left, either trying to stop a 'hard Brexit' or remove the Tory government. A new development in 2017 was several tactical voting websites to help voters decide how to vote, combined with newspaper articles giving advice. The Brexit debate dominated tactical voting in the 2019 election. This resulted in tactical voting websites giving confusing advice depending on if the website's priority was supporting EU remain candidates or best-placed candidates to defeat a Tory MP.

Since the 2019 general election, several by-elections have seen

Labour and the Liberal Democrats quietly cooperating and significant levels of tactical voting to defeat Tory candidates. In 2021, a by-election was held in North Shropshire following the resignation of the disgraced MP Owen Paterson. This was a very safe Tory seat that the Liberal Democrats won, with a combination of tactical voting and help from Labour, not campaigning. Many voters, including Tory supporters, were sick of the Johnson government and wanted to send a clear message by voting for the liberals. The Liberal Democrats had recently not campaigned in a Tory seat by-election for Old Bexley and Sidcup to help Labour. The Tories won this seat but with a reduced majority.[9]

In June 2022, there were two by-elections in Tory-held seats that Labour won in Wakefield and the Liberal Democrats in Tiverton & Honiton. Again both parties quietly stood aside for each other, and there was 'industrial scale tactical voting'.[10]

I am part of the team that launched the https://stopthetories.vote/ tactical voting website for the 2023 local elections, which saw huge levels of tactical voting to remove Tory Councillors. We analysed who would be best to tactically vote for in each area with a local election, which voters could find out by use of a simple postcode search. The site was launched one week before the local election date, and was used by half a million voters during that time. The Tory Party predicted they expected to lose 1,000 Councillors, their worst-case scenario. They will have made this prediction, expecting to lose less, so when they lost 700-800 Councillors, they could claim this as a good result. The Tories lost over 1,000 Councillors due to the high levels of tactical voting, which is a very encouraging sign for the general election.

How to do tactical voting

To remove this Tory government and Tory MPs, you'll need to vote for the Labour or Liberal Democrat candidate that is most likely to beat the Tory MP or Tory candidate in your parliamentary seat. First, you need to check which party your current MP belongs to, and if you live in a safe seat for that party. There are several places to check this information online, including the UK Parliament website.[11]

When thinking about tactical voting, there are five types of seats to consider:

1. Tory MPs in marginal seats with a majority of votes of a few hundred to several thousand;
2. Progressive MPs in marginal seats including Labour, Liberal Democrats, SNP, Plaid Cymru, and Green Party;
3. Tory safe seats;
4. Progressive MP safe seats;
5. Seats where progressive parties are competing against each other. These are normally in urban areas.

Tactical voting is most effective for the next election in marginal seats currently held by Tory MPs. There are several ways to work out which Labour or Liberal Democrat candidate is best placed to beat Tory MPs. First, check to see who came second to the Tory MP at the last election on the UK Parliament website. Second, when the general election campaign starts, check the tactical voting websites, such as https://stopthetories.vote or https://tacticalvote.co.uk/. A third way is to check the bookies or betting shops to see which candidate they think is in second place to the Tories. A fourth way is to check the centre-left newspapers online, such as the Guardian and the Mirror, which print multiple articles during election campaigns on how to tactically vote in that election. I recommend checking a number of these resources so you have the best information.

For those marginal seats with Labour or Liberal Democrat MPs and the Tories in second place, you tactically vote for the incumbent progressive MP to stop the Tories. Tactical voting is less important in Tory safe seats, but it can't hurt. Tactical voting is not recommended for the last two types of seats.

There are two other tactical voting options. First, if you are a student, you can register to vote at your parents' address or if you live in another seat for your studies. Use the method described above to determine which seat your vote will have more impact, then register and vote there. Vote swapping is another form of tactical voting, and there is the website https://www.swapmyvote.uk/ to help people find each other in different seats.

22

HOW TO STOP THE TORIES IN THE LONG TERM

The previous chapters have outlined the superior abilities of the Tories to dominate our politics and country. They have proved too powerful for the Labour Party and the left to defeat in elections without forming alliances with smaller parties, rare periods of Labour strength, or temporary periods of crisis for the Tories. The Tories are now in a crisis, combined with a Labour Party that is focused on winning and looking likely to win the next election. But if the UK's political arrangements are left as they are, then we can be certain that after 2 or 3 elections, the Tories will 'modernise,' with a new fresh-faced leader that appeals to swing voters with 'moderate' policies. Voters will be tired of Labour and forget how bad Tory governments are, and the Tories will then return to power and undo any progressive policies that Labour have introduced. In the same way, the last 13 years of Tory misrule have erased New Labour's domestic achievements in redistributing wealth to a moderate degree.[1]

There are so many problems with British democracy that the country needs significant political and constitutional reform. Most importantly, the political playing field needs rebalancing through electoral reform to represent the majority of the British voters who vote for parties in opposition to the Tories. The majority want progressive governments to grow the economy, redistribute wealth, reduce inequality and poverty, tackle climate change, properly fund public services, create decent jobs, build enough houses, and welcome immigrants. The Tories either fail to do any of this or do the opposite. If democracy can't resolve Britain's ongoing political crisis, more voters might turn away from democracy to right-wing populist politicians. This trend has developed over the last 10 years and will continue unless something is done to reverse it.

Britain desperately needs democratic modernisation through several political and constitutional reforms to fix our broken democracy. We also need a way to weaken the Tories and force them to become more moderate to win power, so as to ensure we don't see the return of extreme Tory governments that have governed over the last 45 years. These reforms are medium-term goals that will take decades to implement and would form the baseline for a decent society.

1. Most importantly, we need electoral reform, specifically proportional representation (PR), so that we have progressive governments that represent the majority of voters;
2. The voting age needs to be dropped from 18 to 16;
3. We need reform of political parties and election spending so that strict donation and election spending limits exist. Ideally, the state would fund political parties to remove the corruption that political donations cause;
4. On media reform, the 2013 Leveson recommendations need to be implemented. The goal would be to create an independent regulatory body to promote higher standards, including the power to investigate serious breaches and sanction newspapers. Legislation would be needed to ensure the new regulator was doing a good job. There would be a legal duty on the government to protect the freedoms of the press. Victims of press abuse and ethical journalists need to be protected. In addition to Leveson, foreign nationals' ownership of British media publications should be banned to stop international billionaires from warping our media and politics;

5. We need the House of Lords reformed into an elected second chamber that represents the whole country. Representatives of this new body should be elected using proportional representation;
6. The centralisation of state power needs to be devolved from the government and Westminster so there is equitable power distribution between the nations; and national, regional and local governments. These devolved powers would need to come with increased funding;
7. The Tories' abuse of government power must be stopped by subjecting executive powers and state bodies to the rule of law and under the power of a reformed Parliament.
8. There need to be robust legal remedies for the abuse of power by the government, its ministers, and national or local government officials;
9. The independence of the judiciary (courts) must be ensured to stop Tory government interference, as we have seen when Johnson was Prime Minister;
10. The Human Rights Act 1998 must be strengthened to protect civil liberties, the right to peaceful assembly, freedom of association, trade union rights, privacy rights, freedom of expression, freedom from discrimination, freedom from detention without trial, and trial by jury;
11. We need all these reforms included in a written, codified constitution.[2]

How Does Proportional Representation Help?

The key reform we need that opens things up to the other essential reforms listed above is electoral reform; Proportional representation (PR) is a broad term for a more proportional voting system where the seats that political parties win in parliament should be in proportion to the way people voted across the country. There are several ways to decide who gets elected to parliament, with some being more proportional than others. The two most proportional systems, Single

Transferable Vote or Party Lists, would mean that a party that got a quarter of the voters would get a quarter of the seats in parliament.

In 1995 Margaret Thatcher was asked if the Tories would benefit from a period in opposition; she replied: "That's crazy... they might change the voting system." The Tories know full well that FPTP benefits them and that the electorate is politically to their left. If Britain had a more proportional voting system, voters would elect more progressive governments.[3]

Why do we need PR?
Our democracy and political system are clearly broken and out of date. They favour the Tories, who repeatedly run the country into the ground. A PR voting system is not a magic fix, but it would help Britain move in a better direction. We need a new social contract to reduce the extreme inequality in Britain and to improve our democracy and living standards. Introducing PR would make this possible, help protect these reforms, and ensure ongoing accountability.

There are many reasons why we need a PR voting system:
1. FPTP disproportionately benefits the Tories, so we need PR to ensure that progressive governments are elected by a majority of votes, which we rarely see in Britain;
2. It would result in more centre-left progressive governments that could implement wealth redistribution and much-needed democratic, political and constitutional reform;
3. PR would force the Tory Party to become more moderate to win power and stop them from introducing highly destructive policies when in power. Under FPTP, the Tories are able to dismantle any progressive domestic policies introduced by the previous Labour government;
4. Political diversity would be represented and not repressed. Britain is now a multi-party democracy based on an out-of-date FPTP electoral system;
5. Each person's vote would have the same value, so each party's MPs would be elected with the same number. This is

in contrast to the current situation under FPTP, when it takes 38,000 votes to elect a Tory MP and 800,000 to elect a Green MP;

6. Votes would matter in every seat, not just marginal constituencies, compared to now, where swing voters in marginals decide elections;
7. Voters would have multiple representatives from different parties to choose to represent them. Whereas, currently voters only have 1 MP, that for millions, is from a party they disagree with;
8. 'Wrong winner' elections would no longer occur; this is when a party that wins a majority of votes across the country fails to win a majority of seats, so does not form the government;
9. PR would end the wasting of votes in 'vote mountains' in safe seats;
10. PR would result in higher turnout and satisfaction with democracy;
11. PR would end the need for tactical voting. Voters could vote for the party they prefer instead of many voting for the party most likely to stop the party they dislike;
12. We can move on from having to choose the lesser of two evils, which can be manipulated by the right-wing press, big business and wealthy interests, so millions vote against their interests. Instead, smaller parties could offer policies that voters want and put pressure on larger parties to do the same;
13. PR would facilitate collaboration and power sharing between parties instead of confrontational tribal politics. Coalition governments encourage consensus and compromise, so more voters get some of what they want and less of what they don't want;
14. PR would result in more women MPs, as shown by other countries that use PR;
15. As proved by other countries using PR, it would result in a

more united and equal society.[4]

Alternative Voting Systems To FPTP

There are broadly seven different electoral systems that can be divided into three groups based on how proportional they are in electing political representatives. The first group are known as 'majoritarian' systems that are not seen as proportional. These include First Past the Post, Two-Round System, Alternative Vote and Supplementary Vote. The second has one voting system combining majoritarian systems and PR: the Additional Member System. The third group are PR voting systems. These include Party Lists and Single Transferable Vote. These 7 voting systems are described below.[5]

First Past the Post (FPTP)
FPTP is the current electoral system for the House of Commons. The UK has 650 seats, each of which elects 1 MP. To win, a candidate must get more votes than the other candidates in that seat, but it does not need an absolute majority of all votes. FPTP is a highly disproportional electoral system, and its problems are detailed in Chapter 1. FPTP is also used in local elections in England and Wales. Wards have 2 or 3 councillors up for election or staggered over different years. The top 2 or 3 candidates are elected.[6]

Alternative Vote (AV)
AV is based on single-member seats, like FPTP, but instead of only voting for one candidate, voters rank candidates in order of preference – 1, 2, 3 etc. Once the votes are counted and if a candidate has not received over 50% of votes, the candidate with the least votes is eliminated, and their votes are redistributed to the other candidates based on voters' second preferences. This process will continue until one candidate has 50% of votes plus 1. This system removes the need for tactical voting but is not proportional and could lead to less proportional results than FPTP. It is used to elect the Australian

Lower House. The UK's referendum on introducing this system in 2011 was rejected.[7]

Supplementary Vote (SV)
This is a simplified version of AV. There are two columns by the candidates' names, one column for the voter's preferred candidate and a second column for their second choice candidates. They put an X in each column instead of a number. Voters do not have to include a second preference vote. Once the votes are counted, and no candidate receives 50% of the votes, all but the top two candidates are eliminated. Of the votes for the eliminated candidates, their second preference votes for the remaining two candidates are counted. The candidate with the most votes from the second round is declared the winner. SV was used for electing Mayors and Police and Crime Commissioners in the UK for the last 20 years, but the Tories reverted these elections to FPTP in 2022 for future elections to benefit their own candidates.[8]

Two-Round System
The Two-Round or Second Ballot system has two separate days of voting with a gap of a few weeks between. On the first day, there is a full list of candidates standing for election, and voters select one candidate. If one candidate gets 50% of the vote, they are elected. The top two candidates enter the second round if no candidates get a majority. On the second day, voters select one candidate from the remaining two candidates. This is a highly disproportional electoral system and artificially boosts large parties. It is famously used in France.[9]

Additional Member Systems (AMS)
Additional Member Systems have several variations, and at their most basic, it combines FPTP with a regional Party List system. The Party List is a top-up to make elections more proportional. Voters have two ballot papers; the first has a list of candidates standing to be a local MP, in the same way, we elect MPs now. The second ballot

paper is to vote for parties within larger regional constituencies. The parties announce a list of candidates in advance. A vote for a party helps elect MPs from the parties' lists in the order the party decides. This electoral system is more proportional than FPTP and keeps the constituency link through a single MP. It is a compromise solution and therefore has its problems. It maintains the current issue of 'safe seats', and parties have a lot of control over who is elected from the Party Lists. It is argued that it creates two classes of MPs resulting in tensions. Local MPs have constituency casework; Party List MPs do not. An advantage is that it gives voters more than one MP to represent them. Another is that parties can win seats in every part of the country, which reduces the possibility that governments will ignore parts of the country. AMS is used to elect the London Assembly and Scottish and Welsh parliaments. In Scotland, they elect 73 local Members of the Scottish Parliament (MSPs) by FPTP and 56 MSPs from the second ballot Party List.

There are some variations of AMS:

1. Mixed Member Proportional (MMP) is used in Germany in broadly the same way, except the top-up Party List is national instead of regional;
2. Mixed Member System (MMS), which is a minimalist form of AMS, proposed to overcome objections from Labour Party supporters of FPTP. This would have 500 local MPs elected by FPTP and 150 Party List MPs. To get a Party List MP, political parties must win at least one constituency MP;
3. AV+ is a form of AMS that elects local MPs with AV instead of FPTP combined with the top-up Party List element.[10]

Party lists

Instead of electing one candidate for each of the 650 seats, Party List systems have a bigger area; for example, there might be 65 larger constituencies, each electing 10 MPs. There are three types of Party List systems.

1. Closed List: parties publish a list of candidates for each area, and the ballot paper only has a list of parties that voters can choose from. Parties will receive seats roughly in proportion to the number of votes. The MPs elected will depend on their position on the list the parties submitted in advance;
2. Open List: each party presents a list of candidates. Voters choose the candidate they support from any point on the list. To determine how many seats each party should receive, a vote for a candidate is counted as a vote to their party. So the more votes a candidate gets, the greater the increase in the number of MPs for their party that get elected overall, and the more likely the chosen candidate will be elected. This version gives voters a high level of candidate choice;
3. Semi-Open List: voters can choose to vote for a party or candidate. A vote for the party is like the Closed List process. Votes for candidates can help them move up the party list.

Party Lists are the most popular electoral system in the world, used by more than 80 countries with slight variations. Countries that use Party List systems generally have multiple parties due to being highly proportional. This results in coalition governments being the norm. Most Party List countries have 4 or 5% legal thresholds to block parties with very low support gaining seats. Some countries have single nationwide constituencies, such as the Netherlands. A downside of large constituencies is this weakens the link between MPs and constituents. Others have very small constituencies, such as Finland and Spain. The advantage of smaller seats is that MPs understand local issues better. The downside is that they will have fewer MPs in a constituency, which makes the result less proportionate as you need more votes to elect an MP.[11]

Single Transferable Vote (STV)
STV has large constituencies with multiple MPs of, say, 5, representing diverse opinions in the area. Parties will stand a maximum of 5 candidates in a seat. Voters rank all the candidates in order of preference and can number as many or as few candidates as they like. To win, candidates must reach a quota, which different countries calculate differently. Votes are transferred from low-ranking candidates that are eliminated or from winning candidates with excess votes. This means no votes are wasted, making it a very proportional system. It also gives voters a lot of choices about how they vote, either block voting for a party or, for specific candidates from different parties based on the candidates' abilities. Voters can also vote for independent candidates without risking wasting their votes. Seats can be created more naturally to include a whole town or county, which creates a strong local link and gives voters several MPs to approach with issues. STV is used in Northern Ireland, the Republic of Ireland, Malta, Scotland and Australia.[12]

Dealing With Criticisms Of PR

General elections have 3 functions:
1. to decide a government;
2. to choose MPs to represent people in a geographical area;
3. to create a parliament that represents the electorate.

Each voting system described above is a trade-off between these three, with different people having different priorities and preferring different systems. FPTP provides one form of representation for local communities and results in governments that millions have voted for, although rarely a majority of voters. But FPTP fails badly at representing the broad range of views of the electorate, resulting in multiple political and societal problems. PR voting systems are designed to create parliaments that reflect voters' opinions better. But it creates concerns about weakening the link between local people and their MP, and people fear weak coalition governments.[13]

Here are five common criticisms of PR voting systems and responses.

Coalition governments mean that policies from minority parties can be implemented

A big fear people have about PR is that it will allow extremist parties to gain MPs that FPTP currently, in theory, blocks from parliament. UKIP won 4 million votes in the 2015 election, and dozens of their MPs would have been elected under PR. My response is that had these UKIP MPs been elected, the Brexit referendum would likely have gone the other way. Instead, tens of thousands of UKIP activists joined the Tory Party, took it over and changed it to the party of Brexit.[14]

PR systems have thresholds where a party cannot win seats unless they have a minimum percentage of the vote, at 4 or 5%. This can be combined with the size of the PR constituency being set, creating a threshold and a barrier to entry to parties with very low support. An example is that 10 large constituencies across the country with 5 Party List seats is a higher barrier to entry for small parties than one 50-seat national constituency. As democrats, we should support all parties with a certain level of support getting representation, even if we don't agree with their views. In addition, once parties get national attention, their policies will be assessed, and these parties will need to moderate and become less extreme to grow beyond their core support base.[15]

PR can lead to unstable and weak coalition governments

FPTP already leads to unstable and weak coalition governments, such as the Labour-Liberal government from 1977 to 1979 or the Conservative minority government from 2017 to 2019. The Tories won a big majority in 2019, but the government has been unstable since 2022, with constant infighting and a lack of direction. Additionally, FPTP leads to many more unplanned elections than countries with PR.

PR results in a different form of government that prioritises power sharing, consensus and collaboration, compared to FPTP, which is about power hoarding and confrontation. Since the devolved Assemblies were established in Wales and Scotland in 2000, a range of progressive coalitions and majority governments have proved effective and stable.[16]

Additional Member System (AMS) can create conflict between the constituency MP and the Party List MPs

It is argued that AMS creates two classes of MPs. This is a valid concern, and the response is that if we want a more proportional voting system, but are not prepared to go with either of the most proportional voting systems (Single Transferable Vote or open Party Lists), then the 'two classes of MPs' problem is something we'd need to live with. No voting system is perfect, but AMS is more proportional and better than FPTP. The second point is that this is actually an argument for STV, which doesn't have these problems.

Closed Regional Party List systems can make parties more powerful than voters

If a candidate for a large party is placed near the top of the list, they will likely be elected. The straightforward way to resolve this is to use either STV or open Party List systems, where there is much more voter choice.

PR systems would lose the MP local or constituency link

The claim is that PR would weaken the link between local people and their MP because it means large multi-member constituencies with several MPs, or has the AMS top-up Party Lists to improve proportionality. However, FPTP does not provide a strong constituency link for millions of voters because their MP is someone they didn't vote for and don't agree with their politics and therefore do not trust them to represent their views in parliament.[17]

Of the PR systems we could get, AMS, STV or Party Lists, each has a constituency link. AMS would have bigger constituencies than at present, but the link is there. STV and Party Lists have larger regional constituencies, with multiple MPs to choose from to represent you in parliament. Many would prefer this choice, compared to now, where we have a single MP who is unlikely to be someone we agree with.

History Of Electoral Reform In Britain

Below is a history of electoral reform in Britain.

Before 1945
Before 1832 less than 10% of the British men (250,000 men) could vote, and this was based on owning property and receiving a minimum of 40 shillings of rent. The 1832 Great Reform Act reduced the property-owning qualification, reorganised electoral boroughs, and created an electoral register. This meant that 14% of the adult male population over 21 could vote. The Chartism Movement was active between 1838 and 1848 with six demands, including universal male voting (franchise) and a secret ballot. Up to this point, how the electorate voted was public knowledge.

The 1867 Reform Act decreased the property-owning qualification again so all men with an address and over 21 could vote. Boroughs were reorganised again to make representation across the boroughs more equal. This act increased the size of the electorate to 32% of the adult male population, including some working-class men. Several parliamentary acts in the 1870s and 1880s introduced more reforms. Open elections were replaced with secret ballots. The amount that could be spent on election expenses was standardised, and it became a criminal act to bribe voters. The electorate increased to 56% of the adult male population in the mid-1880s.

Some women property owners had been able to vote until the 1832 Great Reform Act, but this new legislation specified voters as 'male persons'. The 1869 Municipal Franchise Act gave unmarried women that were ratepayers the vote in local elections. This was extended in the 1894 Local Government Act to include some married women. In 1900, over 1 million women were registered to vote in local elections in England.

During the 1910s, support for PR in the Labour Party and the trade union movement increased. Legislation was proposed in 1917 for PR to be introduced in about a third of seats and AV elsewhere, but both were rejected by parliament. The 1918 Labour Party Conference voted in favour of PR, but this was not included in the manifesto. The Liberal Party only switched to supporting PR in 1924 when it started to worry about its long-term survival. By this point, the Labour Party could see it was replacing the Liberals, so it lost interest in reforming the voting system. Labour did introduce a bill in parliament for AV in 1931 to gain Liberal support and stop a Liberal/Conservative alliance. The Bill passed in the House of Commons with Liberal support, but the Tory-dominated House of Lords weakened it, and then Labour lost power.[18]

The 1918 Representation of the People Act increased the electorate to include all men over 21 and most women over 30. That year, women over 21 were allowed to stand as MPs. The 1928 Equal Franchise Act reduced the age women could vote to 21, the same as for men.[19]

Post-war period 1945-1990s

Following Labour's electoral success in the post-war period, the party forgot about PR. This was helped by the two-party nature of British politics until the 1970s. Labour did enact some mild reform of elections. The 1949 Representation of the People Act removed second votes for graduates and business premises owners, which made up about 7% of the population. The 1969 Representation of the People Act lowered the voting age to 18.[20] Northern Ireland was the first part of the UK to introduce PR in 1973 when it adopted STV for local elections. During the 1980s and 1990s, the pressure for electoral reform increased, following the success of the Tories in elections on a minority of the vote.[21]

At the 1987 Labour Party Conference, there were 25 resolutions calling for the Labour Party to commit to reforming the electoral system. It was rejected by the leadership but got support from some MPs. The New Statesman and Fabian Society supported PR with the launch of Charter 88 campaign for broad constitutional reform. The Labour leadership continued to support FPTP. In 1990, Scottish Labour rejected FPTP for the proposed Scottish Parliament. The Labour National Executive Committee set up a working party to consider voting systems to be used for a Scottish Parliament to be chaired by Raymond Plant. In 1990 Labour leader Neil Kinnock expanded the remit of the Plant Commission to include the voting system for the House of Commons. In 1993 the Plant Commission supported PR, specifically the SV system for the House of Commons and regional party lists for EU and Scottish elections. The Labour leader John Smith stated that this would need to be decided by a referendum during Labour's next government.

During the 1992 election, the Tories and the right-wing media used Labour's new openness to electoral reform to scare voters about hung parliaments and a coalition government. Opinion polls following the election showed that most people were against replacing FPTP with PR.[22]

New Labour electoral reform 1994-2010
Following John Smith's death and during the leadership election, Tony Blair stated his support for a referendum on changing the voting system for the House of Commons. In early 1997 Labour and the Liberal Democrats worked together to agree on a programme of constitutional reform that both parties would support. The Cook-Maclennan Joint Consultative Committee on the Constitution launched its report in March 1997, with the recommendations going into Labour's election manifesto. These included supporting PR for EU elections, a referendum on the House of Commons voting system, a commission to identify an alternative PR voting system for the Commons, and the introduction of PR for the new Scottish and Welsh Assembly and the European Parliament.[23]

Following the 1997 Labour victory, most of these reforms were adopted, except for a referendum on changing the voting system for the Commons. MEPs were elected through a closed Party List system. In Scotland and Wales, AMS was introduced to elected representatives of their devolved Assemblies. In 2007, STV was introduced for Scottish local council elections. New Labour also introduced several single office-holder positions nationwide, including Metro Mayors and Police and Crime Commissioners (PCC). These were elected by SV until the Tories introduced legislation in 2022 so that FPTP will elect future Metro Mayors and PCCs. Unsurprisingly, this will give Tory candidates an advantage.

New Labour established an independent commission to identify a new voting system, chaired by Liberal Democrat Lord Jenkins. The Jenkins Commission report was published in 1998 and recommended a new hybrid called AV+, based on two existing systems. As described above in the voting systems section, this is a form of AMS. Voters have two ballot papers; one elects the local MPs using AV instead of FPTP by ranking the candidates in order of preference. Candidates would be eliminated until one gets 50% of the vote. The second vote is for a party using Party Lists to make the elections more proportional. The Commission recommended that 85% of MPs should be elected by AV, 15% from a Party List. Labour National Policy Forum 2000 report raised concerns about this proposal, and nothing more was done to reform the voting system for the Commons.[24]

21st-century electoral reform

At the 2010 election, the Labour manifesto included a commitment to change the voting system to AV. The Tory/Liberal Democrat Coalition Government ran a referendum on the House of Commons voting system in 2011, based on changing it to AV, but it was rejected. The Tories agreed to this referendum as part of the deal with the Liberal Democrats to form the Coalition government. The 'Yes to AV campaign' was poorly run, and there was a lack of support from much of the Labour Party. On the other hand, the 'no campaign' was effective, dirty, well-funded, based on lies, and backed by the

Tories.[25]

Support for PR in the Labour Party picked up in 2020-1, with hundreds of motions sent for debate at the party conference. It was debated at the 2021 conference, but a motion was not passed due to a lack of trade union support. However, a poll in 2021 found that over 80% of Labour Party members backed changing the voting system to PR. Large trade unions, including Unite the Union and UNISON, supported PR in 2021-2, so the motion was passed when PR was debated at the 2022 Labour Party Conference. Since the conference, local Labour Party branches have been responding to Labour's National Policy Commission consultation on what should go into the next manifesto, with proposals to include PR for House of Commons elections. In 2023, the retail workers union USDAW came out in support of PR.

In November 2022, Labour MP Cat Smith presented a Bill to Parliament to introduce PR for parliamentary elections, Metro Mayors, PCCs and local elections in England and Wales. However, with the Tories in government and control of the parliamentary agenda, there is zero chance of the Bill being debated or put into law. In May 2023, a coalition of democratic groups organised the 'Sort the System' event in Westminster to lobby parliament for equal votes.

Strategy To Get PR

There are four broad ways to get PR for the House of Commons. These are majority imposition, minority bargain, mass revolt and mass disillusionment. Majority imposition is when a large party decides changing the voting system would be in their interests to maintain power. Minority bargain is when a minority party demands electoral reform to join a governing coalition. Mass revolt is when citizen pressure forces a political party to hold a referendum on the voting system. The mass disillusionment route is when years of antipathy towards politics and declining turnout cause a political party to offer constitutional reform to attract votes.[26]

Regarding majority imposition in the UK, the Tories are

committed to FPTP and are against introducing PR, so Labour is the only large party that might change the voting system to PR. We have seen minority bargaining in action with the Liberal Democrats getting a referendum on AV from the Tories in 2011 as part of joining the Coalition Government. Looking ahead, the Liberal Democrats have also stated that if Labour needs their support to govern following the next election, then Labour would need to introduce electoral reform without a referendum. This route may be possible if there is a hung parliament after the next election. The mass revolt and mass disillusionment route looks unlikely in the UK.

Through the 1990s, it was assumed that changing the voting system to a form of PR would require a referendum. Following the dirty and deceitful 'no to AV' and Brexit leave campaign, many PR supporters have understandably gone off referendums. The goal of the PR campaign in Labour is to get electoral reform onto the party Manifesto so Labour can introduce it without a referendum. There is no legal requirement to have a referendum on changing the voting system. A clear manifesto commitment and evidence of public support for the change would be enough.

2022 was a big year for electoral reform. As well as the Labour Party Conference passing a motion in support, this was the first time a majority (51%) of respondents to the British Social Attitudes survey stated that they want the electoral system changed compared to 44% that want to keep the current system.[27]

If Labour were to go down the manifesto route to changing the voting system instead of a referendum, then a public consultation would be needed through constitutional convention to ensure the change is seen as legitimate, and will prevent the Tories, once back in government, from simply switching back to FPTP or holding a referendum on the issue. A constitutional convention comprises randomly selected citizens brought together to deliberate and recommend which PR voting system should be implemented. This could be part of a broader consultation on constitutional and political reform of our democracy.[28]

Challenges To Getting PR In The Labour Party

Broadly there are four challenges to implementing PR via the Labour Party. Although over 80% of members and the main affiliated trade unions are supportive, there is still resistance in the party.

Tribalism and Labourism
Some in the Labour Party see it as the only party of the centre-left and see PR as a threat that will give an advantage to other parties such as the Liberal Democrats, SNP, Greens and Plaid Cymru. This view is shared by both the right-wing of the Labour Party, as well as members who strongly identify with the party and hate other centre-left parties, especially the Liberal Democrats, for going into coalition with the Tories in 2010. These groups would rather Labour get into government every so often with a majority of the seats than share power with other centre-left parties for more of the time. Members with this perspective are in many powerful positions in the party hierarchy, including MPs and party officers in London or around the country, and occupy senior positions in the Constituency Labour Party branches.

Labour shadow cabinet resistance to PR
During the 2020 Labour leadership election, Starmer said he favoured electoral reform and PR.[29] In 2022 and 2023 Starmer has said that changing the voting system to PR is not a priority. The Starmer Labour leadership have not stated they will never introduce PR, just that it is not a priority for the next general election manifesto and their first term in office. This may change if the next election results in a hung parliament and Labour needs the Liberal Democrats' support to form a government. We also can't assume that Labour will include PR in a future manifesto; that is something we will have to apply pressure on Labour to ensure. See more on this at the end of the chapter.

The Labour leadership are focused on winning the next election. Electoral reform does not come up on the doorstep, in focus groups or opinion polls, as a key issue for voters compared to the cost of living crisis or struggling public services. The Labour leadership are taking a pragmatic approach, focusing only on what will help the party win and ignoring everything else. Labour will likely win the next election. Still, there are reports that Starmer repeatedly tells the shadow cabinet that they need to operate as if they are still behind the Tories in the opinion polls to avoid complacency. It is also possible that the Tories will come to their senses, stop fighting each other and introduce popular policies to give them a fighting chance at the next election. This is unlikely, but Starmer is cautious and will work on this basis.

In recent general elections, the Tories have claimed that Corbyn and Miliband would form weak coalition governments with the SNP if there were a hung parliament. This has caused Labour problems with swing voters, many of whom believe coalition governments are unstable. Since the 2023 local elections, Labour looks likely to have the largest number of parliamentary seats at the next election, but might fall short of a majority. Starmer has ruled out an arrangement with the SNP, but has refused to rule out working with the Liberal Democrats. The Tories and their media quickly dusted off their 'coalition of chaos' attacks. If Labour were to announce support for PR for House of Commons elections, this would fuel these claims, so strategically, it is understandable to avoid this.

Labour MPs' Resistance to electoral reform

Introducing PR would change things significantly for current Labour MPs. With AMS, seats would become bigger (combined with a top-up list). With STV and Party Lists, much larger multi-member regional constituencies would be created. Due to the large defeat in the 2019 election, most current Labour MPs are in safe seats or seats that the MP has worked hard for years to maintain. So they understandably see introducing PR as a threat to keeping their seat.

They are right to fear these changes, and any Labour MP with these concerns prioritises their income and career over what is best for the country and the most vulnerable. These Labour MPs are an obstacle to progressive change. Many of these MPs claim that PR would break the constituency link as an excuse to close down the debate on changing the voting system. They either don't understand that PR systems have a local link or are misrepresenting it. Many Labour MPs that are against PR are in favour of AV because this maintains the current seat boundaries, and because these MPs are in safe seats, they will likely win under AV.

Labour Party leftwing resistance to PR
Some on the left of the Labour Party believe it is possible to elect another socialist to lead the party and win a general election instead of just missing out in 2017. I described in chapter 20 how Labour was actually nowhere near winning in 2017, but many on the Labour left believe this fantasy. They therefore want to keep FPTP to make this possible and see PR as giving in to centrist politics, concerned that the Liberal Democrats and Tories will form the majority of the coalition governments under PR. A section of the Labour Party on the 'hard left' advocate revolutionary Trotskyist politics and are against PR because they believe it is possible to take over the Labour Party and then win a majority government several decades in the future. Unrealistic, to say the least, and in the meantime, we have to put up with destructive Tory governments three-quarters of the time.

What Form Of PR Are We Likely To Get In The UK?

Suppose Labour actually were to include PR in a future manifesto and introduce it without a referendum. In that case, the form of PR we would get will depend on recommendations from a constitutional convention and then negotiation with Labour MPs, many of which will strongly resist the reform. The 1997 Labour government introduced AMS, STV and closed Party Lists for different elections around the UK. For the House of Commons, the Plant Commission recommended SV, and the Jenkins Commission recommended AV+. Labour leader Brown backed AV in 2010, and the Liberal Democrats accepted the AV referendum in 2011.

Campaign group Make Voters Matter created the 'Good Systems Agreement' that found consensus from MPs and political organisations across the political spectrum based on ten principles. This narrowed down the choice to AMS combined with AV+ or STV. It concluded that if AMS were chosen, it needs to be more proportional than the Scottish form of AMS. This would ensure a constituency link. The Good Systems Agreement determined that the new system needs to be chosen by a "citizen-led, deliberative process".[30]

Will The Next Labour Government Introduce PR?

As discussed, it is unclear whether Starmer wants to introduce PR. He has made statements supporting PR but has said several times over the last year that electoral reform and PR are not a priority. He is focused on winning the next GE and doesn't see PR as a vote winner. Therefore it is highly unlikely that he will include changing the voting system to PR in the next Labour manifesto.

During Labour's first term in government, they are planning to reform the House of Lords to an elected chamber instead of by appointment from party leaders. If this happens, PR could be used for these elections to introduce PR to voters slowly.

It is still possible that Starmer plans to introduce PR for general elections over the next 10 years, but is too focused on winning the next election to consider it for the next election. However, he could add it to the manifesto for the election after next in roughly 2028. This way, Labour would have two full terms in government to implement their policies. Another benefit is that including PR in a Labour manifesto for the 2028 election would result in Liberal Democrat and Green supporters tactically voting for Labour as they would see how this would benefit their preferred parties. This would give Labour added support for that second election, when their popularity might wane, and the Tories might have regrouped and become more competitive. The third election, say in 2032, would then be run under PR, and Labour would likely form a coalition government with the Liberal Democrats, Greens, and SNP.

There is no way of knowing if Starmer plans to introduce PR, but it is possible. Starmer may want to introduce PR, but he might be blocked from doing this by senior Labour people that are against PR, in the same way Blair was. Starmer, of course, may have no intention of reforming the voting system. Either way, the democracy movement must keep up the pressure on the Labour leadership and MPs to make it more likely.

What Do We Do If Starmer Refuses To Introduce PR?

To get PR, we first need Labour to win the next election. Assuming that's been achieved, the democracy movement needs to pressure the Labour Party to add implementing PR to the manifesto for the next election, likely in 2028. Even though the Labour Party Conference supported the PR motion in 2022, the leadership decides what goes on in the general election party manifestos.

How do we apply pressure on the Labour Party to get PR? Labour governments and MPs are more vulnerable than you may think if people are willing to be strategic and focused. For example, the campaign group Indivisible in the US has shown what is possible by targeting Republican Party Congress representatives during the Trump Presidency to undermine his right-wing agenda. This involved lobbying through mass email and phone call drives, turning up at these representatives' offices and public events, politely holding them to account, and making a fuss on important issues.

This strategy could be used against Labour MPs after the next election. Each Labour MP could be categorised based on their support for PR. There would be those that publicly support PR, those that are publicly against and those that are undecided. Those MPs that support PR can be celebrated. Local groups could be set up in each seat with a Labour MP that does not publicly support changing the voting system to apply pressure to change their position. The Indivisible tactics could be adopted to get large numbers of average local constituents to email and call these Labour MPs. The more committed could turn up at MPs' offices, surgeries and local public events, politely asking them difficult questions about their anti-PR position and how it is not in the interests of their voters.

Another approach is 'deep canvassing', pioneered in the US in response to Californians voting against gay marriage in 2008, with great success. This tactic involves one-to-one conversations with voters that create lasting changes in how people vote by shifting their underlying emotions and attitudes that determine their political views. These conversations generally take place on the doorstep or the phone.[31] Deep canvassing could be used by local democracy groups in Labour seats to knock on doors and have open discussions with voters about the benefits of introducing PR and the need to apply pressure on Labour MPs to get it. Not everyone would be on board, but many would already be supportive or open to being convinced. Some would want to take action, and there would be a range of things people can do: talk to their family and friends, post about it on social media, contact their MP, attend a local meeting, event or protest.

Ideally, pro-PR campaigners would convince enough sections of the Labour Party that introducing PR is in the party's interests because, sadly, being in the country's interests is not enough for them. I prefer this approach, but based on the history of the Labour Party and the powerful groups in the party described above that are against introducing it, I'm doubtful this will be enough. A third strategy takes things a bit further. Once Labour is in power, we must apply pressure in multiple ways to get them to bring in PR.

As well as putting pressure on MPs and the Labour leadership through lobbying, a PR political party could be set up to challenge Labour councillors, MPs, and candidates. This would present a credible threat at the ballot box for the 2028 (ish) general election. It would not target any Labour councillors or MPs (and candidates) who have publicly stated their support for Labour introducing PR in the next parliament. The PR Party manifesto would have one demand: for the Labour Party to make a manifesto commitment for the 2028 general election to introduce PR in the next parliament (2028-2032) without a referendum. Following the 2024 general election when the

Tories have hopefully been removed, PR Party candidates could stand in local elections and by-elections against those Labour councillors, MPs and candidates that don't publicly back PR. If Labour has not committed to including introducing PR (STV/Open Party Lists) into the next general election Labour Party manifesto by the start of 2027, the PR Party could move forwards with standing candidates against Labour MPs and parliamentary candidates that do not publicly support Labour bringing in PR in the next parliament.

Democracy Groups Campaigning For PR

There are several groups you can join to campaign for PR:
- Inside the Labour Party, there is the Labour Campaign for Electoral Reform (LCER),[32] and its campaign Labour for a New Democracy (L4ND);[33]
- Compass is a member organisation that campaigns for PR in local groups nationwide and in political parties (Labour, Liberal Democrats, Greens);[34]
- Make Votes Matter is a cross-party group campaigning for PR, with local groups running street stalls to raise awareness of PR;[35]
- Get PR Done is another cross-party campaign for PR;
- Politics for the Many is a trade union campaign for political reform focusing on PR;[36]
- Two linked campaigns that I'm involved in are the Movement Forwards[37] and www.stopthetories.vote;
- Unlock Democracy campaigns to improve our democracy and for a new constitution.[38]
- The Electoral Reform Society campaigns for increasing our democratic rights.[39]

CONCLUSION

The Tories are driven to win elections, form governments, and hold onto power to maintain the social order and to stop Labour from forming governments that threaten this goal. This is because the Tories want to maintain the power and legitimacy of the elite and the wealthy and stop the redistribution of wealth. They do this in government by forcing their values and interests on society and blocking their opponents, the Labour Party, from promoting their values when in government.

I have two goals for this book: to show why the Tory Party is so good at winning elections, and how we can stop them. I have drilled down into the details of these two topics throughout the book, and below I have summarised the key themes.

Why Has The Tory Party Been So Successful?

Throughout the book, I have identified 18 reasons why the Tory Party has been so successful over the last 123 years. Here is a summary:

1. The British electoral system of First Past the Post (FPTP) benefits the Tories in several ways.
2. The Tory Party has a history of picking more credible leaders who have broad appeal to voters and win elections.
3. The Tory Party stays united in public to keep winning.
4. The Tories are extremely adaptable and pragmatic and will do whatever is needed to win the next election.
5. Through the 20th century, when defeated, the Tory Party quickly devised a strategy to regain power.
6. The Tories have a history of superior party organisation at

the national, regional and local levels.
7. The Tory Party is the political organisation of the rich to protect their interests. The party is, therefore, well funded by corporations, the financial sector and wealthy individuals so it can outspend its opponents on election campaigns, helping the party win more elections.
8. The Tory Party's electoral dominance results in a self-reinforcing perception that they are seen as the natural party of government.
9. The Tory Party have developed a method of statecraft to win elections and hold onto power once in government.
10. The Tories' convincing project governing and economic competence.
11. The Tories have proved effective at manufacturing Tory voters over the long term.
12. The Tories use underhand tactics to explain away their failure to govern in people's interests and keep winning elections. These include distraction and blaming others, inventing domestic and foreign enemies that only the Tories can save the country from, crushing opponents in opposition parties or the trade unions, and using dirty tricks and illegal methods to keep winning.
13. The Tories produce appealing electoral programmes and manifestos.
14. The Tory Party have developed more effective electioneering techniques than their opponents over the last 123 years.
15. There is a direct relationship between the Tories' success at winning elections and staying in power for long periods and the right-wing media bias in their favour.
16. The Tories have proven more effective at building voter coalitions than the Labour Party.
17. The Tories are better at appealing to swing voters than their opposition through emotions and values, creating fear about the Labour Party, and appealing to self-interest.
18. The Tories win more elections because the Labour Party has been a weaker opponent over the long term.

Stopping The Tories

In the final two chapters, I propose how we stop the Tories in the short and long term. Here is a summary.

To stop the Tories in the short term, we need mass tactical voting to remove Tory MPs at the next election. The next election will likely be in 2024 in the Spring or Autumn. This will be a defensive election for the Tories, trying to minimise their losses and an offensive one for the opposition parties. Chapter 21 shows the long history of tactical voting against the Tories that has been getting more pronounced over the years. There are now multiple anti-Tory tactical voting websites, including the one I'm involved in, https://stopthetories.vote/, to help with this. Following the 2023 local elections disaster for the Tories, where they lost over 1,000 Councillors, the consensus is that we're heading for a Labour majority government. But we can't be complacent; the Tories' general election campaign will reduce Labour's opinion poll lead. Combine this with the Tories' boundary changes to the parliamentary seats and the introduction of voter ID at polling stations to help them win more seats. We can't assume anything and must work on the basis that those that oppose the Tories must do everything possible to remove them.

Britain's political system is clearly broken and needs significant reform. It helps the Tories win more elections, who then wreck the country. Electoral reform is the key to bringing in the reforms we need, so they become permanent and weaken the Tories. We need a strong form of proportional representation (PR), either Single Transferable Vote or Open Party Lists. Introducing PR would improve our politics in multiple ways, with more progressive governments and fewer Tory governments. It would force those Tory governments to be more moderate to win power. It would also help reduce the extreme inequality in Britain and improve living standards. Finally, it would help protect new progressive reforms and make governments more accountable to voters.

To stop the Tories long term, we need broad and deep political and constitutional reform, including electoral reform, extending voting to those 16 and over, House of Lords reform and replacement, election spending reform, media reform, devolving powers from our over-centralised state, new laws to hold governments to account for any damaging policies and any abuses of power, protect the independence of the judiciary, strengthen the Human Rights Act to protect our rights, and we need all these reforms included in a written, codified constitution.

The only party that might bring in PR is the Labour Party. The party's membership and the large trade unions have strongly backed PR. However, Labour leader Starmer has said it is not a priority for the next election. There is a rational caution to this, even if it would be better if Labour committed to electoral reform in next year's general election manifesto. Suppose we end up with a hung parliament after the next election. In that case, the Liberal Democrats may make this reform part of a negotiation to support a minority Labour government.

But, if the next Labour government forms and fails to introduce PR as part of their programme, then we must direct all our campaigning and lobbying towards the Labour Party leadership, MPs and Councillors. If by the late 2020s, Labour is still not committed to introducing PR in their second term in government; then it might be necessary to set up a PR Party to run against those Labour MPs and Councillors that do not publicly back PR. The goal would be to create a credible threat at the ballot box.

If there is one thing you take away from this book, it is that although the Tories are in a mess and likely to lose the next election, they will be back in 10-15 years after a period of 'modernisation', with a fresh-faced leader and 'moderate' policies, that appeal to swing voters. Voters will be tired of Labour, whoever replaces Starmer might not be up to the job, and voters will have forgotten how bad the Tories were. This future Tory government will certainly undo any redistributional and progressive improvements that Labour introduced. Labour's current policy proposals around devolution of power from Westminster, votes at 16 and reforming the House of Lords are moving in the right direction. But without electoral reform and replacing FPTP with PR, this future Tory government, in 10-15 years, will have just as much power as the current shameful excuse we call the government to destroy our country all over again.

ACKNOWLEDGEMENTS

I would like to thank Stephen Burley and Ade Williams for their very helpful feedback and encouragement. I would also like to thank my family and friends for their support. Most importantly, I would like to thank my best friend and partner Jay Wilkinson for their feedback, support, encouragement, understanding and love. I could not have published this book without all your help.

NOTES

Introduction

1. Phil Burton-Cartledge, Falling Down: The Conservative Party and the Decline of Tory Britain, Verso, 2021, Introduction.
2. Burton-Cartledge, Falling Down, Introduction.

1 The British Political Playing Field

1. Andrew Heywood, Political Ideologies: An Introduction by, 4th edition, Palgrave Macmillan, 2007, 23-62.
2. Jamie Parker, Painting Britain Blue: Why the Conservatives Keep Winning & How Labour Let Them, Silverwood Books, 2021, Chapter 10.
3. Electoral Reform Society, First Past the Post, https://www.electoral-reform.org.uk/
4. Wikipedia, First-past-the-post voting, https://en.wikipedia.org/wiki/Main_Page
5. Institute for Government, Government majority, https://www.instituteforgovernment.org.uk/
6. Electoral Reform Society, First Past the Post, https://www.electoral-reform.org.uk
7. Electoral Reform Society, First Past the Post, https://www.electoral-reform.org.uk
8. Phil Moorhouse, Are the Tories Poisoning Their Own Well? A Different Bias, 2022, https://www.youtube.com
9. Phil Moorhouse, Live Political Discussion on NYE, A Different Bias, 2022, https://youtu.be/6uRc9L6zsIY

10. Frank Cooney, Gary Hughes, David Sheerin, Higher Modern Studies: Democracy in Scotland and the UK, Hodder Gibson, 2016, 32; Lizzy Buchan, First past the post: What is the UK's voting system and how does it work? The Independent, 2018, https://www.independent.co.uk/
11. Cooney et al, Higher Modern Studies: Democracy in Scotland and the UK, 32; Wikipedia, First-past-the-post voting, https://en.wikipedia.org; Makes Votes Matter, First Past the Post, https://www.makevotesmatter.org.uk; Laura Parker, Why first-past-the-post steals elections for right-wing parties – and how to stop it, The New Statesman, 2021, https://www.newstatesman.com
12. John Ramsden, An Appetite for Power: A New History of the Conservative Party, HarperCollins, 1998, 494.
13. A.J. Davies, We, The Nation: The Conservative Party and the Pursuit of Power, Little, Brown, 1995, 217; Ramsden, An Appetite for Power, 6.
14. Christopher Kirkland, How important is turnout in a UK election? The recent actions of the parties give you a good idea, 2019, https://theconversation.com; Matthew Flinders, Low voter turnout is clearly a problem, but a much greater worry is the growing inequality of that turnout, 2014, https://blogs.lse.ac.uk; Politics.co.uk, Election Turnout, https://www.politics.co.uk
15. Anthony Seldon and Stuart Ball, The Conservative Century: The Conservative Party since 1900, Academic, 1994, Chapter 1, Chapter 15.
16. D. E. Butler and Anthony King, The British General Election of 1964, St. Martin's Press, 1965; D. E. Butler and Anthony King, The British General Election of 1966, Macmillan, 1966; David Butler and Dennis Kavanagh, The British General Election of 1979, Holmes & Meier Pub, 1982; David Butler and Dennis Kavanagh, The British General Election of 1992, Palgrave Macmillan, 1992; David Butler and Dennis Kavanagh, The British General Election of 1997, Palgrave Macmillan, 1997; Philip Cowley and Dennis Kavanagh, The British General Election of 2010, Palgrave Macmillan, 2010; Philip Cowley and Dennis Kavanagh, The British General

Election of 2015, Palgrave Macmillan, 2015; Philip Cowley and Dennis Kavanagh, The British General Election of 2017, Palgrave Macmillan, 2018; Robert Ford, Tim Bale, Will Jennings, The British General Election of 2019, Palgrave Macmillan, 2021.

2 Overview Of Tory Success Since 1900

1. Geoffrey Wheatcroft, The Strange Death of Tory England, Allen Lane, 2005, 21.
2. Stuart Ball and Anthony Seldon, Recovering Power: The Conservatives in Opposition Since 1867, Palgrave Macmillan, 2005, 2.
3. Seldon and Ball, The Conservative Century, Chapter 1; Tim Bale, The Conservative Party: From Thatcher to Cameron, Polity Press, 2016.
4. Bale, The Conservative Party: From Thatcher to Cameron, Chapter 7.
5. Cowley and Kavanagh, The British General Election of 2015, Chapter 14.
6. Burton-Cartledge, Falling Down, Chapter 7.
7. Cowley and Kavanagh, The British General Election of 2017, 464.

Part 2 The Tory Party's Main Objective Is Winning General Elections And Power

1. Samuel Earle, Tory Nation: How one party took over, Simon & Schuster UK, 2023, Chapter 1, Chapter 3.

3 Select Leaders Most Likely To Win General Elections

1. Bale, The Conservative Party: From Thatcher to Cameron, Introduction.
2. Davies, We, The Nation, 97-8.
3. Ramsden, An Appetite for Power, 496-7.
4. Anthony Seldon, Why Liz Truss will fail, 2022, New Statesman, https://www.newstatesman.com/
5. Parker, Painting Britain Blue, Chapter 8.
6. Parker, Painting Britain Blue, Chapter 8.
7. Seldon, Recovering Power, 5.
8. Davies, We, The Nation, 66-67.
9. Davies, We, The Nation, 75.
10. Tess Reidy, Why the Tories Always Win, Vice, 2017, https://www.vice.com/en; John Oxley, Can anyone save the Tory party? The New Statesman, 2022, https://www.newstatesman.com

4 Staying United In Public Above All Else

1. Stuart Ball and Ian Holliday, Mass Conservatism: The Conservatives and the Public since the 1880s, Routledge, 2002, 13.
2. Andrew Gimson, Why the Tories keep winning, The New Statesman, 2017, https://www.newstatesman.com
3. Eric Caines, Heath and Thatcher in Opposition, Palgrave Macmillan, 2017, 282.
4. Andrew Gimson, Why the Tories keep winning, The New Statesman, 2017, https://www.newstatesman.com
5. Andrew Gimson, Why the Tories keep winning, The New Statesman, 2017, https://www.newstatesman.com
6. Phil Moorhouse, Deadline for Next Election Extended by Over Half a Year, A Different Bias, 2022, https://youtu.be/ny68g1-EGgM
7. Anthony Seldon, How Tory Governments Fall: The Tory

Party in Power Since 1783, Fontana Press, 1996, Introduction.
8. John Oxley, Can anyone save the Tory party? The New Statesman, 2022, https://www.newstatesman.com
9. Parker, Painting Britain Blue, Chapter 8.
10. Seldon and Ball, The Conservative Century, 22.

5 Adaptability And Pragmatic

1. Tess Reidy, Why the Tories Always Win, Vice, 2017, https://www.vice.com/en
2. Andrew Gimson, Why the Tories keep winning, The New Statesman, 2017, https://www.newstatesman.com
3. Seldon and Ball, The Conservative Century, 34, 40.
4. Davies, We, The Nation, 449.
5. Bagehot, Britain's Tories are the world's most successful party. Here's why, The Economist, 2019, https://www.economist.com/
6. Steve Ludlam and Martin J. Smith, Contemporary British Conservatism, Palgrave Macmillan, 1995, 5, 67; Parker, Painting Britain Blue, Chapter 8; Tim Bale, Why is the Conservative Party so good at winning? UK in a Changing Europe, 2019, https://ukandeu.ac.uk/; Andrew Gamble, Adapt or die: how the Conservative party keeps power, The Guardian, 2019, https://www.theguardian.com/uk
7. Tim Bale, Why is the Conservative Party so good at winning? UK in a Changing Europe, 2019, https://ukandeu.ac.uk/; Andrew Gimson, Why the Tories keep winning, The New Statesman, 2017, https://www.newstatesman.com
8. Ball and Holliday, Mass Conservatism, 27, Chapter 7.
9. Solomon Hughes, The Tories' War on the NHS, Tribune Magazine, 2019, https://tribunemag.co.uk/
10. Ash Sarkar and Samuel Earle, Why The Tories Keep Winning, Novara Media, 2021, https://www.youtube.com/
11. Tim Bale, Why is the Conservative Party so good at

winning? UK in a Changing Europe, 2019, https://ukandeu.ac.uk/; Samuel Earle, The Sordid Story of the Most Successful Political Party in the World, The New Republic, 2021, https://newrepublic.com/; John Charmley, A History of Conservative Politics Since 1830, Red Globe Press, 2008, 3-4.
12. Seldon, How Tory Governments Fall.
13. Ball and Holliday, Mass Conservatism, 12.
14. Caines, Heath and Thatcher in Opposition, 8.
15. Tess Reidy, Why the Tories Always Win, Vice, 2017, https://www.vice.com/en
16. Ludlam and Smith, Contemporary British Conservatism, 6.
17. Laura Marsh, Alex Pareene, Samuel Earle, Ash Sarkar, The Cousinhood That Still Rules Britain, The New Republic, 2021, https://newrepublic.com/
18. Tim Bale, The Conservatives since 1945: The Drivers of Party Change, Oxford University Press, 2012, Chapter 8.
19. Bale, The Conservative Party: From Thatcher to Cameron, Chapter 1.

6 Quickly Regain Power Following A Defeat

1. Ball and Seldon, Recovering Power, 1-2.
2. Ball and Seldon, Recovering Power, 2-5.
3. Ball and Seldon, Recovering Power, 7.
4. Bale, The Conservatives since 1945, 297, 303; Parker, Painting Britain Blue, Chapter 8.
5. Bale, The Conservatives since 1945, 298.

7 Effective Party Organisation

1. Seldon and Ball, The Conservative Century, Introduction.
2. Seldon and Ball, The Conservative Century, Chapter 7.
3. Seldon and Ball, The Conservative Century, Chapter 7.
4. Seldon and Ball, The Conservative Century, Chapter 5.

5. The Conservative and Unionist Party, Party Structure and Organisation, https://www.conservatives.com; Burton-Cartledge, Falling Down, Introduction; Wikipedia, Conservative Party Organisation, https://en.wikipedia.org/; Seldon and Ball, The Conservative Century, Chapter 5.
6. Seldon and Ball, The Conservative Century, Chapter 6.
7. Tim Bale, Tory leadership: Who gets to choose the UK's next prime minister? BBC, 2019, https://www.bbc.co.uk/; Seldon and Ball, The Conservative Century, Chapter 7; BBC, Conservative membership has nearly halved under Cameron, 2013, https://www.bbc.co.uk/; Burton-Cartledge, Falling Down; Wikipedia, Conservative Party Organisation, https://en.wikipedia.org
8. Davies, We, The Nation, 183-4.
9. Seldon and Ball, The Conservative Century, 281-4.

8 The Party Of The Rich

1. Burton-Cartledge, Falling Down, Chapter 1.
2. Seldon and Ball, The Conservative Century, 52; Seldon, How Tory Governments Fall, Introduction.
3. Sam Bright, Hardeep Matharu, Katie Tarrant, Max Colbert, Daisy Bata, Iain Overton, Mapping the Pandemic: £1 Billion in Contracts Awarded to Conservative Donors, Bylines Times and The Citizens, 2021, https://bylinetimes.com/
4. Davies, We, The Nation, Chapter 7; Joe Mellor, 'Cash-for-access culture:' Leaked docs reveal Tory donors given access to PM's top team, The London Economic, 2022, https://www.thelondoneconomic.com/; Rob Merrick, Conservatives branded 'party of billionaires' as one-third of UK's richest people donate to Tories, The Independent, 2019, https://www.independent.co.uk/
5. Yougov, How close is the Conservative Party to rich people? 2023, https://yougov.co.uk/
6. Ludlam and Smith, Contemporary British Conservatism, Chapter 5.

7. Peter Geoghegan, Why are so many Tory MPs able to get filthy rich? Because we let them, The Guardian, 2021, https://www.theguardian.com/uk; Rowena Mason, At least a quarter of Tory MPs have second jobs, earning over £4m a year, The Guardian, 2021, https://www.theguardian.com/uk; Craig Meighan, Richest Conservative MPs listed as second jobs bring in up to £1m each, The National, 2021, https://www.thenational.scot/
8. Liam Doyle, Tory MPs net worth ranked: The 10 richest Government ministers, The Express, 2022, https://www.express.co.uk/
9. Davies, We, The Nation, Chapter 7; The Electoral Commission, Donations and loans, https://www.electoralcommission.org.uk/
10. Stephen Crone and Stuart Wilks-Heeg, Just 50 'donor groups' have supplied over half of the Conservative party's declared donation income in the last decade, a fact disguised by legal 'fame avoidance' techniques, LSE Blogs, 2010, https://blogs.lse.ac.uk/
11. Rajeev Syal, Jill Treanor and Nick Mathiason, City's influence over Conservatives laid bare by research into donations, The Guardian, 2011, https://www.theguardian.com/uk
12. BBC, Labour was best-funded UK political party in 2013, 2014, https://www.bbc.co.uk/
13. Nicholas Watt and Patrick Wintour, Conservative party 'bankrolled by hedge fund managers', The Guardian, 2015, https://www.theguardian.com/uk
14. The Construction Index, Tories boosted by construction donations, 2017, https://www.theconstructionindex.co.uk/
15. Peter Geoghegan, Seth Thévoz and Jenna Corderoy, Revealed: The elite dining club behind £130m+ donations to the Tories, openDemocracy, 2019, https://www.opendemocracy.net/en/uk/
16. Peter Walker, Tories have unhealthy financial reliance on property developers, says report, The Guardian, 2021, https://www.theguardian.com/uk
17. Peter Geoghegan, Seth Thévoz and Jenna Corderoy,

Revealed: The elite dining club behind £130m+ donations to the Tories, openDemocracy, 2019, https://www.opendemocracy.net/en/uk/
18. Rob Merrick, Conservatives branded 'party of billionaires' as one-third of UK's richest people donate to Tories, The Independent, 2019, https://www.independent.co.uk/
19. The Electoral Commission, Financial accounts published for UK's larger political parties, https://www.electoralcommission.org.uk/
20. Adam Forrest, 'Concentrated power': 25% of Tory Party's individual donations come from just 10 people, The Independent, 2021, https://www.independent.co.uk/
21. Ella Glover and Lamiat Sabin, New Tory sleaze row amid report donors who pay £3m get seats in House of Lords, The Independent, 2021, https://www.independent.co.uk/
22. Mikey Smith, '12 Donors of Tory Christmas' who've found gongs or privileged access under the tree, The Mirror, 2021, https://www.mirror.co.uk/
23. Katie Elliott, The 6 Russian oligarchs who donated £2m to Tory party since Boris became PM, The Express, 2022, https://www.express.co.uk/; Rowena Mason and Harry Davies, Labour writes to Tory chair over donations to 34 MPs by firms named in Pandora papers, The Guardian, 2021, https://www.theguardian.com/uk; Jane Bradley, Major Donation to U.K. Conservative Party Was Flagged Over Russia Concerns, The New York Times, 2022, https://www.nytimes.com/
24. Gabrielle Pickard-Whitehead, Who is Michael Hintze? The Tory funder and climate sceptic about to be made a Lord, The Big Issue, 2022, https://bigissue.com/

Part 3 How Tories Govern To Ensure Winning The Next Election

1. TLDR News, Three Reasons the Conservatives Will Keep Winning Elections, 2021, https://youtu.be/-QHwvxJp-b8

9 The Tory Party Presents Itself As The Natural Party Of Government

1. Ball and Holliday, Mass Conservatism, 2.
2. Ball and Holliday, Mass Conservatism, 11-12.
3. Ludlam and Smith, Contemporary British Conservatism, 38.
4. Earle, Tory Nation, Chapter 2.
5. Ludlam and Smith, Contemporary British Conservatism, Chapter 7.
6. Ash Sarkar and Samuel Earle, Why The Tories Keep Winning, Novara Media, 2021, https://www.youtube.com
7. Seldon, How Tory Governments Fall, Introduction.
8. Ball and Holliday, Mass Conservatism, 11-12; Ash Sarkar and Samuel Earle, Why The Tories Keep Winning, Novara Media, 2021, https://www.youtube.com/
9. Andrew Gamble, The Conservative Nation, Routledge, 2014, Chapter 8.
10. Davies, We, The Nation, Chapter 13.
11. Robert Reiner, Who put politics into the police? LSE Blogs, 2010, https://blogs.lse.ac.uk/
12. Anoosh Chakelian, Why hasn't the Metropolitan Police brought Boris Johnson in for questioning? The New Statesman, 2022, https://www.newstatesman.com
13. Mark Garnett and Philip Lynch, The Conservatives in crisis: the Tories after 1997, Manchester University Press, 2003, Chapter 10.
14. Adam Ramsay, Why does England vote Tory? OpenDemocracy, 2020, https://www.opendemocracy.net/en/uk/
15. Davies, We, The Nation, 350.
16. Davies, We, The Nation, 351-2.
17. Nation Cymru, Conservative Party has become 'the English nationalist party' says former Welsh MP, 2020, https://nation.cymru/
18. Davies, We, The Nation, 360-1.
19. Davies, We, The Nation, Chapter 14.

20. Seldon, How Tory Governments Fall, Introduction.
21. Parker, Painting Britain Blue Chapter 1.
22. Anthony Barnett, Iron Britannia, Allison & Busby, 1982; Andy Beckett, Promised You A Miracle: Why 1980-82 Made Modern Britain, Penguin, 2016.

10 Tory Statecraft

1. Jim Bulpitt, The Discipline of the New Democracy, Mrs Thatcher's Domestic Statecraft, Political Studies, Vol. 34, No. 1 (1986): 19-39.
2. C. Stevens, Thatcherism, Majorism and the Collapse of Tory Statecraft, Contemporary British History, Volume 16, Issue 1 (2002): 119-150.
3. Andrew Gamble, The Free Economy and the Strong State: The Politics of Thatcherism, Duke Univ Pr, 1988, 141.
4. Gamble, The Free Economy and the Strong State, 152-3; Alexander Gallas, Thatcherite Offensive: A Neo-Poulantzasian Analysis, Haymarket Books, 2017.
5. Gamble, The Free Economy and the Strong State, 143-4.
6. Gamble, The Free Economy and the Strong State, 4, 152.
7. Gamble, The Free Economy and the Strong State, 150-1.
8. Gamble, The Free Economy and the Strong State, 162.
9. Gamble, The Free Economy and the Strong State, 167.
10. Bulpitt, The Discipline of the New Democracy, Mrs Thatcher's Domestic Statecraft.
11. Stevens, Thatcherism, Majorism and the Collapse of Tory Statecraft, Contemporary British History.
12. Stevens, Thatcherism, Majorism and the Collapse of Tory Statecraft, Contemporary British History.
13. Stevens, Thatcherism, Majorism and the Collapse of Tory Statecraft, Contemporary British History.
14. Bulpitt, The Discipline of the New Democracy, Mrs Thatcher's Domestic Statecraft.
15. Bulpitt, The Discipline of the New Democracy, Mrs Thatcher's Domestic Statecraft.
16. Peter Dorey, Mark Garnett and Andrew Denham, From

Crisis to Coalition: The Conservative Party, 1997-2010, Palgrave Macmillan, 2011, 19; Ball and Holliday, Mass Conservatism, Chapter 12.
17. Stevens, Thatcherism, Majorism and the Collapse of Tory Statecraft, Contemporary British History.
18. Stevens, Thatcherism, Majorism and the Collapse of Tory Statecraft, Contemporary British History.
19. Ball and Seldon, Recovering Power, 26-30; Richard Hayton, Conservative Party Statecraft and the Johnson Government, The Political Quarterly, Volume 92, Issue 3 (2021): 412-419.
20. Hayton, Conservative Party Statecraft and the Johnson Government.

11 Project Governing And Economic Competence

1. The Politics Shed, Governing competency, 2017, https://thepoliticsteacher.org
2. Parker, Painting Britain Blue, Chapter 6.
3. Ball and Seldon, Recovering Power, 20.
4. Ben Walker, Who do we trust to run the economy? The New Statesman, 2022, https://www.newstatesman.com
5. Ball and Holliday, Mass Conservatism, 222.
6. Ludlam and Smith, Contemporary British Conservatism, 57; Trinh Tu, Britons support paying more tax to fund public services – most popular being a new net wealth tax, Ipsos, 2020, https://www.ipsos.com/en-uk
7. Ball and Seldon, Recovering Power, 20.
8. Parker, Painting Britain Blue, Chapter 8.
9. Ball and Seldon, Recovering Power, 20.
10. Tess Reidy, Why the Tories Always Win, Vice, 2017, https://www.vice.com/en
11. Davies, We, The Nation, 277, 278, 300.
12. Davies, We, The Nation.we the Nation, 278; Phil Moorhouse, Data Shows How Tories Have Suppressed Incomes Over the Past Decade, A Different Bias, 2023, https://www.youtube.com/
13. Phil Moorhouse, Sunak First Impressions and How Labour

May Tackle Him, A Different Bias, 2023, https://youtu.be/ljnr8qdCFe0; Phil Moorhouse, Alternatives to Sunak's Austerity Budget Plans, A Different Bias, 2023, https://www.youtube.com/; Phil Moorhouse, Politics Live: Discussing Rishi Sunak's Government and Brexit, 2023, https://www.youtube.com/
14. Richard Murphy, The Tories have always borrowed more than Labour, and always repaid less: they are the party of big deficit spending, Funding the Future, 2021, https://www.taxresearch.org.uk/Blog/

12 Manufacturing Tory Voters

1. Davies, We, The Nation, Chapter 12.
2. Hugh Bochel, Whatever happened to compassionate Conservatism? LSE Blogs, 2010, https://blogs.lse.ac.uk/
3. Laurie Macfarlane, The Unmaking of the British Working Class, Jacobin, 2019, https://jacobin.com/
4. Davies, We, The Nation, 304.
5. Ball and Holliday, Mass Conservatism, 62.
6. Ball and Holliday, Mass Conservatism, 62-3.
7. Ball and Holliday, Mass Conservatism, 65-7.
8. Laurie Macfarlane, The Unmaking of the British Working Class, Jacobin, 2019, https://jacobin.com/
9. Burton-Cartledge, Falling Down, Chapter 2.
10. Laurie Macfarlane, The Unmaking of the British Working Class, Jacobin, 2019, https://jacobin.com/
11. Parker, Painting Britain Blue, Chapter 1; Laurie Macfarlane, The Unmaking of the British Working Class, Jacobin, 2019, https://jacobin.com/
12. Laurie Macfarlane, The Unmaking of the British Working Class, Jacobin, 2019, https://jacobin.com/
13. Burton-Cartledge, Falling Down.Falling Down, Conclusion.
14. Burton-Cartledge, Falling Down.Falling Down, Chapter 2.
15. Phil Moorhouse, PMQs: Partygate and Cost of Living Questions Deflected by Johnson, A Different Bias, 2022, https://youtu.be/eXWr49C-gjE

16. Davies, We, The Nation, 300-3.
17. Jonquil Lowe, ELECTION 2017: Why the pensions 'triple lock' has become a key general election issue, Bedford Today, 2017, https://www.bedfordtoday.co.uk/
18. Burton-Cartledge, Falling Down, 365.
19. The New Statesman, Leader: The price of Conservative rule, 2022, https://www.newstatesman.com; Annette Hastings, Nick Bailey, Glen Bramley, Maria Gannon & David Watkins, The cost of the cuts: the impact on local government and poorer communities, Joseph Rowntree Foundation, 2015, https://www.jrf.org.uk/; Kate Ogden, David Phillips, Luke Sibieta, Max Warner and Ben Zaranko, Does funding follow need? An analysis of the geographic distribution of public spending in England, Institute for Fiscal Studies, 2022, https://ifs.org.uk/
20. Peter Walker, Pamela Duncan, Steven Morris, Helen Pidd and Jessica Murray, Tories accused of levelling up 'stitch-up' over regional deprivation fund, The Guardian, 2021, https://www.theguardian.com/uk
21. Freddie Hayward, Labour demands investigation into Rishi Sunak's comments on taking money from "deprived urban areas", The New Statesman, 2022, https://www.newstatesman.com
22. Ben Chu and Hannah Barnes, Tory and marginal seats benefit most from PM's spending, data shows, BBC, 2019, https://www.bbc.co.uk/
23. Benjamin Kentish, Government funding for 'left behind' towns being spent in wealthier Tory marginals, analysis reveals, The Independent, 2019, https://www.independent.co.uk/
24. Seldon and Ball, The Conservative Century, Chapter 15.
25. Adam Forrest, Tories will gain 'five to 10 extra seats' with boundary changes, says expert, The Independent, 2021, https://www.independent.co.uk/; Neil Johnston and Elise Uberoi, Constituency boundary reviews and the number of MPs, House of Commons Library, 2022, https://commonslibrary.parliament.uk/
26. Toby James and Oliver Sidorczuk, The next generation of

voters? Getting the 'Missing Millions' back on to the UK's electoral register, LSE Blogs, 2010, https://blogs.lse.ac.uk/
27. Owen Jones, Time for decent Tories to speak up. Our democracy is being rigged, The Guardian, 2015, https://www.theguardian.com/uk
28. Peter Walker, Election bill could cut millions from Labour campaign spending, say unions, The Guardian, 2021, https://www.theguardian.com/uk; Helen Pearce, The elections bill is a brazen attack on our trade unions – it must be stopped, Labour List, 2021, https://labourlist.org/; Naomi Smith, Frances O'Grady, Nick Lowles, Kirsty McNeill, Dr Mary Bousted, Kevin Courtney, Mick Whelan, Ben Stewart, Tom Bruffato, Sam Grant, Iain Smith, Elections Bill branded 'power grab' by charities, unions and campaigners, Best for Britain, 2021, https://www.bestforbritain.org/

13 Distract, Invent Enemies, Dirty Tricks, Crush Opponents

1. Davies, We, The Nation, 239-40.
2. Davies, We, The Nation, 319.
3. Clive Bloom, Thatcher's Secret War: Subversion, Coercion, Secrecy and Government, 1974-90, The History Press, 2021, Chapter 27; Another Angry Voice, The blame the victim fallacy, 2012, https://anotherangryvoice.blogspot.com/
4. Gamble, The Free Economy and the Strong State, 165.
5. Davies, We, The Nation, We the Nation, 339.
6. Stevens, Thatcherism, Majorism and the Collapse of Tory Statecraft, Contemporary British History; Wikipedia, Back to Basics (campaign), https://en.wikipedia.org/
7. Channel 4 News, Cameron unveils immigrant benefits crackdown, 2013, https://www.channel4.com/news/
8. Another Angry Voice, Political Myth Busting: The "always cleaning up Labour's messes" narrative, 2014, https://anotherangryvoice.blogspot.com/; Another Angry

Voice, The "bankrupt Britain" lie, 2016, https://anotherangryvoice.blogspot.com/; Another Angry Voice, The fallacy of "market confidence" in austerity, 2012, https://anotherangryvoice.blogspot.com/
9. Samuel Earle, The Sordid Story of the Most Successful Political Party in the World, The New Republic, 2021, https://newrepublic.com/
10. Hayton, Conservative Party Statecraft and the Johnson Government; Sam Fowles, Conservative Leadership: A Summer of Invented Enemies? Politics.co.uk, 2022, https://www.politics.co.uk/
11. Larry Elliott, Blaming Labour won't work this time – the Tories will have to own this crisis, The Guardian, 2020, https://www.theguardian.com/uk
12. Kate Nicholson, Tories Are Being Called Out For Blaming Labour For The Strikes... Despite 12 Years In Power, Huff Post, 2022, https://www.huffingtonpost.co.uk/; Michael Walker, The Tories Can't Stop Lying About Rail Strikes, Novara Media, 2022, https://www.youtube.com
13. Will Dunn, The Tories are trying to blame the Bank of England for our economic crisis, The New Statesman, 2022, https://www.newstatesman.com
14. Sam Fowles, Conservative Leadership: A Summer of Invented Enemies? Politics.co.uk, 2022, https://www.politics.co.uk/
15. Phil Moorhouse, 6 Urgent Problems for Truss to Deal With, A Different Bias, 2022, https://youtu.be/CUm4Dh9_weY
16. BDB Pitmans, When is a dead cat, not a dead cat? 2021, https://www.bdbpitmans.com/
17. Press Association, Labour urged to reopen Falkirk vote-rigging inquiry, The Guardian, 2013, https://www.theguardian.com/uk
18. George Eaton, PMQs review: Cameron's "bunch of migrants" was a dead cat to distract from Google, The New Statesman, 2016, https://www.newstatesman.com
19. Vox Political, Tories 'dead cat' claim about Corbyn hides huge PMQs defeat for May – over Brexit, 2018,

https://voxpoliticalonline.com/
20. Naomi Smith, Beware Boris's model bus: Daft "dead cat" stories mask real issues, Left Foot Forwards, 2019, https://leftfootforward.org/
21. Bell Gabriel, The Tories' Dead Cat, https://bellgabriel.wixsite.com/ringmybell
22. Jaymi McCann, Dead cat strategy meaning: Why critics claim new Covid rules are a distraction from No 10 Christmas Party row, i News, 2021, https://inews.co.uk/; Adam Forrest, Boris Johnson wants 'dead cat' plan B measures to distract from Christmas party, suggests Cummings, The Independent, 2021, https://www.independent.co.uk/
23. Sorcha Bradley, Is Boris Johnson using 'dead cat' strategy in latest Dominic Cummings row? The Week, 2021, https://www.theweek.co.uk/
24. Andrew Woodcock, Has Boris Johnson's blunder killed the dead cat diversion tactic? The Independent, 2022, https://www.independent.co.uk/
25. Jacob Thorburn, Labour and Tory MPs accuse Boris of rolling out 'unethical' Rwanda migrant plan as 'dead cat' strategy to dodge fury over PartyGate fine, The Daily Mail, 2022, https://www.dailymail.co.uk/home/index.html
26. Davies, We, The Nation., 233, 255.
27. Davies, We, The Nation, 229-30.
28. Davies, We, The Nation, 231-2.
29. Burton-Cartledge, Falling Down, 123.
30. Bloom, Thatcher's Secret War, Introduction; Adam Peggs, How Thatcher's Class War Remade the Tories, Tribune Magazine, 2021, https://tribunemag.co.uk/
31. Davies, We, The Nation, 339.
32. Wikipedia, Rate-capping rebellion, https://en.wikipedia.org
33. Davies, We, The Nation, 340; Wikipedia, Greater London Council, https://en.wikipedia.org
34. Wikipedia, Poll Tax 20th century, https://en.wikipedia.org
35. Burton-Cartledge, Falling Down, Chapter 2.
36. Yali Banton-Heath, Kill All The Bills, Tribune Magazine, 2021, https://tribunemag.co.uk/

37. Greg Barradale, The government's anti-protest bill is back. Here's what you might not know about it, The Big Issue, 2023, https://bigissue.com/
38. Davies, We, The Nation, 256.
39. Davies, We, The Nation, 222-226; Wikipedia, Zinoviev letter, https://en.wikipedia.org/wiki/Zinoviev_letter)
40. Davies, We, The Nation, 224.
41. Davies, We, The Nation, 240-54.

14 Appealing Electoral Programmes And Manifestos

1. Davies, We, The Nation, Chapter 8; Phil Moorhouse, Are Tory MPs in Too Deep With Johnson Now? A Different Bias, 2022 https://www.youtube.com
2. Phil Moorhouse, Sunak's Asylum Policy is Dangerous and Self-Defeating, A Different Bias, 2023 https://youtu.be/krnUy_nfTow; Phil Moorhouse, 30p Lee May Not be a Brilliant Strategist After All, A Different Bias, 2023, https://youtu.be/bTQXZHOzhp4; Phil Moorhouse, Live Political Discussion, A Different Bias, 2022, https://youtu.be/J1FFgGUjxFk
3. Kitty S Jones, Austerity, socio-economic entropy and being conservative with the truth, Politics and Insights, 2014, https://politicsandinsights.org/
4. Phil Moorhouse, Some Tories Worried About Truss Government, A Different Bias, 2022, https://www.youtube.com Phil Moorhouse, Brexit Protocol Helps Northern Ireland Recover from Covid, A Different Bias, 2022, https://www.youtube.com
5. Phil Moorhouse, Politics Live: Discussing Dishonest Politics, A Different Bias, 2022, https://youtu.be/W1xG1f4SSPQ; Phil Moorhouse, Labour Considering Abolishing House of Lords, A Different Bias, 2022, https://youtu.be/7tuU8_jWW9E; Biden Discusses Northern Ireland Protocol With Truss, A Different Bias, 2022, https://youtu.be/FBeBE4mP53Q
6. Greg Heffer, Cameron's 10 years as Tory leader: the highs, the lows & the broken promises, The Express, 2015,

https://www.express.co.uk/; Michael Savage, Cameron's decision to cut 'green crap' now costs each household in England £150 a year, The Guardian, 2022, https://www.theguardian.com/uk
7. Yvette Cooper, Nine Broken Promises From the First 100 Days of This Conservative Government, Huff Post, 2015, https://www.huffingtonpost.co.uk/
8. Dawn Foster, The Tory Lie Machine, Jacobin, 2019, https://jacobin.com/
9. BBC, Boris Johnson resignation: Did he meet his pledges as prime minister? https://www.bbc.co.uk/

15 Effective Electioneering Techniques

1. Phil Moorhouse, Live Political Discussion, A Different Bias, 2022, https://youtu.be/7keAa9O-5AY; Cowley and Kavanagh, The British General Election of 2015, 274; Cowley and Kavanagh, The British General Election of 2017, 411-413.
2. Davies, We, The Nation.We the Nation, 200, 240; Ludlam and Smith, Contemporary British Conservatism, 56.
3. Parker, Painting Britain Blue, Chapter 6.
4. Phil Moorhouse, Politics Live - Discussing the Stormont and Local Election Results, A Different Bias, 2022, https://youtu.be/WhD9fOu_Td4
5. Ivor Gaber, Strategic lying: the new game in town, Election Analysis, 2019, https://www.electionanalysis.uk/
6. Davies, We, The Nation, 196-7.
7. Davies, We, The Nation, Chapter 8; Ball and Holliday, Mass Conservatism, Chapter 5; Seldon and Ball, The Conservative Century, Chapter 14; Bale, The Conservatives since 1945, Conclusion; Ludlam and Smith, Contemporary British Conservatism, Chapter 3; Michael Pinto-Duschinsky, Paying for the Party Myths and realities in British political finance, Policy Exchange, 2008, https://policyexchange.org.uk/
8. Bale, The Conservative Party: From Thatcher to Cameron,

Chapter 7.
9. Cowley and Kavanagh, The British General Election of 2015, Chapters 2, 6, 10, 14; Andrew Mullen, Political consultants, their strategies and the importation of new political communications techniques during the 2015 General Election, Election Analysis, 2015, https://www.electionanalysis.uk/; Aisha Gani and Rowena Mason, Tories pumping £100,000 a month into Facebook advertising, The Guardian, 2015, https://www.theguardian.com/uk
10. Cowley and Kavanagh, The British General Election of 2017, Chapters 3, 12, 16; Joey D'Urso, Who spent what on Facebook during 2017 election campaign? BBC, 2018, https://www.bbc.co.uk/
11. Another Angry Voice, Is it time for Britain to adopt "geniocracy", 2023, https://anotherangryvoice.blogspot.com/
12. Ford et al, The British General Election of 2019, Chapters 3, 6, 15; Jay Blumler, What's the election communication system like now? Election Analysis, 2019, https://www.electionanalysis.uk/; The Economist, How the Conservatives won the social media campaign, 2020, https://www.economist.com/

16 How The Right-Wing Media Helps The Tories Win Elections

1. Raymond Kuhn, Politics and the Media in Britain, Red Globe Press, 2007, 237.
2. John Street, Mass Media, Politics and Democracy, Palgrave Macmillan, 2001, 161.
3. Sheerin, Higher Modern Studies: Democracy in Scotland and the UK Higher, 129.
4. Bill Jones, Philip Norton, Isabelle Hertner, Politics UK, Routledge, 2021, 218-20; Davies, We, The Nation, 203.
5. Sheerin, Higher Modern Studies: Democracy in Scotland and the UK Higher, 56.
6. Jones et al, Politics UK, Chapter 10; Samuel Earle, The

Sordid Story of the Most Successful Political Party in the World, The New Republic, 2021, https://newrepublic.com/
7. Sheerin, Higher Modern Studies: Democracy in Scotland and the UK Higher, 131.
8. Tom Chivers, Britain's Media Monopoly Is a Threat to Democracy, Tribune Magazine, 2021, https://tribunemag.co.uk/
9. Street, Mass Media, Politics and Democracy, Chapter 4; Jones et al, Politics UK, Chapter 10.
10. Wikipedia, Elections in the United Kingdom, The media influence debate, https://en.wikipedia.org
11. Kuhn, Politics and the Media in Britain, 259.
12. Street, Mass Media, Politics and Democracy, Chapter 4; Mass Media, Politics and Democracy; Kuhn, Politics and the Media in Britain, 177.
13. Kuhn, Politics and the Media in Britain, 259.
14. Ludlam and Smith, Contemporary British Conservatism, 44; Ralph Negrine, Politics and the Mass Media in Britain, Routledge, 2016, 172.
15. Owen Jones, The Establishment: And how they get away with it, Penguin, 2015, 88-9.
16. Butler and Kavanagh, The British General Election of 1992, 207.
17. Cowley and Kavanagh, The British General Election of 2010, 305.
18. Bart Cammaerts, Did Britain's right-wing newspapers win the election for the Tories? LSE Blog, 2015, https://blogs.lse.ac.uk/
19. Samuel Earle, The Sordid Story of the Most Successful Political Party in the World, The New Republic, 2021, https://newrepublic.com/
20. Sara Badawi, Murdoch's Long Shadow, Tribune Magazine, 2020, https://tribunemag.co.uk/
21. Alex Williams and Jeremy Gilbert, Hegemony Now: How Big Tech and Wall Street Won the World (And How We Win it Back), Verso, 2022, Chapter 5.
22. Silvo Lenart, Shaping political attitudes: the impact of interpersonal communication and mass media, SAGE

Publications, Inc, 1994, 16.
23. Williams and Gilbert, Hegemony Now, Chapter 5.
24. Natalie Fenton, How the British media helped Boris Johnson win, Aljazeera, 2019, https://www.aljazeera.com/
25. Street, Mass Media, Politics and Democracy, 113-117.
26. Negrine, Politics and the Mass Media in Britain, 177.
27. Phil Moorhouse, Will Elon Musk Knacker Twitter? A Different Bias, 2022 https://youtu.be/na_HZZDhp0M
28. Jones, The Establishment, 96.
29. Zarah Sultana, The Free Press Fantasy, Tribune Magazine, 2021, https://tribunemag.co.uk/
30. Jones, The Establishment, 98-99.
31. Natalie Fenton, Media policy, power and politics, Election Analysis, 2015, https://www.electionanalysis.uk/
32. Jones, The Establishment, 97-8.
33. Justin Schlosberg, Rupert Murdoch at 90, Tribune Magazine, 2021, https://tribunemag.co.uk/
34. Davies, We, The Nation, 203, 330.
35. Seldon and Ball, The Conservative Century, 560.
36. Davies, We, The Nation, 337-8.
37. Jones, The Establishment, 115-6.
38. Samuel Earle, The Sordid Story of the Most Successful Political Party in the World, The New Republic, 2021, https://newrepublic.com/; Jones, The Establishment, 101, 111.
39. Natalie Fenton, Media policy, power and politics, Election Analysis, 2015, https://www.electionanalysis.uk/
40. Nigel Norris, Revealed: Cameron's 26 meetings in 15 months with Murdoch chiefs, The Independent, 2011, https://www.independent.co.uk/
41. Justin Schlosberg, Rupert Murdoch at 90, Tribune Magazine, 2021, https://tribunemag.co.uk/
42. Hacked Off, Hacked Off The Press and The People with expert panel, YouTube, 2022, https://youtu.be/gMtUNnWie8k
43. Jones, The Establishment, 90.
44. Bart Cammaerts, Did Britain's right-wing newspapers win the election for the Tories? LSE Blog, 2015,

https://blogs.lse.ac.uk/
45. Sara Badawi, Murdoch's Long Shadow, Tribune Magazine, 2020, https://tribunemag.co.uk/
46. Davies, We, The Nation, 339.
47. Wikipedia, British Broadcasting Corporation (BBC), https://en.wikipedia.org/wiki/BBC; Freddy Mayhew, BBC warns decriminalising TV licence-fee evasion would cost it over £1bn and lead to cuts, Press Gazette, 2022, https://pressgazette.co.uk
48. Connor Parker, The Sun's Losses Triple As The Times Turns A Profit, Latest Figures Show, Huff Post, 2019, https://www.huffingtonpost.co.uk/
49. Steven Barnett, Four reasons why a partisan press helped win it for the Tories, Election Analysis, 2015, https://www.electionanalysis.uk/; Owen Jones, When Tory lies go unchallenged, democracy itself is in danger, The Guardian, 2020, https://www.theguardian.com/uk
50. Politics Theory Other, Hegemony Now (part two) - w/ Jeremy Gilbert, 2022, https://soundcloud.com
51. Butler and Kavanagh, The British General Election of 1992, 181.
52. Politics Theory Other, Hegemony Now (part two) - w/ Jeremy Gilbert, 2022, https://soundcloud.com
53. Politics Theory Other, Hegemony Now (part two) - w/ Jeremy Gilbert, 2022, https://soundcloud.com
54. Tom Blackburn, How GB News Will Shift our Media Further to the Right, Tribune Magazine, 2020, https://tribunemag.co.uk/
55. Williams and Gilbert, Hegemony Now, Chapter 5.
56. Steven Barnett, Four reasons why a partisan press helped win it for the Tories, Election Analysis, 2015, https://www.electionanalysis.uk/
57. Steve Barnett, Press distortion of public opinion polling: what can, or should, be done? Election Analysis, 2019, https://www.electionanalysis.uk/
58. Another Angry Voice, Analysing the Daily Express budget analysis, 2021, https://anotherangryvoice.blogspot.com/
59. Phil Moorhouse, Did Sunak Help a Russian Oligarch Evade

UK Sanctions? A Different Bias, 2023, https://youtu.be/Br-JvNzcj9w
60. Another Angry Voice, Theresa May and the British propaganda problem, 2017, https://anotherangryvoice.blogspot.com/
61. Samuel Earle, The Sordid Story of the Most Successful Political Party in the World, The New Republic, 2021, https://newrepublic.com/
62. Simon Wren-Lewis, Strong on the economy? The Tories are weak – and the media should say so, The Guardian, 2019, https://www.theguardian.com/uk
63. Another Angry Voice, Why do Tory MPs get a total free pass on their astounding anti-business attitudes? 2018, https://anotherangryvoice.blogspot.com/
64. Phil Moorhouse, Weak Pound Could Cause Problems for Truss's Energy Plan, A Different Bias, 2022, https://www.youtube.com
65. Phil Moorhouse, Braverman Caught Out in Asylum Lies, A Different Bias, 2022, https://youtu.be/HXr7gi7iras
66. Jones, The Establishment, 86; Samuel Earle, The Sordid Story of the Most Successful Political Party in the World, The New Republic, 2021, https://newrepublic.com/
67. Katie Hoare, What is media gaslighting? Happiful, 2021, https://happiful.com/
68. Lee Salter, 'This is cloud cuckoo': radical alternatives to public debt, Election Analysis, 2015, https://www.electionanalysis.uk/
69. Simon Wren-Lewis, Strong on the economy? The Tories are weak – and the media should say so, The Guardian, 2019, https://www.theguardian.com/uk

17 Factors Influencing Voting Behaviour

1. David Edgerton, Labour didn't lose its 'red wall' – it never had one, The Guardian, 2021, https://www.theguardian.com/uk
2. Selina Todd, The People: The Rise and Fall of the Working

Class, 1910-2010, John Murray, 2015, Introduction.
3. Seldon and Ball, The Conservative Century, Chapter 15.
4. Ramsden, An Appetite for Power, 353; Davies, We, The Nation, 217.
5. Politics Theory Other, Hegemony Now (part two) - w/ Jeremy Gilbert, 2022, https://soundcloud.com; David Edgerton, Labour didn't lose its 'red wall' – it never had one, The Guardian, 2021, https://www.theguardian.com/uk; Brendan O'Neill, Labour lost the working-class vote a long time ago, The Spectator, 2015, https://www.spectator.co.uk/
6. Butler and King, The British General Election of 1966; David Butler and Michael Pinto-Duschinsky, British General Election of 1970, Macmillan, 1971; David Butler and Dennis Kavanagh, The British General Election of October 1974, Macmillan, 1975; Butler and Kavanagh, The British General Election of 1992; Ford et al, The British General Election of 2019.
7. Butler and King, The British General Election of 1966, 264; Butler and Pinto-Duschinsky, British General Election of 1970, 342; Butler and Kavanag, The British General Election of October 1974, 278; Butler and Kavanagh, The British General Election of 1979, 343; Butler and Kavanagh, The British General Election of 1992, 277.
8. Seldon and Ball, The Conservative Century, 583; Sheerin, Higher Modern Studies: Democracy in Scotland and the UK Higher, 48.
9. Ball and Holliday, Mass Conservatism, 219-20; Sheerin, Higher Modern Studies: Democracy in Scotland and the UK Higher, 48.
10. Seldon and Ball, The Conservative Century, 581.
11. Seldon and Ball, The Conservative Century, 583; George Arnett, UK became more middle class than working class in 2000, data shows, The Guardian, 2016, https://www.theguardian.com/uk
12. Butler and King, The British General Election of 1966; Butler and Pinto-Duschinsky, British General Election of 1970; Butler and Kavanag, The British General Election of October 1974; Butler and Kavanagh, The British General

Election of 1992.
13. Sheerin, Higher Modern Studies: Democracy in Scotland and the UK Higher, 50-1; Ford et al, The British General Election of 2019, 532.
14. Ford et al, The British General Election of 2019, 532; The Economist, Who are the Conservatives' new voters in the north? 2019, https://www.economist.com/
15. Cowley and Kavanagh, The British General Election of 2017, 419.
16. British Election Study, Age and voting behaviour at the 2019 General Election, 2021, https://www.britishelectionstudy.com/
17. Seldon and Ball, The Conservative Century, Chapter 16.
18. Ford et al, The British General Election of 2019, 501; Jessica Smith, Boris's missing women, Election Analysis, 2019, https://www.electionanalysis.uk/; The Economist, Who are the Conservatives' new voters in the north? 2019, https://www.economist.com/; Sheerin, Higher Modern Studies: Democracy in Scotland and the UK Higher, 51.
19. Davies, We, The Nation, 217.
20. Davies, We, The Nation, 145.
21. Lucy Skoulding, General Election 2019: Why London votes Labour when the rest of the UK votes Conservative, My London, 2019, https://www.mylondon.news/
22. Parker, Painting Britain Blue, Chapter 8.
23. Cowley and Kavanagh, The British General Election of 2017, 427.
24. Rachel Wearmouth, Tories Resurgent In Post-Industrial Towns As Brexit Redraws UK Political Map - New Report, Huff Post, 2017, https://www.huffingtonpost.co.uk/; Ross McGuinness, Labour losing ex-industrial and university towns to Conservatives ahead of general election, says poll, Yahoo News, 2019, https://uk.news.yahoo.com/
25. Peter Kellner, Why Northerners don't vote Tory, YouGov, 2013, https://yougov.co.uk/; Ryan Swift, Why did Labour lose in the north of England? The Conversation, 2019, https://theconversation.com/uk; Gamble, The Free Economy and the Strong State, 218.

26. Jonn Elledge, How demographics explains why northern seats are turning Tory, The New Statesman, 2019, https://www.newstatesman.com; Phil Moorhouse, re the Tories Poisoning Their Own Well?, A Different Bias, 2022, https://www.youtube.com
27. Ludlam and Smith, Contemporary British Conservatism, 46, 51-2.
28. George Eaton, How Tory dominance is built on home ownership, The New Statesman, 2021, https://www.newstatesman.com
29. Parker, Painting Britain Blue, Chapter 6.
30. The Economist, The truth behind the Tories' northern strongholds, 2021, https://www.economist.com/; The Economist, Who are the Conservatives' new voters in the north? 2019, https://www.economist.com/
31. Ford et al, The British General Election of 2019, 530.
32. BBC, The puzzle of the people least likely to vote Tory, 2018, https://www.bbc.co.uk/; Alex Massie, Why does the Tory party have a problem with ethnic minority voters? Because it deserves to, The Spectator, 2015, https://www.spectator.co.uk/

18 The Tories Are Better At Building Voter Coalitions

1. Parker, Painting Britain Blue, Chapter 8.
2. Gamble, The Free Economy and the Strong State, 164; Seldon and Ball, The Conservative Century, 53.
3. Gamble, The Conservative Nation, 202-6.
4. Parker, Painting Britain Blue, Chapters 1, 8.
5. Ramsden, An Appetite for Power, 353-6.
6. Ball and Holliday, Mass Conservatism, 94.
7. Davies, We, The Nation, 218.
8. Gamble, The Free Economy and the Strong State, 219.
9. Politics Theory Other, Hegemony Now (part two) - w/ Jeremy Gilbert, 2022, https://soundcloud.com; Ball and Holliday, Mass Conservatism, 224.
10. David Butler and Dennis Kavanagh, The British General

Election of 1987, Palgrave Macmillan, 1988, 275.
11. Parker, Painting Britain Blue, Chapter 8.
12. Parker, Painting Britain Blue, Chapter 6.
13. Bale, The Conservative Party: From Thatcher to Cameron, Chapter 8.
14. Parker, Painting Britain Blue, Chapter 6.
15. Cowley and Kavanagh, The British General Election of 2015, 380.
16. Parker, Painting Britain Blue, Chapter 6.
17. Burton-Cartledge, Falling Down, 473.
18. Cowley and Kavanagh, The British General Election of 2017, Chapter 16.
19. Parker, Painting Britain Blue,Paint Britain Blue, Part 2.
20. Parker, Painting Britain Blue, Introduction.
21. Parker, Painting Britain Blue, Chapter 8.
22. Parker, Painting Britain Blue, Chapter 8.
23. Ford et al, The British General Election of 2019, 526.
24. Parker, Painting Britain Blue, Chapter 5.
25. The Economist, Who are the Conservatives' new voters in the north? 2019, https://www.economist.com/
26. Politics Theory Other, Hegemony Now (part two) - w/ Jeremy Gilbert, 2022, https://soundcloud.com
27. Ford et al, The British General Election of 2019, 541.

19 Why Do People Vote Tory?

1. Jonathan Haidt, Why working-class people vote conservative, The Guardian, 2012, https://www.theguardian.com/uk
2. Jonathan Haidt, The Righteous Mind: Why Good People are Divided by Politics and Religion, Penguin, 2013, Part 1.
3. Haidt, The Righteous Mind, Part 2.
4. Haidt, The Righteous Mind, Chapter 9.
5. Haidt, The Righteous Mind, Chapter 10.
6. Haidt, The Righteous Mind, Chapter 11.
7. Claire Ainsley, The new working class: How to win hearts, minds and votes, Policy Press, 2018, 34-38.

8. Haidt, The Righteous Mind, Chapter 8.
9. Drew Westen, The Political Brain The Role Of Emotion In Deciding The Fate Of The Nation, PublicAffairs, 2008, 639.
10. Chris Mooney, 5 Ways to Turn a Liberal Into a Conservative (At Least Until the Hangover Sets In), Discover Magazine, 2012, https://www.discovermagazine.com/
11. Alex Syrpis, Why Do People Vote Tory? The Redcliffe Report, 2021, https://www.theredcliffereport.com/
12. Heywood, Political Ideologies Heywood, 65-98.
13. Luke Doherty, The electability of social conservatism: a viable force in British politics, Orthodox Conservatives, https://www.orthodoxconservatives.uk/
14. Phil Moorhouse, Have Red Wall Tories Learned Nothing? A Different Bias, 2022, https://www.youtube.com
15. Parker, Painting Britain Blue, Chapter 8.
16. Duncan Weldon, Britain's big squeeze, The New Statesman, 2022, https://www.newstatesman.com
17. Parker, Painting Britain Blue, Chapter 6; James Tilley, Hard Evidence: do we become more conservative with age? The Conversation, 2015, https://theconversation.com/uk
18. Ball and Holliday, Mass Conservatism, 51.
19. Samuel Earle, The Sordid Story of the Most Successful Political Party in the World, The New Republic, 2021, https://newrepublic.com/

20 The British Labour Party

1. Jeremy Gilbert, Get PR Done: Why PR will be good for the Labour Party, YouTube, 2021, https://www.youtube.com
2. Jeremy Gilbert, History is clear: Labour must lead an alliance for democratic reform, openDemocracy, 2020, https://www.opendemocracy.net/en/uk/
3. Get PR Done, Questions – Why PR will be good for the Labour Party, with Prof. Jeremy Gilbert, YouTube, 2021, https://www.youtube.com; Jeremy Gilbert, The End of the Road: From Bennism to Corbynism, South Atlantic Quarterly, Volume 120, Issue 4 (2021): 879–891.

4. Pinto-Duschinsky, Paying for the Party Myths and realities in British political finance, https://policyexchange.org.uk/
5. Ian Dunt, Why do the Tories keep winning elections? politics.co.uk, 2021, https://www.politics.co.uk/
6. Get PR Done, Why PR will be good for the Labour Party, with Prof. Jeremy Gilbert, YouTube, 2021, https://www.youtube.com
7. Alan Finlayson and Jeremy Gilbert, Keir Starmer's 'The Road Ahead', Culture Power Politics, 2021, https://culturepowerpolitics.org
8. Jeremy Gilbert, The only way Labour can win is by ditching 'Labourism', The Guardian, 2019, https://www.theguardian.com/uk
9. Bale, The Conservative Party: From Thatcher to Cameron.
10. Phil Moorhouse, Sunak's Troubles and Party Politics, A Different Bias, 2023, https://youtu.be/qWTakBk_MXY
11. Moorhouse, Sunak's Troubles and Party Politics, https://youtu.be/qWTakBk_MXY
12. Des Freedman, Election 2015: it's the press wot won it? Election Analysis, 2015 https://www.electionanalysis.uk/; Lee Salter, 'This is cloud cuckoo': radical alternatives to public debt, Election Analysis, 2015, https://www.electionanalysis.uk/
13. Pinto-Duschinsky, British Political Finance.
14. A. J. Davies, To Build a New Jerusalem: The Labour Movement from the 1880s to the 1990s, Michael Joseph, 1992, 451.
15. Julian Glover, Explained: Labour party funding, The Guardian, 2002, https://www.theguardian.com/uk
16. Labour Unions, What is a 'Political Fund'? https://labourunions.org.uk/
17. Matthew Burton and Richard Tunnicliffe, Membership of political parties in Great Britain; House of Commons Library, 2022, https://commonslibrary.parliament.uk/
18. Andrew Miles and Mike Savage, The Remaking of the British Working Class, 1840-1940, Routledge, 2017, 87.
19. Brian Brivati and Richard Heffernan, The Labour Party: A

Centenary History, Palgrave Macmillan, 2000, 178-182.
20. Phil Moorhouse, Politics Live: How Long Will Jeremy Hunt Last as Chancellor?, A Different Bias, 2022, https://youtu.be/6SVX_yukz78
21. Matt Beech, Kevin Hickson and Raymond Plant, The Struggle for Labour's Soul: Understanding Labour's Political Thought Since 1945, Routledge, 2018, 190; Patrick Diamond, The British Labour Party in Opposition and Power 1979-2019: Forward March Halted? Routledge, 2021, 371.
22. Diamond, The British Labour Party in Opposition and Power 1979-2019, 375.
23. Get PR Done, Why PR will be good for the Labour Party, with Prof. Jeremy Gilbert, YouTube, 2021, https://www.youtube.com
24. Jeremy Gilbert, History is clear: Labour must lead an alliance for democratic reform, openDemocracy, 2020, https://www.opendemocracy.net/en/uk/
25. Geoff Norcott, Triggernometry: Why Labour Keep Losing with Geoff Norcott, YouTube, 2021, https://www.youtube.com

Part 6 Stopping The Tories

1. Samuel Earle, The Sordid Story of the Most Successful Political Party in the World, The New Republic, 2021, https://newrepublic.com/
2. Phil Moorhouse, Labour Still Resisting Proportional Representation, A Different Bias, 2022, https://www.youtube.com
3. Ash Sarkar and Samuel Earle, Why The Tories Keep Winning, Novara Media, 2021, https://www.youtube.com
4. Andy Beckett, History shows that the Conservatives can't hold back social change, The Guardian, 2021, https://www.theguardian.com/uk

21 How To Stop The Tories At The Next General Election

1. Jeremy Gilbert, History is clear: Labour must lead an alliance for democratic reform, openDemocracy, 2020, https://www.opendemocracy.net/en/uk/; Wikipedia, Lib–Lab pact, https://en.wikipedia.org; Seldon, How Tory Governments Fall, Chapter 5.
2. Butler and King, The British General Election of 1964, 347-8.
3. Martin Linton and Mary Southcott, Making Votes Count: The Case for Electoral Reform, Profile Books, 1998, 31.
4. Butler and Kavanagh, The British General Election of 1979, 407.
5. Butler and Kavanagh, The British General Election of 1987, 58, 97, 266.
6. Butler and Kavanagh, The British General Election of 1992, 280, 336.
7. Duncan Brack, Lessons from the Ashdown-Blair 'project', in Lisa Nandy, Caroline Lucas and Chris Bowers, The Alternative: Towards a New Progressive Politics, Biteback Publishing, 2016, 211-12; Linton and Southcott, Making Votes Count, 35-6; Butler and Kavanagh, The British General Election of 1997, 251-2, 309-13.
8. Cowley and Kavanagh, The British General Election of 2015, 409-10.
9. Peter Madeley, Return of tactical voting spells bad news for Tories - Labour MP, Shropshire Star, 2021, https://www.shropshirestar.com/
10. Chris Jarvis, 'Industrial scale tactical voting' behind Tory by-election defeats leads to calls for proportional representation, Left Foot Forward, 2022, https://leftfootforward.org/
11. Search for UK MPs at https://members.parliament.uk/

22 How To Stop The Tories In The Long Term

1. Jeremy Gilbert, History is clear: Labour must lead an alliance for democratic reform, openDemocracy, 2020, https://www.opendemocracy.net/en/uk/
2. Wikipedia, Charter 88, https://en.wikipedia.org/wiki/Charter_88; BBC, Leveson report: At a glance, 2012, https://www.bbc.co.uk/news/uk-20543133
3. Linton and Southcott, Making Votes Count, 115.
4. Make Votes Matter, Proportional Representation, https://www.makevotesmatter.org.uk; Labour for a New Democracy, Everything but the Commons, https://www.labourforanewdemocracy.org.uk; Sheerin, Higher Modern Studies: Democracy in Scotland and the UK Higher, 37; Katie Ghose, Embracing Electoral reform in Lisa Nandy, Caroline Lucas and Chris Bowers, The Alternative: Towards a New Progressive Politics, Biteback Publishing, 2016, 273-289; George Monbiot, The Oligarch that Took Over Britain, Double Down News, https://www.youtube.com; Make Votes Matter, PR and Equality, https://www.makevotesmatter.org.uk/equality
5. Electoral Reform Society, Proportional Representation, https://www.electoral-reform.org.uk
6. Neil Johnston, Voting Systems in the UK, House of Commons Library, 2023, https://commonslibrary.parliament.uk
7. Labour Campaign for Electoral Reform, Alternative Vote (AV), https://labourforelectoralreform.org.uk
8. Electoral Reform Society, Supplementary Vote, https://www.electoral-reform.org.uk
9. Electoral Reform Society, Two-Round System, https://www.electoral-reform.org.uk
10. Linton and Southcott, Making Votes Count, 133; Electoral Reform Society, Additional Member System, https://www.electoral-reform.org.uk
11. Electoral Reform Society, Party List Proportional Representation, https://www.electoral-reform.org.uk

12. Electoral Reform Society, Single Transferable Vote, https://www.electoral-reform.org.uk; Linton and Southcott, Making Votes Count, 136.
13. Peter Kellner, Be careful what you wish for… voting reform could kill Labour, The New European, 2021, https://www.theneweuropean.co.uk
14. Stephen Bush, Andy Burnham: "I'm prepared to go back but as something different", The New Statesman, 2021, https://www.newstatesman.com
15. Katie Ghose, Embracing Electoral reform in Lisa Nandy, Caroline Lucas and Chris Bowers, The Alternative: Towards a New Progressive Politics, Biteback Publishing, 2016, 282.
16. Katie Ghose, Embracing Electoral reform in Lisa Nandy, Caroline Lucas and Chris Bowers, The Alternative: Towards a New Progressive Politics, Biteback Publishing, 2016, 283.
17. Make Votes Matter, First Past the Post, https://www.makevotesmatter.org.uk
18. Lynne Armstrong and Mary Southcott, Trade Unions in the vanguard, The Chartist trade union supplement 2022, https://www.chartist.org.uk; Linton and Southcott, Making Votes Count, Chapter 9; André Blais, To Keep or To Change First Past The Post? The Politics of Electoral Reform, Oxford University Press, 2008, 67.
19. Karl McDonald, Millions of working-class men got the vote 100 years ago too, i News, 2018, https://inews.co.uk/; Wikipedia, Elections in the United Kingdom, Expansion of the franchise, https://en.wikipedia.org
20. Wikipedia, Elections in the United Kingdom, Expansion of the franchise, https://en.wikipedia.org
21. BBC, Electoral reform, 2001, http://news.bbc.co.uk
22. Linton and Southcott, Making Votes Count, Chapters 11 and 12.
23. Linton and Southcott, Making Votes Count, Chapter 12; Lynne Armstrong and Mary Southcott, Trade Unions in the vanguard, The Chartist trade union supplement 2022, https://www.chartist.org.uk
24. BBC, Electoral reform, 2001, http://news.bbc.co.uk
25. Tom Clark, 10 reasons the AV referendum was lost, The

Guardian, 2021, https://www.theguardian.com/uk
26. Alan Renwick, How Likely is Proportional Representation in the House of Commons? Lessons from International Experience, Government and Opposition, Vol. 44, No. 4 (2009), 366-384.
27. Electoral Reform Society, Long running survey finds majority support proportional representation, 2022, https://www.electoral-reform.org.uk
28. Katie Ghose, Embracing Electoral reform in Lisa Nandy, Caroline Lucas and Chris Bowers, The Alternative: Towards a New Progressive Politics, Biteback Publishing, 2016.
29. Electoral Reform Society, Keir Starmer announces support for constitutional convention and proportional representation, 2021, https://www.electoral-reform.org.uk
30. Lynne Armstrong and Mary Southcott, Trade Unions in the vanguard, The Chartist trade union supplement 2022, https://www.chartist.org.uk; Make Votes Matter, Good Systems Agreement, https://www.makevotesmatter.org.uk
31. To learn more about deep canvassing go to https://deepcanvass.org/
32. https://labourforelectoralreform.org.uk/
33. https://www.labourforanewdemocracy.org.uk/
34. https://www.compassonline.org.uk/
35. https://www.makevotesmatter.org.uk/
36. https://getprdone.org.uk/
37. https://themovementforward.com
38. https://unlockdemocracy.org.uk/
39. https://www.electoral-reform.org.uk/

THE TORY WINNING MACHINE

Printed in Great Britain
by Amazon